Crime News in Modern Britain

Portraits of Celebrities at Different Times of their Lives.

AGE 36.
*From a Photo. by
Maull & Co.*

AGE 50.
*From a Photo. by
Watkins & Haigh.*

Judge of the High
Court of Justice in the
Queen's Bench Division
at sixty, the age at which
the fourth of our por-
traits represents him.

AGE 45.
*From a Photo. by
Whitlock,
Birmingham.*

From a Photo. by]   AGE 60.   *[Lock & Whitefield.*

SIR HENRY HAWKINS.
BORN 1816.

HE HON. SIR HENRY
HAWKINS is a son of Mr. J. H.
Hawkins, solicitor, and was born
at Hitchin. He was called to
the Bar at the Middle Temple at
the age of twenty-seven, becoming a Q.C. at
forty-two. He enjoyed one of the largest
practices ever known, his power of cross-
examining witnesses and of addressing the
jury being unrivalled. He was engaged in
the prosecution of the Claimant in the memor-
able Tichborne Trial. He was appointed

From a Photo. by]   PRESENT DAY.   *[Elliott & Fr y*

Frontispiece: The Lawyer as Pin-Up

Crime News in Modern Britain

Press Reporting and Responsibility, 1820–2010

Judith Rowbotham
Director, SOLON: Promoting Interdisciplinary Studies in Law, Crime and History

Kim Stevenson
Professor in Sociolegal History, University of Plymouth, UK

and

Samantha Pegg
Senior Lecturer in Law, Nottingham Trent University, UK

First published 2013 by
PALGRAVE MACMILLAN

Palgrave Macmillan in the UK is an imprint of Macmillan Publishers Limited,
registered in England, company number 785998, of Houndmills, Basingstoke,
Hampshire RG21 6XS.

Palgrave Macmillan in the US is a division of St Martin's Press LLC,
175 Fifth Avenue, New York, NY 10010.

Palgrave Macmillan is the global academic imprint of the above companies
and has companies and representatives throughout the world.

Palgrave® and Macmillan® are registered trademarks in the United States,
the United Kingdom, Europe and other countries

ISBN: 978–0–230–30359–1

This book is printed on paper suitable for recycling and made from fully
managed and sustained forest sources. Logging, pulping and manufacturing
processes are expected to conform to the environmental regulations of the
country of origin.

A catalogue record for this book is available from the British Library.

A catalog record for this book is available from the Library of Congress.

Contents

Foreword

This is an auspicious time for a book about criminal reporting. When the authors started work, their book was to be about the reporting of crime. By the time they finished, people were more interested in the alleged criminality of reporters.

The 190 years it covers have seen the rise and fall of crime reporting. If the authors can be persuaded to update their work in a decade from now, they may well find themselves chronicling its demise. There may well be more crime to report in 2020 but there are likely to be fewer printed newspapers in which it can be reported.

Until I read this well-researched book, I had no idea that many nineteenth-century crime reporters were trained lawyers, writing anonymously. The authors explain how lawyers working in and for the press transformed the trade of journalism, making it a respectable career for educated, middle-class young men. Those lawyers replaced the 'penny-a-liners' – freelances who had a financial incentive to make things up. *Plus ça change.*

The late nineteenth century saw the rise of investigative journalism, with W.T. Stead finding himself arrested for demonstrating how easy it was to buy a girl of 13. Many of his successors have found themselves living life on the edge and there is every chance that some of them will be following him to prison.

For others, though, journalism is a nobler calling. From Stead onwards, reporters and commentators have played an important part in exposing miscarriages of justice and promoting law reform. Without the campaigning work of the press, it is unlikely that the government would have established the Court of Criminal Appeal in 1907. Many other reforms have followed.

During the twentieth century and into the twenty-first, there were increasing restrictions on what journalists could report. Most of these restrictions were arguably in the interest of justice. But, by the second decade of the twenty-first century, the judges were opening up their courts, recognising the public's right to know. A ban on taking photographs in the courts of England and Wales was introduced in 1925. It was lifted, very slightly, in 2013 when television cameras were allowed into the Court of Appeal. The courts began to welcome bloggers and tweeters, citizen journalists using new methods of communication.

Despite what some people may believe, journalism is not a profession. Nobody can license me to report the news and so nobody can take my reporter's licence away, even if the Leveson plans for press regulation proceed apace. Freedom of expression is the mark of a free society. However ill informed some of the press may be, I would not have it any other way.

Joshua Rozenberg
April 2013

Preface and Acknowledgments

This book has been longer than expected in the making, but the instigation of the Leveson Inquiry, coming as we completed an early outline of the book, forced us to rethink and recontextualise our approach to this survey. At that point, we felt that it provided a convincing, compelling and timely framework against which to present and review the historical development of crime news, in that we had identified a significant decline in the quality of that news in terms of its legal accuracy. In writing this book, we wished to explore the reasons for and the impact of differences in the reportage of crime on popular understandings of crime and criminality, and consequently of the ways in which justice was (or was not) meted out to offenders. The events of 2011 demanded that we also highlighted and reflected upon the pre-existing causational factors that occasioned such a high profile denouement to our retrospective review.

In 2013, crime reportage features in the news in ways that were unexpected in 2010 when we started to write this book. A conviction of the need for a better understanding of the presentation of crime through the media was the original impetus, because it is through that lens that the majority of citizens obtain their understanding of crime and justice. We were aware that there was a contrast between the levels of public support for the criminal justice system in the post-1850 Victorian era and the more negative attitudes found at the start of the nineteenth century. What role has the media played in creating, and then sustaining or undermining, that support, especially in the late twentieth and early twenty-first centuries? Having used newspapers as sources to understand historical and modern attitudes towards types of crime including murder, rape, burglary and domestic violence, we were conscious that the attitude of the media towards the criminal justice system at least mirrored, if it did not create, public support (or lack of it) for the daily operation of that system. Media presentations of individual trials, at all levels of the court hierarchy, could suggest, explicitly or implicitly, whether or not 'justice' was being appropriately delivered.

We had become very conscious that there was a significant difference in the legal content (and accuracy) of such daily reportage of crime, intended for popular consumption, between the post-1850 Victorian era and the modern era. But was that simply an inevitable corollary, as many have implicitly assumed, of an increasingly complex legal system? We did not think the reason for this diminution in legal quality was so simple. But seeking to explore any wider complexities meant that we had to think about the strategies for reporting law from the perspective of the law as well as taking into account the different demands and expectations of the criminal justice process from a historical perspective. In planning this text, we were consequently driven by a sense of the need for a genuinely interdisciplinary approach which would incorporate a historical perspective, paying appropriate attention to cultural contexts, but also a real and substantial appreciation of the criminal law. Only in that way, we believe, is it possible to comprehend the complexities of the issues involved from all sides.

What we could not have imagined was how our historico-legal analysis of the production and dissemination of crime news would suddenly be overtaken by the unprecedented events of the summer of 2011: events that would set up fundamental questions about the integrity and morality of the British press, reflecting on both its crime reportage and the actual criminality of its editors and journalists. This persuaded us to expand certain aspects of our book to consider the implications for the future of crime intelligence in the media in the light of these disclosures.

Much has been, and will continue to be, written about the Leveson Inquiry, its Report and the ways in which the press, overall, might be regulated. But this is not a book about Leveson. What we realised is that we were writing a book which illuminated how the scenario of 2011 had evolved. It was widely known that phone-hacking figured as one of the investigative tools being used by journalists in the decade before 2011. Generally, the public was largely unconcerned at the sensationalising of often mundane incidents through reporting the involvement of celebrity figures in them. Consumers continued to buy, not boycott, titles accused of invading their privacy by a range of celebrity figures, tacitly tolerating the strategies that led to such enjoyably 'juicy' news about individuals already in the public eye.[1] Equally, the political community (once the security-laden issue of hacking into royal phones had been dealt with) was largely uninterested in the embarrassment and distress of people like Hugh Grant or Max Clifford at having their privacy invaded by illegal means.

---

[1] We do not, here, deal with the issues of privacy – clearly of importance to debates over responsible journalism, partly because this had already been comprehensively dealt with, in ways that do invoke a historical dimension. See J. Rozenberg (2005) *Privacy and the Press* (Oxford University Press).

However, this text is *not* an attack on investigative journalism or on any other agency implicated in some way in the inquiry. We need the safeguards it provides in a flourishing modern democracy. The 2013 proposals to revive the Justice and Security Bill's clauses to make it illegal to reveal certain aspects of official dealings when tested in government hearings in the interests of 'state security' are being widely challenged in the press because of the implications they would have for investigative journalism. Such legislation would, for instance, almost certainly have prevented much of the Profumo scandal from emerging into the media spotlight – good for politicians; bad for justice and for a sound public comprehension of the justice delivery system. History also shows that investigative journalism can flourish as enjoyable reading and in the public interest *without* resorting to the strategies and illegalities of recent years.

Over the decade before we started to write this book, the authors looked exhaustively and intensively at a wide range of newsprint, national and local, from the early nineteenth century to the present day. We have consistently contextualised this against the background of developments in the criminal justice system and in-depth studies of lawyers, as professionals and as people. Our knowledge of the history of publishing, as well as of the broader cultural and political history of Britain, has provided a further framework to our considerations. A consciousness of the need to maintain both coherence and legal accuracy has meant that we have not considered the whole of mainland Britain in this survey. Scotland has been excluded for the purely practical reasons of avoiding extending this volume by at least another two chapters in order to account, properly, for the differences between Scottish and English (and Welsh) law. This does not mean we are unaware of Scottish newsprint and criminal cases, but their coverage and consideration must be the work of another volume.

Recognising, but deliberately not repeating, the conclusions in the myriad of texts interrogating the issues of crime and the media from the perspectives of criminology and media studies has meant that the landscape for our exploration has been framed by a consciousness established by that scholarship of the consumer expectations which, at different periods, have governed how news is presented for differing reading audiences. Equally, we acknowledge that the production of crime news, and its management through the criminal justice process, is significantly influenced by the ways in which newspaper proprietors and editors believe individuals and communities respond to that reportage: again something addressed by other scholarship, particularly for the last half of the twentieth century.

We believe that, for this to be an effective survey of the delivery of crime news in the media, we need to be interdisciplinary, acknowledging the legal as well as the historical dimensions in equal measure. In developing our approach, we were very conscious of the complexities of bringing together the two sophisticated disciplines of law and history; both with different agendas, albeit they share complementary interests. Interdisciplinary work, if done well, respects the integrity of each discipline in sharing knowledge and understanding across disciplinary boundaries. With one author a historian by first discipline, another a lawyer and the third a legal historian in terms of her PhD (supervised by the first two), there was a wealth of experience in managing the tensions involved in bringing together law and history and working out practical strategies for complementing and enhancing work done by both historians and lawyers in this area. This will also, we hope, make it a useful text for other relevant academic disciplines that we have looked to, notably criminology, media and journalism studies.

We are grateful to many people, especially to our fellow Directors and the other members of the SOLON network (www.pbs.plymouth.ac.uk/solon), who have listened to us, read other work by us and reflected back to us usefully critical comment. Other legal and crime historians and criminologists, particularly those who have attended our SOLON conferences, have also provided a fruitful arena in which we could evolve the ideas we put forward here. We are honoured as well as grateful that Joshua Rozenberg agreed to write the Preface for us, pointing us to the way we should go in the future as well as reflecting so kindly on what we have done here. We owe thanks also to the staff at the British Newspaper Library at Colindale, who have, over the past decade, been a consistent and helpful resource, as have our own institutional libraries. Family, friends and colleagues who have put up with us insisting on discussing gory details and legal minutiae, and constant references to Serjeant Ballantine, 'Hanging' Henry Hawkins or Lord Wolfenden (not to mention Bodkin Adams, and Sweet Fanny Adams!) are also due a debt of gratitude. We are grateful also to our publishers for accepting the delayed appearance of this work.

Introduction: A History of Crime News

Of compelling newsworthiness?

This is a book about crime intelligence – intelligence in the sense both of the information provided through media formats (principally newspapers) and of the way in which it has been received, understood and used. Our focus here is an exploration of the ways in which crime has been presented in the media, using the print format for the obvious reason that newspapers were an important feature of the media landscape throughout the key period under discussion – the mid-nineteenth century to the present day. Essentially, the media are a means of mass communication that can purvey 'news' to a series of audiences. What has always made some events 'newsworthy' and others not is a combination of 'values', notably danger and conflict, the involvement of a well-known individual, scandal (in other words that which is morally if not actually legally offensive to society), and that which is 'out of the ordinary' in some way. Crime has always manifested several of these 'news values' and so has long been a media staple, as both criminologists and media studies experts recognise. But this is not primarily either a criminology or a media studies text, though it is certainly informed by both these disciplines.[1] It is, rather, an interdisciplinary text drawing mainly on both history and law for its methodology and its analysis and

---

[1] Key texts notably include E. Carrabine (2008) *Crime, Culture and the Media* (Cambridge: Polity Press); S. Cohen and J. Young (eds) (1973) *The Manufacture of News: Deviance, Social Problems and the Mass Media* (London: Constable); P. Mason (ed.) (2003) *Criminal Visions: Representations of Crime and Justice* (Cullompton: Willan); Y. Jewkes (2004) *Media and Crime* (London: Sage); S. Cohen (2011) *Folk Devils and Moral Panics* (London: Routledge Classics); C. Critcher (2003) *Moral Panics and the Media* (Buckingham: Open University Press); D. Garland (2001)

focusing on newsprint rather than on drama (stage and film), television, radio or internet as media formats.[2]

Decisions on the presentation of crime narratives and representations of the perspectives taken by various titles set the framework through which we learn to understand the realities of the everyday legal world, something that is not simply of concern to legal specialists (academic or professional). This is one basic reason why, in any society, what is defined as crime is always 'newsworthy', however that news is delivered. Crime is defined by behaviour which challenges our boundaries of what is acceptable conduct within society. There is a long-standing and universal desire to know (in detail) the features of a crime, and whether there is any contextualising information which could mitigate its seriousness. This involves adding a human dimension to the pure legalities of the criminal justice process, and this is what makes crime newsworthy. At times that human dimension so changes our basic comprehension of a crime in the strict legal sense, making our perception of it more or less serious, that it automatically becomes an event of compelling newsworthiness. Thus is crime news born. Understanding this is crucial to a comprehension of the moral panic surrounding the Leveson Inquiry and its 2013 Report (for moral panic, in Cohenian terms, we certainly believe it will come to be labelled).

Print journalism and Leveson

Any modern exploration of crime reportage in the media must take account of the Leveson Inquiry and the reasons it was set up. Revelations during the trial in June 2011 of Levi Bellfield for the murder of Milly Dowler informed the public that an investigative journalist working for the *News of the World* had hacked into the victim's voicemail, apparently in order to enhance the sensationalism of his coverage of her story. It was charged that his actions had hindered police investigations, given her family false hope and, ultimately, had aided the defence in a trial where the overwhelming public sympathy was on the side of the victim and her bereft family. The sense of public outrage was so great that it was

---

The Culture of Control (Oxford University Press); A. Young (1996) *Imagining Crime: Textual Outlaws and Criminal Conversations* (London: Sage); R. Surrette (1998) *Media, Crime and Criminal Justice: Images and Realities* (Belmont, CA: Wadsworth).

[2] This means in particular that we do not consider radio and television media reportage except in passing to contextualise changes in newspaper policy. To have given that dimension proper value would have resulted in this book being at least another third longer.

not enough for the newspaper itself, one with a venerable pedigree, to be closed: the Government was forced into action.

This was the background to Lord Justice Leveson's appointment in July 2011 to chair a public inquiry, originally intended mainly to investigate the professional conduct of, and the nature and extent of interconnections between, the press, the polity and the police when producing popular journalism.[3] The public alarm that forced the inquiry was rooted in fear that intrinsic to the modern activities of investigative journalists was the potential regularly to distort the delivery of justice. However, the Leveson Inquiry was, in many ways, taken over by a broader agenda concerned more with the range of illegality (including intrusions into personal privacy) that had become, it seemed, integral to investigative journalism generally rather than with the potential for investigative journalism to derail or distort the criminal justice process.

Certainly investigative journalism had long intruded on the personal privacy of figures deemed of interest to a variety of readerships. It seems that it was tacitly agreed by readers of the papers publishing such stories that, since celebrities sought publicity on their own account, they were 'fair game' for additional unsought publicity. Because of this, most newspapers could afford to pay little attention to earlier police operations (in 1999 and 2003) to investigate the illegal dimensions to investigative journalism, which had simply led to prosecutions of private investigators used by journalists, not those employing them and using the illegally acquired information in news stories.[4] Only *The Guardian* had cared, after 2002, to keep alive the story of phone hacking and the issue of illegal acquisition of information and the implications for a broader sense of 'justice' within society. That campaign had acquired greater vehemence after 2006, with items arguing regularly that the police had prematurely shut down their inquiry during which Clive Goodman and

---

[3] Lord Leveson (2012) *Leveson Inquiry: Culture, Practice and Ethics of the Press* http://www.levesoninquiry.org.uk/.

[4] Operation Nigeria, 1999, was little reported except by *The Guardian*, which noted it implicated 'Tabloid journalists' (from the *News of the World*, *Daily* and *Sunday Mirror*) in purchasing information from private detectives, who had in turn 'paid corrupt officers for confidential police material'; no journalists were prosecuted, as it was then agreed they had not committed any criminal offences in acquiring or using the material: 'Journalists caught on tape in police bugging', *The Guardian*, 21 September 2002. Operation Glade, 2003, again involved the interviewing of tabloid journalists but no arrests, and it went virtually unnoticed even by *The Guardian* until the Leveson Inquiry gave it a retrospective relevance. See *Press Gazette*, 12 May 2012.

Glenn Mulcaire had been convicted of hacking into royal household phones.[5]

The revelations during the trial of Bellfield situated the tactics of phone hacking as a way of gleaning information which could be converted into 'news' into an entirely new landscape. Particularly shocking was the fact that the targets were not those who had in any way placed themselves willingly in the public eye. It also could not be argued in justification (as with some earlier twentieth-century investigative journalism) that journalists or the private investigators they employed were doing a job the police could, or would, not do. This dramatically shifted public perceptions of how the print media were operating. When it emerged that the phones of the victims of the 7/7 bombings in London in 2005 had also been hacked, public disgust and outrage intensified.[6] It meant that other news-gathering tactics used by journalists that had long been tacitly accepted by the public and politicians came under active scrutiny and, as a result, were viewed in a new, and far more censorious, light. Crucially, the fact that individual members of the police were not just selling information to private investigators working for journalists, but also were in direct contact with paying journalists, tainted both professions. It led to suspicions that the police had shut down the 2006 inquiry as a means of self-protection.

However, such suspicions, allied to the decision to allow evidence from those identified as victims of newspaper stories about them based on information gained by illegal means, meant that journalism in general, and not crime reportage, became the key target for Leveson. Even the ongoing police investigations became wider, and more focused on the accompanying illegalities of investigative journalism rather than on the potential to distort the criminal justice process.[7] Consequently, the focus on journalistic illegalities in general, and the moralities involved in investigative journalism (how, when and where to limit this in the interests of 'victims' and the general public), has become the most important element in public debate as well. But, while a will to explore how far there has been, in recent years, any regular impact by crime reportage on the workings of the formal legal process and its ability to deliver justice has been eclipsed elsewhere, that consideration has remained central to the authors of this book.

---

[5] See *The Guardian*, 29 November 2006; 7 July 2011.

[6] 'News International Rebekah Brooks is linked personally to private eye News of the World used in Milly Dowler phone scandal', *Daily Mail*, 6 July 2011; 'Phone hacking: families of 7/7 victims "were targets" ', *The Guardian*, 6 July 2011.

[7] Investigations such as Operations Weeting, Tuleta and Elvedon are predicted to remain ongoing into 2015. See 'Operation Weeting: arrests and charges timeline', *The Guardian*, 2 November 2012.

Crime journalism in historical perspective

The objective of this book is the provision of a history of journalism's relationship with the criminal justice process in the modern era (tracing the story back to the late eighteenth century). In so doing, it illuminates just how predictable, from that long-term perspective, the revelations of 2011 were. Investigative journalism had long intruded on the criminal justice process, and it was, we would argue, only a matter of time before the increasing scale of this (enabled by new technologies in the last decades) was recognised as causing a problem. If not the Bellfield trial, some other trial would soon have uncovered the objectionable journalistic tactics that shocked the public into an awareness of how extensive (and how unjustified) were the illegal intrusions into the lives of victims of crime made by some popular investigative journalism.

This text explores the impact of a gradual accumulation of shifts in popular expectation and the boundaries of popular tolerance plus commercial pressures and, above all, a widespread lack of appreciation of the role played by the law in society. The consequent failure by the media to promote a proper understanding of the criminal law created the dangerous scenario that was in place in 2011. This background to twenty-first-century investigative journalism arose accidentally over the previous century. There was a mixture of in-house complacency about their own standards and importance to the public interest on the part of the press even when faced with very real commercial pressures to remain financially viable. This was combined with a lack of political will to tackle press excesses (often for party political electoral motives). There was also a disengagement between the ordinary citizen and the processes of the criminal law resulting from an increasing exclusion of the citizen from the daily business of the criminal justice process. This meant that the involved spectator became a voyeur of the justice system in action. We illustrate the ways in which crime reportage has developed in modern times, to show how, over a sustained historical period, it has unintentionally contributed to a diminishing popular understanding of the law and its workings. A lack of comprehension of the criminal law and its justice delivery processes has real implications for poor management of the fear of crime in modern Britain.[8]

---

[8] See S. Farrall, J. Jackson and E. Gray (2009) *The Social Order and the Fear of Crime in Contemporary Times* (Oxford University Press).

The text can also, we hope, aid a reassessment of the role of crime reportage, contributing to informed debate on what constitutes journalistic responsibility and also stimulating a will on the part of politicians and legal professionals to make the law, particularly the criminal law, more accessible to the general public. We have, in today's Britain, the most ill-informed society (in terms of its comprehension of law) in modern history. In the past, crime intelligence in the shape of interesting and accurate reportage of crime and criminality was available because it was necessary. The development of institutions like the Crown Prosecution Service demolished that necessity. However, without turning back the clock, the model of Victorian reportage reminds us that it is possible to provide entertaining reportage which is also legally informative and accurate.

Throughout the periods we address, there has been an enduring public thirst for crime news narratives, presented through the frames of investigation and arrest, followed by trial and punishment. Treating criminal acts as unfolding drama in terms of their presentation on the news pages is nothing new, as is the case with tactics to sensationalise that news, through use of investigative journalism. Stead's 1885 series, 'Maiden Tribute of Modern Babylon', provides both example and warning in that the articles were avidly read, but their author was prosecuted for his illegal news-gathering techniques.[9] Late Victorian newspaper proprietors and investigative journalists learned useful lessons. By the start of the twenty-first century, those lessons were long forgotten. From a criminal justice perspective, what currently is particularly damning is the publishing of sensational information careless of whether that could prejudice a defendant's right to a fair trial. It has become easier to ignore the line between legality and illegality when 'success' apparently follows at least some investigative journalism, as in the case of the *Daily Mail*'s front page public accusation of Stephen Lawrence's killers, which undoubtedly contributed to the eventual conviction of two of those involved in Lawrence's murder.[10] But that does not make such tactics serve the public interest generally. It is also fair to say that the lack of willingness on the part of politicians to ensure the press policed itself effectively, and a degree of disengagement on the part of the legal system (witness the diminishing seriousness of fines and other penalties in contempt of court cases since the 1960s), bear responsibility in enabling current realities.

---

[9] See Chapter 4.
[10] See Chapter 7.

Approaches and methodologies

It has been pointed out that understanding the functions of journalism depends on the ability to construct and utilise adequate critical methods of research.[11] In constructing our chapters and to provide a basis for assessment of the extent to which the newspaper press had the ability to influence public understandings of the criminal justice process, we address a number of key questions for each period. Who is actually responsible for generating the basic copy used in the final print production? Here the shift from the legally qualified reporters (lawyer–reporters being the term we chose to use) to newspaper professionals who conflated the role of reporter and journalist has proved to be fundamental. Twentieth-century journalism may have produced 'specialist' crime reporters, but few of them were legally qualified. The issue, then, became the extent to which there was or remained a sound relationship between criminal justice professionals and professional journalists. The importance of the relationship between journalists and the police became apparent during our research into twentieth-century crime reportage. Of slow growth, and largely unregulated in practice, this grew to be the most significant relationship in the production of crime reportage by the end of the twentieth century. The demise of specialist crime reporters with their specialist contacts has meant that a new intermediary agency has been used in the last quarter century, in the shape of the private investigator, employed by journalists to act as the 'go-between' in accessing information. But the pattern of closeness between police officers and journalists has remained at the core of crime reportage, as recent events underline. We have also consistently asked what seems to have been the purpose or objective of a title in publishing crime news at any one time. Was it simply to inform or to educate as a matter of public record and dissemination of the truth, or to dissuade and prevent individuals from committing crime in the greater public interest? Or was it, rather, to entertain and sensationalise readers with a view to increasing or maintaining sales levels? What role, if any, was played by a consciousness of a need to invoke the public legitimisation of crime control practices?

Media historians and criminologists have identified a number of concerns and issues about the potential methodological approaches that could be utilised in such a study. In terms of chronological continuums, for example, Joel Wiener has commented that, as a significant facet of

---

[11] L. Brake, A. Jones and L. Madden (eds) (1990) *Investigating Victorian Journalism* (Basingstoke: Macmillan) p. xi.

popular culture, the coverage of crime matter in Victorian newspapers has not yet been analysed adequately.[12] To remedy this deficit, the first three chapters provide a more detailed exploration which it has not been necessary to use in the later chapters. It has also been important to pay particular attention to the last half of the nineteenth century because of the need to reveal the crucial role in the development of modern crime reportage played by the lawyer–reporter, and the consequent expectations of the legal profession of the style and content of reportage into the twentieth century. By contrast, we have chosen to pay less attention to the detail of crime news from the 1960s on. Instead of repeating what has been covered in real and challenging depth in other texts, we have covered that period in a single chapter by taking a fresh perspective on the framing developments in that period.

The extent to which existing scholarship has effectively promoted a genuine interdisciplinary approach also requires consideration. As noted by Osborne, 'the historical problems of crime reporting and images of crime, in print and electronic media, have always been seen as minor questions on the fringes of other disciplines'.[13] We agree that has been the case, and here strongly assert that crime news history necessarily requires an unambiguous commitment to interdisciplinarity so that the legal issues involved are not marginalised. It is for this reason that we take account of the detail of relations between the press and the various agencies of the criminal justice system.

We would also suggest that, as attention increasingly turns to crime reportage in the online environment, as discussed in Chapter 8, this is a crucial time to reflect back on the production and dissemination of crime news by the print press. There are questions about the possible survival of such print productions in the face of challenges from various electronic media formats including Twitter, personal websites and blogs. Their use by established crime news journalists suggests a crucial shift in the location of crime news for the future, bringing with it new challenges in maintaining accuracy and legality, interrogating facts and sources in the clamour to break stories. This text offers a balancing perspective on what is needed to avoid the mistakes of the recent past through its *longue durée* approach to crime news.

---

[12]   J. Wiener (ed.) (1988) *Papers for the Millions. The New Journalism in Britain, 1850s to 1914* (Westport, CT: Greenwood Press) p. 60.

[13]   R. Osborne (1995) *Crime and the Media: From media studies to post-modernism* in D. Kidd-Hewitt and R. Osborne (eds) *Crime and the Media: The Post-Modern Spectacle* (London: Pluto Press) p. 25.

Contextualising the history of crime news

Leveson convincingly situates this discourse in a contemporary context, but our initial, and still powerful, rationale for undertaking this enterprise was the gap in the historiographical and legal literature dealing with crime news over a sustained period. Curran has suggested that, at the expense of a more conventional historical approach, most discourse on media history has tended to focus on the chronology of individual *mediums* such as newspapers, books, radio, television, films and more recently the internet, often combined with a media-centric approach concentrating on their respective content and institutions. He argues that such methodologies may limit any effectual understanding of the relationship between the growth of the media in the context of wider social trends. A more innovative and desirable approach, in his view, is to 'insert' or contextualise British media history within broader narratives on the development of modern society. This will 'produce a more contingent view of ebb and flow, opening and closure, advances in some areas and reverses in others' that should help to 'dissolve linear narratives – whether progress or regress – in favour of complexity'.[14] Our aim with this book is, therefore, to contextualise the history of crime news in the press and examine the nature, and the 'ebb and flow', of specialist crime reportage within the framework of the modern development of the criminal justice system from the late eighteenth century to the present day.

The chapters identify, interrogate and rationalise the shifts in the priorities, narratives, style and content of newspaper coverage of crime news, printed in broadsheet, quality and tabloid publications. Evidence in support is provided from the reported detail of the prosecution of criminal offences and trial proceedings conducted in both the summary courts (magistrates courts, police courts, petty sessions) and the higher courts (Quarter-sessions, Assizes, Crown Court). Specifically, the main focus is an exploration of why, and how, different newspaper titles selected, constructed and presented particular crime reportage for popular consumption. What factors and which individuals constructed and took responsibility for the quality, volume, authorship, authenticity and placement of crime news within individual publications and across the genre more generally? What has been the relationship between these issues and conceptualisations of what constitutes the public interest in

---

[14]   J. Curran (2002) 'Media and the Making of British Society, c.1700–2000', *Media History*, 8(2), 135–154 at 149.

terms of public knowledge of and support for the criminal justice process? And to what extent did this affect (or was it affected by) prevailing social, political and legal contexts? What emphasis is given, in the reportage, to the decisions of magistrates, judges and juries? To the arguments, speeches and cross-examinations articulated by barristers and solicitors? How have the police and their actions been regarded, and how has that been dependent on their identified role as witness, prosecutor, investigator or press informant? How did the portrayal of witnesses and victims compare with the representations of those accused? To what extent do the demands of the readership influence how crime news is packaged and presented?

It has been argued not just that 'The press is the medium by which the public becomes informed' but also that 'The general reader cannot translate the language of the courts without taking the time to become a specialist.'[15] What our early chapters reveal is that this conclusion is too simplistic: the Victorian and Edwardian audiences for crime news were much better equipped to comprehend the 'language of the courts' than their modern counterparts, because they had a greater need to know it *and* because crime reportage in that period reflected that need in the language and orientation of the various news items. How far do we assume a modern impossibility here because the will to do so is lacking? Audiences are capable of understanding complex political, scientific and philosophical debates in television documentaries, for instance – why not complex legal ones?

We here demonstrate that it is the intrinsic and contingent relationship between the newspaper industry, the law and the legal profession, and the public readership that is fundamental to enabling a process of translation and interpretation to best effect. In their explorations of the current scenarios in terms of crime reportage, criminologists such as Barak have suggested that, while crime information can represent some of the 'most potent imagery the media can present', there is always the underlying problem that 'full or incomplete interpretations of reality are not presented'.[16] After all, as Cohen and Young conclude, 'The media do not just transmit neutral information; they present a particular set of images about what the social world *should* be like.'[17] Media representations of crime news have unequivocally shaped public attitudes towards

---

[15]   J. Gerald (1983) *News of Crime. Courts and Press in Conflict* (Westport, CT: Greenwood Press) p. vii.

[16]   G. Barak (ed.) (1994) *Media Process and the Social Construction of Crime* (New York: Garland) p. ix.

[17]   S. Cohen and J. Young (eds) (1981) *The Manufacture of News* (London: Constable) p. 429.

the criminal justice system. But we would argue that the levels of mutual esteem existing between the criminal justice system (including the police), the media process and the public necessarily determines how well informed and educated any particular readership may be about the criminal law and criminal justice matters.

Practicalities and choices

It was necessary to make certain choices of newspaper title, in order to make this volume manageable. The decision was to concentrate throughout on the national titles rather than the provincial or local ones so that a greater consistency of titles used could be maintained across our chronology. *The Times* has thus been a key resource, because it was and is a marker of the way in which the law (including the criminal justice process) has been presented for mass consumption. We advisedly use the term mass consumption here, because, though we agree that it has, in the period we have examined, never been the leading title in terms of circulation figures, it has provided a model copied by others. Indeed, at times even its content has been effectively copied by other papers (particularly provincial ones); further enhancing its value as a source for both historians and lawyers.

By contrast, *The Guardian*, being a more party political title from the start, manifested only minor interest in crime news in the nineteenth and early twentieth centuries, when there was minimal party-inflected debate over crime management. It only developed into a significant title in terms of its law (and consequently its crime) coverage in the last decade of the twentieth century. But, over the last quarter century, it has located itself at the cutting edge of discussions on law and reform, state responsibility and policy, while addressing also the issue of how the law should be properly reported through its sustained campaign to explore the dimensions of phone-hacking within investigative journalism and its impact on the criminal justice system. We have, therefore, made increasing use of that title in the final two chapters. In some ways, its nineteenth-century equivalent in terms of both its challenging attitude to law in action and its willingness to campaign was the *Pall Mall Gazette*, especially when leading Victorian jurist James Fitzjames Stephen and later radical campaigner and journalist W.T. Stead were making important contributions to its law and crime coverage.[18]

---

[18] The merging of the title with *The Globe* in 1921 and its final demise in 1923 ensured it was not substantially used in the twentieth century.

We have also made heavy use of the *Daily Telegraph* from its early days as a daily aimed at a mass working-class audience, and using crime news from the start to attract and keep that audience, something it managed through substantial changes in target audience and political orientation. Another title used consistently, up to its demise in 2011, has been the *News of the World*, as a representative of the Sunday reading market – always directed at a working-class audience, though its sensational coverage of crime (and later other stories) ensured that it got attention from wider audiences. The development of the tabloid newspaper at the end of the century brought three more titles under our scrutiny, in the shape of the *Daily Mail*, *Daily Express* and *Daily Mirror*. The new styles of journalism that these titles promoted had an ongoing radical impact on crime reportage, and, with *The Times*, they became our most regularly used sources for the twentieth-century chapters. But we have also drawn on reports from other titles when there seemed good reason to do so (including particularly extensive coverage of a crime story), such as the *Morning Post* in the nineteenth century and the *Sun* in the twentieth.

Increasingly, it has been important to make a distinction between the 'quality' or broadsheet press and the 'popular' or tabloid press. In the nineteenth century, there was (because of the use of lawyers to produce crime reports) a high degree of homogeneity of approach towards the coverage of crime across all titles, as discussed in Chapters 2 and 3 in particular. This broke down with the development of the so-called New Journalism and the tabloid press. A real distinction appeared between how crime was reported, and the criminal law referred to, in the quality and the popular press. The former was less sensational (and so less emotional) in its coverage of crime and criminality; the latter turned to shorter (and less informative) sentences and fewer column inches, accompanied by large headlines and illustrations to replace text.

In making such judgments, we have drawn heavily on the existing literature on journalism, past and present, particularly in our understanding of the term 'sensationalism' and its implications for how newsprint seeks to make crime news ever more 'unusual' to enhance emotional appeal.[19] Equally, we draw on our own previous work and that of others when using terms such as public opinion or discussing issues such as circulation and readerships.[20] We have, where there was

---

[19] For instance, D. Berry (2008) *Journalism, Ethics and Society* (Aldershot: Ashgate) pp. 24–26.

[20] J. Rowbotham and K. Stevenson (eds) (2005) *Criminal Conversations: Victorians Behaving Badly* (Columbus: Ohio State University Press).

a point to make about how crime news was read and comprehended, provided some comment on newspaper layout, formats and styles, but this has not been our major preoccupation. Nor have we felt it necessary to provide a comprehensive history of journalism throughout the book's chronology, since well-written texts addressing the broad picture are widely available; the same holds true for other areas of law touching on this, including libel law, media law and the 'law of privacy'.[21] While, because of the expansion of investigative journalism, these have all (especially the latter) become increasingly significant to individuals who may also be subject to criminal proceedings for their actions and seek to use the law to protect themselves, we have used contempt of court proceedings to keep our focus on the issue of justice delivery. We have noted the ebbs and flows in the coverage of legislation dealing with crime, however, because that has an important role in estimating levels of crime knowledge in the community, but, again, this is not a history of criminal legislation. Finally, it would have been possible for us to have written a monograph on every chapter in this survey, but we believed it more important to provide an overall perspective to highlight themes that could otherwise have been lost in a series of micro-studies. While aware of the flaws and omissions we have had to make to keep this volume within bounds, we believe that we have managed to provide a useful survey of crime reportage in the modern era; something which can shape a better understanding of how it might develop in the rest of the twenty-first century.

---

[21] For instance, D. Rolph (2008) *Reputation, Celebrity and Libel Law* (Aldershot: Ashgate); T. Crook (2010) *Comparative Media Law and Ethics* (Abingdon: Routledge); R. Wacks (1995) *Privacy and Press Freedom: Rights in Conflict* (Oxford: Blackstone Press); J. Rozenberg (2005) *Privacy and the Press* (Oxford: Oxford University Press).

1
The Beginnings of Crime Intelligence: 1800–1860

'A Lawyer is an honest Employment, so is mine. Like me too he acts in a double Capacity, both against Rogues and for 'em; for 'tis but fitting that we should protect and encourage Cheats, since we live by them.'[1]

Introduction

If modern crime intelligence is constituted by a public audience informed by the media about crime and (at least to an extent) about the legal processes contextualising it, its origins lie within the development, in the sixteenth century, of the printed broadside or broadsheet ballad. These early print productions emerged as powerful cultural factors shaping how crime (particularly murder) was popularly understood within and between communities. While not addressing the legal process directly, they helped establish its importance as the key tool for managing crime and protecting the community.[2] In broadsheet ballads, offenders, once caught, were tried, convicted and suitably punished, and increasingly that punishment was mediated through or at least sanctioned by a formal legal process.[3] However, they made no attempt to portray the legal 'truth' of any criminal proceedings, concentrating only on their outcomes. Yet, for the first time, news of criminal events managed

---

[1] John Gay, *The Beggars Opera* (1728), Act 1, Scene 1.

[2] T. Pettit (2010) 'Journalism vs Tradition in the English Ballads of the Murdered Sweetheart', in P. Fumerton, A. Guerrini, K. McAbee (eds) *Ballads and Broadsides in Britain 1500–1800* (Aldershot: Ashgate) p. 80.

[3] See J. Rowbotham, D. Nash and M. Muravyeva (eds) (2012) *Blame, Shame and Culpability* (Abingdon: Routledge SOLON) in which various chapters explore the connections over time between formal and informal justice punishment strategies.

within a formal legal context could be spread with some uniformity to a mass, if not (strictly speaking) a contiguous, market. Broadsheets narrating crimes which caught the imagination could be copied and recopied; they helped to fuel the demand for more information about criminal activity, which resulted in productions such as the *Newgate Calendar* with its retrospective and moralistic framing of the more sensationalist narratives of crime.[4]

As Malcolm Gaskell has pointed out, it was that narrative (establishing the event and its outcome), rather than the precise details of the actual crime or the role of the law, which was initially important in the creation and reception of such productions. The 'symbolic content' rather than any 'precision of reporting' was what characterised the broadsheet approach to crime reportage.[5] The law was there, but not in detail. This emphasis on the symbolism of a crime is unsurprising given the lingering tradition which conflated crime and sin even into the early nineteenth century.[6] Moral dimensions to offending were managed increasingly by groups such as the Society for the Reformation of Manners, with links to religion but working in secular society by the end of the eighteenth century. The legacy of sin and consequent shame remained central to popular understandings of law-breaking well into the nineteenth century, thanks to the continuing production of these broadsheets.[7]

The quality of the crime intelligence gleaned from broadsheets was limited. Reports of crimes were formulaic to a high degree, repeating the same messages in the context of the different criminal narratives. Their emphasis was on events leading to the scaffold, and the allocation of the respective blame; since the purpose behind broadsheets was to package even moral warnings in an entertaining way, there was no need for precise, informative detail on any particular case. Thus, the legal process was depicted with a broad brush up to the eventual outcome, especially if that involved the scaffold.

The development of the newspaper press from the late eighteenth century into recognisably modern news deliverers took place against

---

[4] For a flavour of the criminal biographies of this type, see P. Rawlings (1992) *Drunks, Whores and Idle Apprentices* (Abingdon: Routledge).

[5] M. Gaskell (2000) *Crime and Mentalities in Early Modern England* (Cambridge University Press) p. 214.

[6] P. Friedland (2012) *Seeing Justice Done. The Age of Spectacular Capital Punishment in France* (Oxford University Press).

[7] For further comment on shame, see Rowbotham, Muravyeva and Nash, *Shame, Blame and Culpability*; D. Nash and A.M. Kilday (2010) *Cultures of Shame. Exploring Crime and Morality in Britain 1600–1900* (Basingstoke: Palgrave Macmillan).

the background of this broadsheet ballad provision. Initially, titles were mainly local or provincial, though a few began to acquire a national importance amongst the emerging middle and established upper classes, notably *The Times* and the *Morning Post*. But, whether national or regional, the importance of the newspaper press was that it provided increasing scope for innovative ways of reporting crime at length, providing detail that was impossible in the broadsheet format and a different emphasis from the *Newgate Calendar* with its greater immediacy. Crime was a regular feature in most titles. Coming at a time when the adversarial criminal trial format was prioritising the role of the lawyer, the growing audiences for newspapers rapidly created a demand for crime intelligence, enabling a consequent growing popular interest in the trial process. For both editors and proprietors, a single trial involving a sensational crime offered much greater scope than the intrinsically shorter scaffold event. It might last more than a day at the Assizes (an execution, with all the preliminaries and aftermath, rarely occasioned more than a morning or afternoon), whereas even a sitting of the summary courts could provide several items likely to entertain and engage readers. Broadsheets remained a popular resource for mass reading up to the middle of the century, but the growing importance of newspapers as a source of crime news by the late 1820s is effectively illustrated by the coverage of the famed Red Barn murder: an event which caught the national imagination, resulting in substantial coverage in local and national titles from the first reports of the discovery of the body to the eventual execution of the perpetrator.

Murder always commanded interest. Like many other titles in April 1828, the *Morning Post* announced to its readers the discovery of a 'Horrid Murder'.[8] The body of Maria Marten was found buried in the Red Barn (a local landmark), reportedly after she had appeared in a series of dreams to her stepmother indicating that she had been murdered instead of running away with her lover, and obvious suspect, William Corder. After his arrest, following the opening of the inquest in Bury St Edmunds, Suffolk, newspapers continued to speculate on his character and liability well into May, highlighting in lengthy news items the numbers making journeys, from as far afield as London, to view the Red Barn.[9] Corder's trial at the Summer Assize in August (though the result was generally advised in the press as being a forgone conclusion) was also covered

---

[8] 'Horrid Murder', *Morning Post*, 24 April 1828.

[9] See, for instance, *Ipswich Journal*, 17 May 1828; 'The Red Barn at Polstead', *Morning Post*, 1 August 1828.

in detail by national as well as provincial titles throughout the United Kingdom (including Ireland).[10] In addition, an execution broadsheet, which according to sources such as Mayhew was highly popular, sold 1.65 million copies. All of this indicates that, for a variety of reasons, this was a crime narrative which caught the imagination of all classes, high and low, regardless of location. But a comparison with the information in the single-side newssheets is telling; it was the newspapers that provided the most titillating detail, which was subsequently absorbed into popular melodrama, performed well into the twentieth century. It was the newspaper coverage *before* the execution that attracted around 10,000 spectators to travel to witness Corder's execution. Equally, after the trial, it was only in the newspapers that the extensive details of Corder's eventual confession were to be found, courtesy of the eccentric but respected Old Bailey reporter James Curtis, reporting for *The Times* on this occasion.[11]

The demise of the old broadsheets

The principle that dissemination of crime intelligence in the form of print productions was fundamentally a matter of public interest was already firmly embedded in the popular and the political psyche by the 1830s, thanks to the increasing literacy of the British reading public.[12] The newspaper coverage of this high-profile event demonstrated the potential of the press to take over from broadsheets as the favoured form of communicating detailed crime intelligence. Corder himself described the press as a 'powerful engine for fixing the opinions of large classes of the community'.[13] Fatefully, another 'Horrible Murder', perpetrated in November 1828 just seven miles away from Polstead, where a 10-year-old

---

[10] See 'Trial of Corder', *The Times*, 12 August 1828; 'The Polstead Murder', *The Hull Packet and Humber Mercury*, 12 August 1828; 'Suffolk Assizes', *Derby Mercury*, 13 August 1828; 'Confession and Execution of Corder', *Belfast Newsletter*, 19 August 1828. See also J. Rowbotham, 'The Shifting Nature of Blame. Revisiting Issues of Blame, Shame and Culpability in the English Criminal Justice System', in Rowbotham, Muravyeva and Nash (eds) *Shame, Blame and Culpability* pp. 63–79.

[11] Later published in book form. See J. Curtis (1834) *An Authentic and Faithful History of the Mysterious Murder of Maria Marten: With a Full Development of All the Extraordinary Circumstances which Led to the Discovery of Her Body in the Red Barn; to which is Added, the Trial of William Corder, Taken at Large in Short Hand Specially for this Work* (London: T. Kelly).

[12] D. Mitch (1992) *The Rise of Popular Literacy in Victorian England* (University of Pennsylvania Press).

[13] 'Summer Assizes', *The Times*, 9 August 1828.

boy was found in a field with his throat cut, led the Coroner to observe: 'if doubts ever arise as to the policy of publishing the proceedings of coroners' inquests, the impolicy of doing so was clearly manifest'.[14] However, this reality, particularly for political and social elites, was also a matter of concern. The expanding ability to read enabled the masses to engage not only with texts which were considered desirable for them, promoting social conformity and cohesion, but also ones which challenged the *status quo*. At the end of the eighteenth and the beginning of the nineteenth century, when the emerging Evangelical revival was seeking to make the masses 'respectable' by boosting their moral consciousness, figures like Mrs Hannah More feared the impact of traditional popular literature, such as broadsheets and chapbooks, often with their bluntly worded and sensationally described crimes and bad behaviour. Of even more concern to such figures, though, were the politically radical productions of that period, from writers and journalists such as Thomas Paine and his populariser, Daniel Eaton, and William Cobbett.

Mrs Hannah More's enterprise in publishing the Cheap Repository Tracts was intended to counter the effects on the masses of such unfortunate reading matter.[15] While she achieved considerable success in supplanting chapbooks, broadsheets and radical journalism were little touched by this and similar exercises, as the publishing enterprises associated with Chartism underline.[16] It was the greater detail of sensational crime that newspapers contained that brought about the eventual demise of broadsheets, as the affection of figures like Sam Weller for the papers, and the police reports in them, in Dickens' *Pickwick Papers* indicates.[17] But, as the satirical comment in *Pickwick Papers* suggests, this was by no means an improvement from the point of view of the concerned respectable classes of the 1830s and 1840s; especially given the challenge to both the established provincial press and the mainstream nationals provided in the shape of the growth of Chartist newspapers during that period. The *Northern Star*, for example, was a commercial enterprise comparable to mainstream newspapers such as *The Times*. While, as the title suggests, it had the profile of a provincial paper, it had a much wider circulation than most such papers. It was, of course, primarily

---

[14] 'Horrible Murder', *The Times*, 10 November 1828.
[15] A. Stott (2004) *Hannah More: The First Victorian* (Oxford University Press) pp. 169–177.
[16] Ibid.
[17] See C. Dickens (1838) *The Posthumous Papers of the Pickwick Club* (London: Chapman and Hall) especially ch. xlv.

concerned with providing a diet of political news with a radical edge, but, ominously, it was a title which also devoted real space to crime reportage and comment on the law, presenting the same challenge to the established system.

For instance, the *Northern Star* announced: 'Dewsbury riot created by the Government, through the medium of their tools "Justice" Ingham and Police Magistrate Greenwood'. Under this headline were powerfully inflammatory statements against the recently amended Poor Law, the Government and the 'bad law' produced by men like Ingham and Greenwood.[18] In 1840 the *Chartist Circular* challenged government policy and the criminal justice system as a whole, arguing that laws needed to be 'as simple and as few as may be; for an extensive and obscure code multiplies occasions of offence and brings the citizen unnecessarily into collision with the state'. It insisted that 'Arbitrary and oppressive laws invite offence and take from disobedience the consciousness of guilt.' The column pointed to the hypocrisy of the difference in treatment by the criminal justice system of the petty thief and the socially respectable but 'criminally' insolvent debtor; and allocated responsibility for the majority of crime to governmental neglect.[19] The *Northern Star* was even more vehement and direct in its attack on the 'wanton injustice' perpetrated by magistrates in Halifax for sentencing a destitute lad to a month's imprisonment simply (according to its interpretation) for the unfortunate 'crime' of poverty.[20] According to the same title, the Government pursued 'a system which made the people poor – then vicious. "Crime" is the result'. The accusation was that there was no will to remedy the system because it gave employment to 'Judges, Sheriffs, Criers, Barristers, Lawyers ... and all the other machinery relating to crime'. It would have to be a 'consolation' to the poor to know that 'it finds "good work" and comfortable livings for a vast number of people who would otherwise have to handle a spade or attend upon the loom'.[21] Excoriating newspaper reportage like this was bolstered by other Chartist productions, such as G.W.R. Reynolds with his highly sensational and enormously popular serial, *Mysteries of the Courts of London*, with its depiction of corrupt law courts and duplicitous officials where the main 'mystery' was the strategies

---

[18] *Northern Star and Leeds General Advertiser*, 18 August 1838. The Dewsbury Riot was an anti-Poor Law protest.

[19] Channing, 'Punishment and Prevention of Crime', *Chartist Circular*, 11 January 1840.

[20] 'Poverty Punished as a Crime', *Northern Star and Leeds General Advertiser*, 16 May 1840.

[21] 'Cost of "Crime" ', *Northern Star and Leeds General Advertiser*, 11 December 1841.

used by the upper classes and the legal profession in a collusion aiming to destroy the morality and innocence of honest working-class men and women, bringing them to doom and misery.[22]

Not only were the legal profession, as well as other establishment figures, attacked by this arm of the popular press; they were themselves concerned about the coverage of crime and law in even the mainstream, less radical, national press. As *The Times* reported in 1828, the newspaper coverage surrounding Corder from the time of his arrest was, according to Lord Chief Justice Cockburn, to 'the manifest detriment of the prisoner at the bar' and thoroughly 'unjust'. Corder had first brought up the debatable impact of newspaper coverage when he had entreated that the jury dismissed from their minds the 'publications of the public press from the first hour of its promulgation to this hour'.[23] In the same edition of *The Times* which included Corder's final confession and execution, there were also a number of reports from the London police courts. These reports covered a dispute concerning an application for a licence, included because it related to new legislation, but making it difficult to get a sense of the law contextualising the dispute, as the focus is on the personalities of the interchange between the disputants and the magistrate. The reason for inclusion reads more as a condemnation of the way in which the law managed disputes than anything else.[24] That approach, with or without an accompanying 'human interest' dimension, was typical of the treatment of cases from both the summary and the higher courts in the early 1830s. Where some detailed coverage of the actual progress of the case was provided it was often, as in the coverage of the prosecution for keeping an illegal gaming house at the Middlesex Quarter Sessions in January 1833, incoherent, unnecessarily lengthy and lacking in sense.[25]

At a time when the proprietors and editors of a burgeoning national press needed, in order to provide a 'respectable' character for their titles, to expand their readership, the legal profession was becoming increasingly conscious of its own poor reputation and the extent to which that was fostered in the press. One correspondent to the *Morning Chronicle* reflected that the magistracy, for instance, was, 'like all public functionaries', much better for 'the surveillance of the press'.[26] Thus, a key

---

[22] G.W.R. Reynolds (1856) *Mysteries of the Courts of London* (London: John Dicks). This was published in serial form between 1848 and 1856.

[23] 'Summer Assizes', *The Times*, 9 August 1828.

[24] 'Police', *The Times*, 11 August 1828.

[25] 'Middlesex Intermediate Sessions', *The Times*, 1 January 1833.

[26] 'Repression of Crime', Letter to the Editor from T.B., 22 May, *Morning Chronicle*, 26 May 1840.

element in the process of restoring the public, or popular, reputation of the justice process and the legal profession was necessarily their rehabilitation in that medium. Increasingly, as a result of initiatives by editors and consent from the legal profession, that involved the direct participation of lawyers in the production of text. This enabled the establishment of a new, more detailed or forensic (which might also be described as a more professional) approach to presentations of crime and the criminal justice process in the media, starting with national titles such as *The Times*. For example, by the late 1830s, its coverage of legal issues increasingly became more informed and informative.

One consequent development was a popular acceptance of a separation between the presentations of the information (the news-gathering aspects) from the opinion piece, in the interests of creating a fact-based 'truthful' (in the legal and the everyday sense) criminal narrative as it was played out in the courtroom. By the early to mid-1850s, reporters and journalists were becoming established as separate occupations. Generally, mid-Victorian journalism did not involve news-gathering, leaving that to the less well-paid reporters.[27] In the hierarchy of the day, journalists ranked higher than reporters, since the process of opinion-giving was linked to the self-advertised role of the press of helping to form a unified public opinion about a whole range of matters in the public domain. Conboy refers to this 'normative integration' as the remedy for a dangerous radicalism, threatening to both the state and the rule of law.[28] The old style of newspaper journalist, the so-called penny-a-liner (effectively freelance writers paid quite literally by the line),[29] was being dispensed with by modernising newspaper editors and proprietors. It was in the provision of crime intelligence that editors sought particularly to avoid using the penny-a-liners. This enabled the increasing focus of public interest, events *in* the courtroom (rather than on the outcomes of a trial, particularly executions), to be accurately reported. As Michael Wolff has pointed out, during the mid-nineteenth century, journalism became 'the most important vehicle in the information of

---

[27] See J. Rowbotham and K. Stevenson (2002) 'Causing a Sensation: Media and Legal Representations of Bad Behaviour', in (same eds) *Behaving Badly: Visible Crime, Social Panics and Legal Responses – Victorian and Modern Parallels* (Aldershot: Ashgate) pp. 31–46; L. Brown (1985) *Victorian News and Newspapers* (Oxford: Clarendon Press).

[28] See M. Conboy (2002) *The Press and Popular Culture* (London: Sage).

[29] According to James Grant, their pay per line in London at least had risen to 'three half-pennies' per line by 1837. J. Grant (1837) *The Great Metropolis* (London: Saunders and Otley).

public opinion', providing a channel for both information and opinion. Wolff has commented on the ways in which, through journalism, 'the urban population' was able 'to influence events' and to 'articulate their developing group and class consciousness', adding that there was 'a need and hunger for greater communication at pretty well all social levels and among and within pretty well all cultural groups'.[30]

The introduction of legal specialism in newspaper reportage

An understanding of the significance of a legal specialism in reportage from the courts in the mid-Victorian period requires some comprehension not just of the preceding history of the press but also of the law, and the reputation of the legal profession. It was not only political radicals like Chartists who provided critical commentary on the criminal justice system. Charles Dickens, for instance, in works from *Oliver Twist* (1838) to *Bleak House* (1853), delivered excoriating detail of the negativities he associated with the criminal law. Such narratives did little to enhance the reputation of a legal system still reforming itself, and of legal professionals seeking to establish themselves as respectable and honest members of society.

What had underpinned the high degree of public disaffection with the criminal justice process had been the impacts associated with the operation of the Bloody Code during the eighteenth and early nineteenth century. With its dismantling, and the move towards a greater emphasis on the summary courts at a time when there was increasing distaste amongst the 'respectable' classes for the execution spectacle, the model provided by the Chartist press of a focus on those summary courts offered a new approach to crime reportage for the mainstream national press. Previously, what reportage there had been from the courts had focused on events in the higher courts or Assizes. But there was a realisation by mainstream editors, and by the legal profession, that the reportage of activities in the magistrates' courts in radical titles like the *Northern Star* was popular with that readership.[31] Thus, it made sense to capitalise on that appeal within the mainstream press, especially given

---

[30] M. Wolff (1979) 'Urbanity and Journalism. The Victorian Connection. H.J. Dyos Memorial Lecture', (Leicester: Victorian Studies Centre) p. 8.

[31] J. Allen and O. Ashton (eds) (2005) *Papers for the People: A Study of the Chartist Press*, (London: Merlin Press); G. Geis (1961) 'Preliminary Hearings and the Press', *UCLA Law Review*, 8, 397–414.

that, after the enactment of the Jervis Acts 1848, over 90 per cent of all offences were concluded at the summary level.

This prospect for a fresh approach to the content and style of crime narratives came at a time when scaffold events were being reduced dramatically. Between 1828 and 1837 executions fell permanently to significantly under 100 a year in England and Wales; and, from 1838, the numbers fell to under 20 per annum. There was, thus, not even a weekly execution to focus on; nor were lesser punishment events such as public whippings or putting individuals in the pillory or stocks available for reportage either.[32] This aided a new will to concentrate on events in the courtroom, where the development of adversarial practices and the increased use of counsel for defence and prosecution had made even the summary courts more exciting to witness and report. All of this confirmed the emphatic shift in focus for crime reportage to events in the courtroom; something accompanied by a shift from floridly written and frequently inaccurate sensationalist reportage to an emphasis on legal accuracy, acting as a new frame for a continuing sensationalism. This new style of reportage sought to maintain the excitement associated with the criminal justice process while enhancing the public image of the rule of law and of lawyers themselves: reflecting changes not just to the criminal justice process itself but also to the practices and standards of the legal profession.[33]

Yet it was by no means predictable that lawyers should have become so intimately involved in the production of newspaper crime intelligence. The majority of the first reporters for crime stories, as for other stories in the press, had been the penny-a-liners. This practice had proved damaging to the reputation of the legal process and lawyers, and undermined the ability of the press to deliver factually accurate news about crime. For example James Grant, in 1837, recounted how James Perry, proprietor of the *Morning Chronicle*, had been fooled by one penny-a-liner into publishing an entirely false, but very long and so very profitable, account of a 'most horrible murder', which had caused a local and totally unfounded panic.[34] The penny-a-liners were regularly inclined to launch into thunderous declamations against both individual

---

[32] G. Smith (1996) 'Civilized People Don't Want to See That Kind of Thing: The Decline of Physical Punishment in London 1760–1840', in C. Strange (ed.) *Qualities of Mercy. Justice, Punishment and Discretion* (Vancouver: University of British Columbia Press) pp. 21–50.

[33] A. May (2003) *The Bar and the Old Bailey, 1750–1850* (Chapel Hill: University of North Carolina Press).

[34] Grant, *The Great Metropolis*.

lawyers and the injustice of the legal process. From the perspective of consumers, such condemnation was not without justification. The press revealed, in its coverage of the Courvoisier trial in 1840, that the leading defence barrister Charles Phillips had known of his client's guilt but had continued to defend him. This was greeted with public outrage, largely aimed at the legal profession, in the light of this unexpected consequence of the Prisoners' Counsel Act 1836.[35] However, the regularly hostile rhetoric of the penny-a-liners was additionally shaped by a desire for financial profit (lengthy condemnations of barristers, judges or magistrates were anticipated stylistic flourishes), and partly because the majority of them were working-class men, often with radical inclinations.[36] Drawing an analogy with Gresham's Law, the result was, as Grant put it, that where the bad worked side by side with the good, the effect was to drive out the good.[37]

The conscientiousness with which the mid-Victorian generation of newspaper editors believed in the moral dimension of their mission to provide their ever-increasing readership with the 'right' kind of information must not be underestimated. One reason for this was that such editors were increasingly members of respectable society themselves, and, if not, they were increasingly reliant on commercial backing from middle-class entrepreneurs.[38] The costs involved in buying into new, but expensive, technological advances such as the steam press meant that titles had, for the first time, to be sure of appealing to a mass circulation within society; they could not afford even a temporary drop in circulation that might result from a reputation for poor or inaccurate reportage.[39] Undoubtedly the advent of the steam press in the 1840s and 1850s was the basis of a greater general accessibility of periodicals and literature, and confirmed the decline of the broadsheet, thanks partly to clearer type-faces and better typesetting techniques, which made it

---

[35] May, *Bar and Old Bailey.*

[36] L. James (1974) *Fiction for the Working Man 1830–1850* (Harmondsworth: Penguin).

[37] See Grant, *Great Metropolis.* Sir Thomas Gresham argued that, where good coinage and bad coinage existed together, the principle was that the bad would always taint the good.

[38] F.M.L. Thompson has pointed out that 'respectability' as a concept was a unifying factor that transcended class boundaries; the respectable working class had more in common with the respectable middle and upper classes than they did with the *un*-respectable working classes; see Thompson (1987) *The Rise of Respectable Society 1830–1900* (London: Fontana).

[39] The example of the failure of Colonel Sleigh, the first proprietor of the *Daily Telegraph*, was a warning, for instance.

worth the extra outlay for these new productions. Given that crime was one of the staple attractions of newspaper and broadsheet formats, editors swiftly looked to improve the quality, at least factually, a development aided by the reality that, by the 1840s, the possible profits and clear potential for shaping opinion had encouraged a number of legal professionals to become proprietors or editors of provincial titles.

The earnings of John Forster (barrister and writer) perceptibly increased in 1830 when he undertook an amount of 'fugitive literary work'.[40] Such experience was clearly advantageous, helping him secure the editorship of *The Examiner* in 1846 and an approach to take over Dickens' chair at the *Daily News*. Further examples include Lord Brougham, who was founder and chief editor of the hugely influential and respected *Edinburgh Review*,[41] and Lord Brampton, who with William Torrens, who also edited *The Examiner*. As a consequence of this new 'respectability' of the press, and some titles like *The Times* at least, the attitudes of legal professionals towards the newspaper industry began to shift away from a traditional resentment and distrust and towards an increasingly enthusiastic collaboration. It was barristers, rather than solicitors, who took the lead in writing for the everyday, rather than the professional, press, partly because of their access to greater opportunities in the courts.

With more Victorians than ever reading about the 'actual' truth of police news and court cases in both fiction and press accounts, the desire of the legal profession to change popular attitudes towards the criminal justice system found an appropriate outlet in the reshaping of crime reportage. This involved not only an emphasis on events within the courts but (through leaders and opinion columns) education about the ongoing reform of the legal process. Public fears about corruption, professionalism and the expense of going to court vied with respect for and trust in the specialist expertise of some qualified lawyers. One of the earliest law reformers was Lord Brougham, whose earnest dedication to improving the practical and moral education of young men in particular, as well as in reforming his own profession, was very apparent throughout the late 1830s, and well into the 1850s.

Men like Brougham had been pioneers in the use of popular printed messages to inform the public about the 'reality' of the law and the legal process. As early as 1839, an anonymous 'Student at Law' (who very

---

[40] R. Renton (1912) *John Forster and His Friendships* (London: Chapman and Hall).
[41] Founded in 1802 by Francis Jeffrey, Sydney Smith and Henry Brougham, published until 1929. Brougham was also a writer on the *Morning Chronicle*.

possibly went on to become a well-known lawyer of repute) had been convinced by Brougham and wrote a pamphlet for his fellow lawyers promoting the potential educational powers of the press. In *The Fourth Estate: or the Moral Influence of the Press*, he exhorted the public to respect the press and to be indebted to the newspapers for the knowledge and sense of moral duty they promote. In his view, the papers could teach the law to the public better than 'even Lord Brougham himself'. He argued that the press in many respects was a popular parliament, testing and informing public opinion on legislative proposals, as well as a popular court of justice, commenting upon all questions of public conduct and private and public morals, and thereby exerting a significant influence.[42]

With advice such as this, it is hardly surprising to find that judges, barristers and stipendiary magistrates began to agree that they could use the power of the press to draw public attention to a vast array of legal issues and topics. These ranged from the highly academic and technical to the more straightforward and accessible; from the esoteric and philosophical to the moral and ethical; from treatises and essays to tracts and pamphlets. Above all, though, it gave an opportunity to draw attention to the increasingly professional legal content. Why, then, has this been overlooked by historians of the press and legal historians generally? Certainly, historians of the press have not appreciated the growing legal sophistication of reportage from the courts from the last half of the nineteenth century, while legal historians have tended to look to more traditional sources in their histories of nineteenth-century criminal law. Equally, while many crime historians have used the press, they have not focused on the wider legal dimensions to the reportage, including how and why it was generated, and why it was so different from earlier reportage.

A major reason for this is the evidential obscurity provided by the tradition of anonymous reportage and journalistic comment, which was the normal practice of the day, now surviving only in leader or editorial comment. This disguised the intimate involvement of lawyers in the writing of crime reports from the courts, both at the time and from subsequent scholarship. It has, at times, been possible to recognise the authors of legal journalism, but identifying which legal reporter generated specific pieces of court reportage will always be guesswork. As highlighted already, it is important to realise that in the mid-century a clear distinction was made between 'reporters' and 'journalists'. Reporters were those who literally reported news. They were the men who gleaned the information

---

[42] A Student at Law (1839) *The Fourth Estate: or the Moral Influence of the Press* (London: Ridgeway) pp. 9–12.

and transcribed it. In terms of legal reporting, 'reporters' typically meant the men who sat in the law courts on a daily basis and recorded events to provide a legally accurate 'true crime' narrative. Journalists were writers with a wider mission, being the men who reflected on issues and stories, and commented on them. Most also had a better reputation than the penny-a-line reporters, partly because they were better educated and came from better social backgrounds. Henry Mayhew, for instance, was the son of a lawyer who started training in law himself until he abandoned it for journalism. Charles Dickens also was a journalist before becoming a famous author. Indeed, there was a long-standing cross-over between journalism and law. One of the most important and influential groups of the early journalists were legal professionals first and journalists second, as in the case of James Fitzjames Stephen, the great Victorian jurist.

For editors and proprietors, then, reliance on lawyers as reporters in the magistrates' courts was firmly established as a successful and attractive policy by the end of the 1850s.[43] It was also a feasible use of lawyers, because it was an age when more and more cases, even in the summary courts, were featuring the use of counsel, especially for the prosecution but also increasingly for the defence (particularly if there was a charge of assault with a sexual dimension!). There were also many more barristers; by the mid-century the profession was undoubtedly overcrowded.[44] Of course, particularly in the provinces, the penny-a-liners continued reporting as well as providing the initial crime news narrative, but by the end of the 1850s there was a growing recognition of the need for legal reporters in the courts, even by the legal profession. The *Law Times*, for instance, pointed out (when commenting on the Road murder case in 1860: the last nationally notorious case where penny-a-liners wrote contributions, but only for the provincial readership) that, when 'notorious cases' occurred, reporters would always set to work 'to obtain all the information they can obtain, good, bad and indifferent'. But for 'a man of no special legal training...to comment upon the preliminary investigation', and later 'to assess and review the decision of the Queen's judges' was something which was, 'offensive and improper'.[45] Such reaction from within the profession helps to explain its acceptance of this expansion of a 'specialist' genre of legal reporting and journalism,

---

[43] Rowbotham and Stevenson, 'Causing a Sensation', pp. 31–33.

[44] J. Lewis (1982) *The Victorian Bar* (London: Robert Hale) p. 39.

[45] This was an initially unsolved murder, finally resolved by the 1865 confession of Constance Kent to the murder of her half-brother. See N. Kyle (2009) *A Greater Guilt. Constance Emilie Kent and the Road Murder* (Salisbury: Boolarong Press).

undertaken by 'qualified' men.[46] Lawyers could be trusted to comprehend the nuances involved in preparing material of acute public interest
which avoided overstepping the mark of legal propriety. In this, the
established tradition of journalistic anonymity, covering also the work
of the reporters, was seen as an indispensable asset.

Undoubtedly because of the number of legal professionals who were in
positions of power as owners and editors, they were increasingly identified as the preferred choice of reporter in the courts at all levels, from the
middle of the century on. Indeed, the first editor of the *Pall Mall Gazette*,
Frederick Greenwood, reportedly kept a 'keen lookout' for promising
talent in the Inns of Court, recruiting men like Robert Campbell, the
Chancery barrister, to his ranks.[47] When such men went looking for
qualified lawyers they found it easy to recruit: something which was to
hold true for the rest of the century.[48]

The Victorian legal profession was never to be one for those without
means or the ability to generate means. The expenses of practice were
considerable, and even those who had the necessary wherewithal could
expect to spend a number of years in penury, a truth which endured
well into the twentieth century. The coincidence of demand and supply
meant that more barristers were prepared to attend on a regular basis
that apparently humble venue, the magistrates' courts (especially those
presided by a stipendiary magistrate)[49] in order to learn their trade
and pick up work, where they could also hope to earn an amount by
reporting interesting cases for the newspapers.

Refreshing the legal stereotype

While there was a clear mutual interest between editors, legal journalists and reporters, relations in these early stages were not always cordial.

---

[46] *Law Times*, reported in *County Courts Chronicle*, 1 August 1861, pp. 210–211.

[47] T. Escott (1911) *Masters of English Journalism. A Study of Personal Forces*
(London: T Fisher Unwin) pp. 246–247. While the *Pall Mall Gazette* started publication in the 1860s, this point is relevant to this chapter.

[48] A. Baker (c.1888) *Pitmans Practical Journalism, an Introduction to Every
Description of Literary Effort in Association with Newspaper Production, with Notes
on Newspaper Law by Edward A Cope* (London: Pitman & Sons) p. 45. See also
L. Brake (1988) 'The Old Journalism and the New: Forms of Cultural Production
in London in the 1880s', in Wiener (ed.) *Papers for the Millions*, p. 20.

[49] Stipendiary magistrates were themselves qualified lawyers, and were paid to
sit regularly in the summary courts; they were a particular feature of urban areas
like London.

From the point of view of a legal profession in the 1840s and early 1850s, still seeking to define its proper role within the criminal justice process,[50] there was a real potential for a conflict of interests when it came to closer relations with the press. The long-standing habit of press critique of the legal profession was one contributory factor, which it was not yet willing to forfeit in exchange for the more individual attacks which later came to characterise legal journalism. For instance, during the highly charged and controversial process of the reformation of the Bar during the 1850s, *The Times* had few positive things to say about lawyers and was highly critical: 'its attacks had a savage intensity which make today's criticisms of the Bar look very mild indeed'.[51]

It has to be admitted that the public stereotype of the traditional barrister, especially after passage of the Prisoners' Counsel Act 1836, had remained largely negative. In its aftermath, barristers were regarded not just as corrupt hacks but also as figures unjustifiably profiting from the public purse.[52] The trial of Courvoisier in 1840 for the murder of his employer Lord William Russell had not helped the reputation of barristers. It was not just that his counsel, Charles Phillips, had continued to defend Courvoisier despite knowing of his guilt; it was more the strenuous efforts made by Phillips to throw responsibility for the crime upon the housemaid or the police in a powerful concluding speech to the jury.[53] It was this which made the subsequent revelation of Phillips' awareness of his client's guilt so shocking to public opinion, as comment in, and letters to, the press underlines. It highlighted the issue of professional morality and responsibility: was this an individual breach of judgment, or was the profession as a whole morally tainted, so that the Courvoisier trial had simply revealed an ongoing reality?[54] Many journalists of the day took the latter view, and, consequently, barristers were even more

---

[50] A point made by May, *Bar and Old Bailey*, as well as by J. Langbein (2003) *The Origins of Adversary Criminal Trial* (Oxford University Press) and D. Cairns (1998) *Advocacy and the Making of the Adversarial Criminal Trial, 1800–1865* (Oxford University Press).

[51] R. Cocks (1983) *Foundations of the Modern Bar* (London: Sweet and Maxwell) pp. 88–90.

[52] See, for instance, Cocks, *Modern Bar*; also D. Bentley (1998) *English Criminal Justice in the Nineteenth Century* (London: Hambledon Press).

[53] J. Hostettler (2006) *Fighting for Justice. The History and Origins of the Adversary Trial* (Winchester: Waterside Press)

[54] 'The Political Examiner', *The Examiner*, 28 June 1840. See also 'The Licence of Counsel', Manlius, Letter to the Editor, *Morning Chronicle*, 22 June 1840; 'Licence of Counsel', A Templar, Letter to the Editor, *Morning Chronicle*, 25 June 1840; 'From One of the Profession', Letter to the Editor, *The Times*, 25 June 1840.

frequently the butt of condemnatory jokes and caricatures, particularly in newspapers and periodicals, whether aimed at the well-educated or the more popular reading classes. Echoing Reynolds' satirical depictions of legal figures in *Mysteries of the Courts of London*, for instance, were savage characterisations in *Punch* from the start of its publication in 1841, and into the 1850s. *Punch* featured not only the bitingly satirical 'Comic Blackstone' (from 1843) but also the figure 'Mr Briefless' (from 1841). Interestingly, Gilbert á Beckett, the creator of both of these, was himself a lawyer and later a police magistrate, and an ardent supporter of the reform of the Bar in this period.[55]

In the latter half of the 1850s, however, and after various vicissitudes, there was finally a greater concordance between the legal profession and the press, due mainly to the changing attitudes of judges and magistrates (driven particularly by older reformers and newcomers to the Bench, and a new breed of police magistrate) towards the practice of advocacy in the courtroom and its public coverage.[56] The basis for this was the gradual acceptance by both the legal profession and 'respectable' newspaper editors and proprietors of the parameters of what constituted a 'fair trial' (effectively, the modern adversarial version). For many lawyers, the continuing discussion concerning Charles Phillips' strategy did raise issues about their own conduct, but it highlighted even more strongly the negative coverage of their profession in the press. Where should the line be drawn between full coverage of all material that might be of interest to a reading public, and comment on the requirements of a 'fair trial' in terms of policies to be pursued by prosecution and defence in the courts?[57] With the development of a new consensus between the proprietors and editors and the legal profession that it was in the public interest to support the rule of law, the use of lawyers to write about themselves and their work became a more credible enterprise. The establishment of lawyers as reporters or journalists promoted a more constructive attitude, which still allowed opportunities for individual attacks on unpopular or incompetent lawyers provided by anonymous

---

[55] M. Spielman (1897) *The History of 'Punch'* (London: Cassell and Co.). The character of Mr Briefless was regularly revived in ways that, as later chapters will reveal, show how public attitudes towards lawyers and the criminal law changed over the latter half of the century.

[56] May, *Bar and Old Bailey*, Conclusion.

[57] A retrospective of the debate formed part of Phillips' obituary: see 'The Death of Mr Commissioner Phillips', *The Standard*, 3 February 1859. See also Rowbotham and Stevenson, 'Causing a Sensation', p. 43; May, *Bar and Old Bailey*, pp. 176–190.

reportage of events in the courts while promoting a vision of a generally competent criminal justice process, especially within the courtroom.

However, it is important to realise that it was not all positive when it came to publicly presenting legal individuals. A willingness to attack certain individuals was good for sensationalism, and so reputations could be as easily broken as made by the media. The danger of such infighting was that the public anonymity of such reportage was less than secret within legal circles. Effectively, 'The Press' was now controlled by a very small group, and, if you knew who owned a particular title, you knew what to expect of it and who worked for it. Barrister E.F. Pigott, though little known or remembered now, was, nevertheless, an extremely well-connected and influential member of this group, founding *The Leader*, the forerunner of the influential *Saturday Review*. Sir John Campbell, the Attorney General, reported for the *Morning Chronicle* when edited by Mr Serjeant Spankie, and Farrer Herschell was also a reporter for a short time on *The New Reports*. Theodore Hook, editor of the distinctly conservative *John Bull* newspaper, was a close friend of that skilful manipulator of juries, Serjeant Ballantine. Many legal reporters were conscious of their future careers and might wish to curry favour or destroy perceived competitors. Lord Brougham often found favour with the press for being in touch with the groundswell of public opinion, but others were less popular. Lords Westbury and Lyndhurst, active political lawyers, clearly did not endear themselves to *The Spectator*'s lawyer–journalists, for example. An 1864 byline ('Lord Westbury's "saponaceous" Side') headlined a diatribe against his 'unctuousness' and capacity 'for exuding at pleasure a certain tone and temper of feeling at all pores, secreting it from minute glands all over the surface of his conversation'.[58] A later critique compared the relative merits of the intellectual capacity of Lord Brougham and the late Lord Lyndhurst, acidly asserting that 'We purposefully choose the comparison in intellect with Lord Lyndhurst because we do *not* admire Lord Lyndhurst's career. Lord Brougham's ambition has been far more useful to the world than Lord Lyndhurst's.'[59] The extent to which this represented a high degree of infighting within the legal profession is indicated by Lyndhurst's obituary in *The Times* in 1863, which proffered a very different opinion

---

[58] *The Spectator*, 23 July 1864 p. 843.
[59] *The Spectator*, 1 October 1864 p. 1120. Lyndhurst was three times Lord Chancellor and made many enemies – though Brougham became an ally of his in the 1840s. Lyndhurst had supported Jewish emancipation and improving women's rights to divorce.

of his contribution to the world, concluding that 'No man was more free from corrupt notions or acted more independently of sordid influences. A great, free and clear spirit.'[60]

This involvement of legal professionals as journalists was undoubtedly the main basis for the rehabilitation of the profession that marked the crime reportage of the rest of the century. The traditional anonymity of writing for press and journals disguised the self-interested nature of this promotion, and modified any possible public disquiet about too intimate a relationship between the legal profession and the press. Indeed, the tradition of unattributed authorship in newspapers was identified by those within it as 'the true secret of its power, for it may be observed that the less we know of the writers of a paper, the more powerful or influential is the paper'.[61] Using that anonymity, legal professionals took an active role in seeking to educate the public about the 'science' of law, promoting an understanding of the legal process. They used popular fascination with real crimes to actively engage with the man on the street, advising him on how to behave and react towards the law, and what to expect from it. By puffing the comments of individual judges and barristers, they could draw public attention to an extensive array of legal issues and topics.[62] For example, Stephen was ready to assume a responsibility, through his anonymous contributions to organs such as the later publication the *Pall Mall Gazette*, for promoting a positive image of legal *professionals*, even though, as a law reformer in outlook, he regularly criticised aspects of the current English legal process.

Establishing the relationship

There is clear evidence that, despite anonymity, numbers of the older members of the legal profession were initially somewhat uneasy about the increasing involvement of lawyers as reporters and journalists, fearing that it would lead to an even fiercer light being shone upon the profession, to its detriment. Austin, the provincial reporter for *The Times*, recollected that in the late 1850s 'Resolutions were passed by the members of the Oxford and Western Circuits declaring it to be incompatible with the status of a barrister to report proceedings for the public

---

[60] 'Lord Lyndhurst: the Friends of the Noble', *The Times*, 8 October 1863.

[61] J. Dawson (1885) *Practical Journalism. How to Enter Thereon and Succeed* (London: Upcott Gill) p. 41.

[62] See, for example, Anon (1872) 'Trial by Judge, and Trial by Jury', *Westminster Review*, April, 289–324.

press.'[63] Mr Cooke Evans and Mr H.T. Cole QC, for *The Times* and the *Morning Chronicle* respectively, were the targets of these resolutions.[64] The reaction of the press is particularly interesting. The newspapers concerned were not prepared to accept the dictum, and the reporters on all circuits supported the press position when, 'by way of retaliation' as Austin put it, the instruction was given to those reporting the two offending circuits that they should 'suppress the names of all the barristers who appeared in cases reported in that paper'. It was 'a serious matter for the bar', who could not afford the loss of free advertising of their skills, and brought about the withdrawal of the offending resolutions.[65]

A belief amongst proprietors and editors that the use of lawyers, genuinely informed about the way that the criminal process operated, had enhanced the reputation of both the press and the legal profession was very visible by the end of the 1850s.[66] One manifestation of this was the high degree of homogeneity in reportage from the law courts. Across the newspaper industry, dedicated sections, variously entitled Crime Intelligence or Police News, for example, were major staples in the newspaper core, and examination of the content of the columns shows a considerable and regular uniformity in the choice of cases reported.[67] In these columns, while the material included reports from the higher courts (Assizes and Quarter Sessions), the daily diet continued to be from the magistrates' courts, continuing the model set by the Chartist papers such as the *Northern Star*.

What this underlines is that, following the model provided by the broadsheets, mid-century reportage continued the presentation of a largely undifferentiated criminal justice narrative, which, despite some occasional diversity, was more characterised by its commonalities and homogeneity. There was surprisingly little inflection attributable to the expression of interests nuanced by class or gender, let alone regionality. As the national 'popularity' of Maria Marten's murder had shown in the 1820s, the locality of a crime, particularly a murder, was incidental to the national interest, so long as there were universally appealing and sensational aspects to the crime. If relatively rare crimes like murder

---

[63] E. Austin (1872) *Anecdotage, or Stray Leaves from the Note Books of a Provincial Reporter* (London: F. Pitman) p. 153.

[64] Ibid.

[65] Ibid pp. 153–154.

[66] J. Grant (1871) *The Newspaper Press, Its Origin, Progress, and Present Position* (London: Tinsley Bros.) vol. 1, p. iv.

[67] Rowbotham and Stevenson, *Criminal Conversations*, introduction.

were always certain to be popular reading, there were other, more apparently mundane topics which also attracted regular attention, if fewer individual column inches, such as domestic violence and petty theft.

Public and professional perspectives: the example of domestic violence

A feature of local and national newspaper coverage of cases from the police courts in the 1850s was concern about what *Lloyds Weekly* described in September 1853 as the 'prevailing crime' of the day: wife-beating.[68] In that year, the Aggravated Assaults Act 1853 had been enacted. As the full title of the Act (The Better Punishment of Aggravated Assaults on Women and Children), and the accompanying debates in Parliament during its passage, make plain, politicians were very conscious of the critical reportage of the current management of the problem by the criminal justice system.[69] Henry Fitzroy spoke in the Commons of the 'numerous reports' in the press of 'cases of cruel and brutal assaults perpetrated upon the weaker sex by men who one blushed to think were Englishmen', and, in the Lords, Lord Granville echoed his sentiments about the reportage of these 'numerous cases of cruelty' reported in the daily newspapers.[70]

There was little will, however, to focus specifically and precisely on such domestic violence by enabling more speedy punitive responses, despite the wider acceptance of the need for women and children to receive greater protection from male violence perpetrated against them, whether in public or in private. Palmerston commented that the 'main object was to increase the punishment to be summarily awarded to every man brutal enough to commit violent assaults on women and children'; and, while he acknowledged that he 'did not at all admit that a man was more entitled to commit these injuries upon his own wife, than upon another man's wife', he thought it wiser to proceed on the basis of general principles. Where he took notice of the domestic scenario, it was to argue against the use of flogging, for instance, which could, counterproductively, stigmatise the wife of the flogged man, exacerbating his resentment against her. Palmerston preferred the solution subsequently

---

[68] *Lloyds Weekly*, 18 September 1853.

[69] For further details of this and similar legislation, see M. Shanley (1993) *Feminism, Marriage and the Law in Victorian England 1850–1895* (Princeton University Press).

[70] *Hansard*, 6 March 1853; 12 March 1853.

passed into law, which 'gave to the magistrate power to increase the duration of imprisonment, to add to it hard labour, and in other cases, which he apprehended would not be very frequent, to add a pecuniary fine'. This had the merit of avoiding offending public opinion; in fact, he hoped it would resonate with public feeling.[71]

However, as the press noted, in practice the Act had little real impact in reducing the level of assaults, in terms of the 'propensity of the lower classes to beat their wives'.[72] What the press presentation of cases also indicates is the continuing complexity of popular and official attitudes towards domestic violence. It is an examination of this reportage which helps to explain the shape of the later Divorce and Matrimonial Causes Act 1857. Along with enabling divorce (if on a differential gender basis), this Act sought to provide practical help for women who were the victims of violence. It eased divorce provisions, and, more importantly, incorporated cruelty as grounds for divorce for women; it also provided an opportunity for financial independence, identified as one of the factors restraining wives from bringing prosecutions for aggravated assault against their husbands. Like the Aggravated Assaults Act 1853 or the subsequent Offences Against the Person Act 1861, though, the 1857 Act specifically avoided identifying *domestic* violence as being criminal. Violence of some form was the basis on which the civil law matter of a divorce for women could be enabled.

Even so, cultural assumptions and associated mitigating factors prevailed. In law, the absorption of the married woman into her husband's *persona* was popularly interpreted as leading to an assumption of ownership of the wife by her husband, and similar attitudes were held towards children in relationship to their fathers (not mothers).[73] As the *Morning Chronicle* commented, 'it is the universal belief of the labouring class, that the law permits them to beat their wives, and the wives themselves share the general error'.[74] Politicians and lawyers arguing for a reform of the law showed themselves unwilling to combat the general principle in order to avoid outraging public feeling, while encouraging a better prosecution rate and more effective management of individual cases of brutality.[75] But, when it came to individual cases, both public

---

[71] Ibid per Palmerston.

[72] *Trewman's Exeter Flying Post or Plymouth and Cornish Advertiser*, 1 December 1853.

[73] Shanley, *Feminism*.

[74] *Morning Chronicle*, 31 May 1850.

[75] Aggravated Assaults Bill, *Hansard* HC Debate, 12 March 1856, 141, cols 24–28.

feeling and the attitudes of the criminal justice system meant that there were many prosecutions for domestic violence in which male brutality towards their spouses was mitigated by some contextual factor, as the reportage makes plain.

For instance, in media coverage, drink was regularly identified as a key causal factor in male-on-female violence. The issue for the courts and the reporters was whether it was a mitigating factor, as defendants often pleaded in their defence, or not. Much depended on whether the husband was a regular drunkard or not, and what had led him to take to drink, something which could include a presumed racial propensity (Irishness)[76] or some manifestation of unwifely or more generally unfeminine behaviour as provocation for aggrieved husbands. The reportage in *Reynolds News* of the prosecution of Peter Judge by his 'common law' wife Bridget Connor demonstrates the interplay of such considerations. In a drunken rage, Judge blackened both Bridget Connor's eyes; then went on a rampage destroying Connor's 'chaney' [china] and other belongings, including her bonnet. The destruction of property which was not legally his, as they had not formally married, counted against him; however, that the 'injured "lady"' had chosen to live with him in sin counted against her. He was 'a little, squint-eyed, bandy-legged man'; she was a 'plump' young woman, indicating a certain match of physical proportions. Both were Irish, which, to their contemporaries, explained both his propensity for drink and her immoral inclinations. It also added the opportunity to inject a degree of humour to the reportage of the proceedings, since Irishness was commonly held to be funny, and the defendant's surname helped the humour still further (the headline was: A Judge As Drunk As a Lord). Ultimately, Mr Hardwicke, the stipendiary at Marlborough Street police court, decided it had been a 'cowardly' but not a drunken assault, emphasising the property aspect. He fined Judge five guineas or three months in default (but *without* hard labour).[77]

By contrast, the reportage of Hannah Broderick's prosecution of her husband Dennis underlines the reality that, in the national and metropolitan press at least, domestic violence where the woman fulfilled appropriate gender stereotypes was presented by the legal profession as morally and legally offensive. Here, the headline was 'Brutal Assault on Wife – Ruffian Punished'. The reportage was careful to stress that Mrs

---

[76] R. Swift (2005) 'Behaving Badly? Irish Migrants and Crime in the Victorian City', in Rowbotham and Stevenson (eds) *Criminal Conversations* pp. 106–125.

[77] *Reynolds News*, 12 October 1851.

Broderick was a legally married woman, but use of the term 'ruffian', with its implications of lawlessness and bullying, damned a man who was, by trade, a carpenter and so normally entitled to respectable status. This would have enabled readers to understand why Broderick received three months, but this time *with* hard labour. The content of the report further sought to bring out the inappropriateness of Broderick's regular violence to his wife. He was described as a 'tall, powerfully-built man', while she was not only physically slight but had just given birth (she carried a three-week-old infant in her arms). Further, as well as drinking, the press was careful to include evidence that he regularly refused to work, bringing wife and children to the brink of starvation, locating him as one of the 'undeserving' and feckless. Care was taken to include the comment of Mr Corrie, the Clerkenwell stipendiary, that there was no doubt of his 'very cruel conduct' towards his wife, and of his regular drunkenness.[78] Press reportage in this period was used to indicate to readers that magistrates would not accept drink as a mitigating factor in cases of domestic violence. The comment of Mr Yardley, the Thames Police Court stipendiary, in 1858 that 'drunkenness was no excuse for crime, but an aggravation of it' was widely reported.[79]

Nonetheless, this cannot be taken too far. The possibility of feminine provocation was a regular factor in the reportage. Mrs Broderick was a stereotypical good woman in terms of her representation in the media, but the wife who had provoked her beating by being 'given to habits of intoxication, smoking and other filthy personal habits', and consequently neglecting the amenities of home and so the comfort of her husband, could not expect sympathy from the courts. Nor could she expect, even if severely beaten, that the reportage would be critical of such lack of legal sympathy, something which clearly had more to do with the ways in which the cultural contexts of offending shaped legal reactions than with the strict letter of the law.[80] Nor was this attitude present only in reportage from the summary courts: in this period, the reportage of cases of domestic violence serious enough to be referred to the Quarter Sessions or Assizes was equally uncritical of the clear reluctance of juries to convict the male defendants in such cases.[81] Under such circumstances, even drunken violence from a husband was treated sympathetically, with the subtext being that the man felt driven to

---

[78] *Morning Chronicle*, 9 August 1856.
[79] *Morning Chronicle*, 12 November 1858.
[80] *Daily Telegraph*, 7 July 1856.
[81] See, for example, *The Times*, 14 July 1855; *Lloyds News*, 20 March 1853.

drink by his wife's actions, and so she bore considerable culpability for her own beating. Such cases were rarely referred up from the summary courts, and the reportage emphasises that neglect of domestic duties by the wife was a regular and generally accepted provocation to violence which could be used effectively as mitigation for the defence. In practice, this meant that the reportage warned women that a wife who either went out to work or worked at home to earn income, consequently not spending enough time making home comfortable for the 'real' breadwinner, remained an acceptable target for understandable male frustration. The lawyer who was the editor of the *Hull Packet* commented that such actions by wives were 'unnatural and pernicious'.[82] It is worth noting that female-on-male domestic violence was still generally treated in the courts and in the reportage as a much more serious matter!

Conclusion

What the development of Victorian crime reportage indicated was that the legal establishment could use newspapers to send very powerful messages to the public about the criminal justice system and the profession in general, often through a depiction of the relative merits and culpabilities of each party involved in a particular case. The transition of legal professionals as journalists and reporters was to the advantage of both the press and the law, and it involved none of the dubious transactions that had marked the careers of penny-a-liners, who had at times improperly paid officials (including the early uniformed police) for information about a particular crime. Lawyers related privileged information as a professional courtesy and not for pay, assured that fellow professionals would not publish anything improper or detrimental to the legal process, no matter how sensational.

---

[82] *Hull Packet*, 7 October 1853.

2
A 'Golden Era'? 1860–1885

Introduction

During the 1860s, the expectation that legally crafted reportage from the courts could work to improve the authority of newspapers and the public standing of the criminal justice process was firmly entrenched. Plainly, it was held to have proved its worth in the eyes of politicians and the legal profession as well as newspaper editors and proprietors, as witnessed by the increasing use of legally trained and active figures as key journalists, writing opinion pieces, including leaders. Early concerns on the part of the legal profession had been essentially allayed, and the parameters of both the habits of good law reportage and legally sound journalism were well established. Crucially, this came at a time when the newspaper press was expanding rapidly due to the repeal of stamp duty and technological advances, allied to a growing market for interesting newsprint, which was where crime reportage came in. Thanks to the increasing importance of the trial as the locale where the fullest, most accurate information was provided, it had proved possible to combine legal accuracy with a sensationalism that, if more sober than the reports of the penny-a-liners, was still attractive enough to readers of all classes to ensure newspaper circulations continued to rise.

In this sense, the respective successes of the *Daily Telegraph* and the *Pall Mall Gazette* are particularly interesting in the ways that they reveal the complexities of the appeal of reportage from the courts. The *Daily Telegraph*, essentially aimed at a working-class readership, attracted wider attention because of the readability and substance of its crime reportage. The *Pall Mall Gazette*, launched in 1865, rapidly became a widely read evening paper amongst the professional and political classes, and again the quality and authority of its legal commentary (generally provided or at least shaped by legal luminaries such as James Fitzjames Stephen) played a crucial part in this. In general terms, though, the increasing reliance of the press on legal journalism as well as reportage is underlined by the following anecdote. Sir William Harcourt started his journalism career in 1849, mainly contributing leaders to the *Morning Chronicle*. He recalled, in 1862, that he had been surprised to learn that an unpublished letter he had sent to *The Times* on transportation appeared in only 'slightly modified form' as the (unattributed) leader; meaning he was able to extract due payment from them for his services.[1] The desire to publicise legal reforms, changes to existing legislation and new procedures provided a substantive legal context to crime reportage for the middle and upper classes, those who were likely to read the *Pall Mall Gazette*. Crime was in itself often sensational in being mysterious, but could also be soberly sensational news in that it promoted critical debate on individual aspects of the justice delivery process.[2] Equally, the more emotionally sensational aspects of crime reportage, allied to the crime narrative, which enthralled the working-class reader of the *Daily Telegraph* and the Sunday titles, were being tempered and focused through clearer messages that explained the new rules and legislation as the best way of ensuring 'justice'. Such public comprehension at all levels would, it was believed, ensure popular support for and confidence in the criminal justice system.[3]

It is impossible to quantify the results of this shift to legally informed crime reportage, but there are qualitative indications that the engagement of the public with both the courts themselves (particularly the summary courts) and such reportage expanded during this period. This is suggested on a number of indirect counts, such as the statistics[4] on the

---

[1] S.M. Ellis (1923) *A Mid Victorian Pepys*, p. v. As well as his editorship, Hardman penned a biography of William Cobbett, enjoyed a close friendship with the poet George Meredith, consorted with a number of publishers, including the proprietors of *Punch*, *Once a Week* and *The Parthenon*, and the editor of the *British Medical Journal*, and contributed to their publications.

[2] See D. Liddle (2004) 'Anatomy of a "Nine Days' Wonder": Sensational Journalism in the Decade of the Sensation Novel', in A. Maunder and G. Moore (eds) *Victorian Crime, Sensation and Madness* (Aldershot: Ashgate), pp. 94–96. Note, however, that William Hardman was a lawyer–journalist, not a professional journalist.

[3] For further discussion of individual titles and crime reportage, see J. Rowbotham and K. Stevenson (eds) (2005) *Criminal Conversations: Victorians Behaving Badly* (Columbus: Ohio State University Press).

[4] See the tables in B.R. Mitchell (1988) *British Historical Statistics* (Cambridge University Press) pp. 779–787, and the general discussion in ch. 15.

increased use of the summary courts, which are amplified by the importance, in daily press coverage, of cases and other incidents from those
courts. Another useful indicator is the content of published correspondence in the press.[5] Equally, there is corroborative comment which can
be derived from a variety of other print formats, which testifies to the
development of the legal professional as a popular media 'personality'.
Leading lawyers such as Serjeant Ballantine or Henry Bodkin Poland were
familiar enough to feature in biographical profiles in widely read periodicals or as figures in a range of cartoons. Finally, it should be remembered
that successful newspaper proprietors were hard-headed business men
with good commercial instincts, who would not have carried on using
lawyers as reporters and journalists if it had not made financial sense to
them in terms of maintaining and expanding their readerships.

The lawyer–reporter and the lawyer–journalist

As the previous chapter underlined, the lawyer–journalist was not a
totally new phenomenon, undoubtedly one reason why men like John
Delane of *The Times* sought to use their input in their titles.[6] Mr Serjeant
Spankie wrote for the *Morning Chronicle* from its heyday in the 1830s
into the 1850s. Lord Brougham was a particularly prolific journalist,
as well as being an active politician and lawyer, from the 1820s to the
1850s, and author of no fewer than 80 articles in the first 20 volumes
of the *Edinburgh Review*. At that time, journalism was not a reputable
occupation.[7] Brougham had turned to it out of financial need, which
makes it hardly surprising that, to preserve his separate professional
status, he had rarely written on the law and legal issues. Even so, the
output of men like him alerted editors such as Delane to the advantages
of recruiting men who were, simultaneously, trained to be persuasive
and credible but also accurate in their presentation of the facts. Through
John Walter II, and his own family background, Delane had the right
contacts within the legal profession; and this, of course, was the man

---

[5] This is a complex area; while it is clear that many letters published in the
correspondence columns were penned within the newspaper, such effusions did
generally reflect what suited the expectations of the readership: see L. Brake and
M. Demoor (2009) *A Dictionary of Journalism in Great Britain and Ireland* (Gent:
Academia Press).

[6] See A. Dasent (1908) *John Thadeus Delane, Editor of "The Times": His Life and
Correspondence* (New York: Scribner's Sons).

[7] A. Aspinall (1945) 'The Social Status of Journalists at the Beginning of the
Nineteenth Century', *Review of English Studies*, 83, 216–232.

who sought to develop reporting specialisms, as with the use of war correspondents.[8] For a man who desired for his paper the accolade of accuracy, the use of men who were genuinely informed about the way that the criminal process worked seemed an obvious strategy to advance the quality and authority of law reporting.

Certainly, in the mid-century, the use of lawyer–reporters expanded rapidly, and by 1867 'three out of every five reporters attached to our chief London newspapers are Inns of Court men', suggesting that such legally trained men may not have confined their reporting work to the courts.[9] It is plain from a range of memoirs and other sources that junior barristers eagerly took up the opportunity to work for one or other of the organs of the press as reporters. It generated income, offered the opportunity of making themselves known to more established figures in the legal profession, and almost certainly alleviated the tedium of hanging around waiting for a case to materialise.[10] Becoming a lawyer, especially a barrister, was also an expensive enterprise. Typically, the mid-century costs involved in being called to the Bar and undertaking pupillage were about £450, and for the first ten years of practice a young, aspiring barrister needed to find at least £300 a year to cover his living and practice costs.[11] Such costs steadily increased as the century went on, and so did the need to generate an income outside the actual practice of the law. J.A. Strahan, who entered Middle Temple in the 1880s, recalled that he spent almost 12 years on the reporting staff of a law paper, spending nearly every day in Court but practising very little law. He confirmed that 'Literature', in the shape of reportage or journalism, was the most common means by which most 'Templers' supplemented their income.[12] Plowden recalled that 'assiduous attendance in the Courts had its uses from a professional point of view as well as that of mere reporting... I had the best opportunity for studying the methods of the ablest advocates at the Bar.'[13] Sir William

---

[8] Dasent, *Delane*.

[9] J.C. Jeaffreson (1867) *A Book About Lawyers* (London: Hurst and Blackett) p. 370.

[10] The importance of the financial contribution to a junior barrister's income of acting as a reporter is referred to in D. Duman (1983) *The English and Colonial Bars in the Nineteenth Century* (London: CroomHelm) p. 148.

[11] W. Rouse Ball (1879) *The Student's Guide to the Bar* (London: Macmillan); Rater (1905) *How I Became a Judge, being the reminiscences of the Honourable Mr Justice Rater* (London: J.B. Nichols and Sons) p. 33: 'Smith and Eldon, both of whom were poor men, subsisting on the meagre profits to be derived from journalism.'

[12] J.A. Strahan (1919) *The Bench and Bar of England* (Edinburgh: Blackwood).

[13] A. Plowden (1903) *Grain or Chaff, The Autobiography of a Police Magistrate* (London: T. Fisher Unwin) p.108.

Harcourt started his journalistic career in 1849, contributing leaders to the *Morning Chronicle*, and becoming one of *The Saturday Review*'s best contributors in 1855. He only removed himself from active journalism after 1875, when his work as a Recorder and magistrate increased to an extent that he claimed to have little time for it (though he remained editor of the *Morning Post*). As this underlines, despite the opportunities in journalism and literature that such experience opened up, law remained the prime focus for most involved as either reporters or journalists.

The contemporary factors for their remaining essentially 'hidden from history' appear complex, but they certainly have helped to disguise the seriousness with which many legal professionals addressed their relationships with the press. A key factor seems to have been a determination to be identified, by their peers, as remaining primarily legal professionals. The example of W.S. Gilbert is telling here: despite his constant legal references in works from 'Trial by Jury' to 'The Mikado', few who discuss his career emphasise the reality that he was a trained barrister. Equally, E.F. Pigott, best known now in his quasi-legal capacity as the Lord Chamberlain's examiner of plays, abandoned his profession as barrister to concentrate on journalism and dramatic censorship.[14] Thus, outside the laws of libel, the links between the nineteenth-century press and the legal profession, and the implications of this association, have rarely been highlighted. One clear reason was the reluctance of the lawyers themselves to be identified as acting also as reporters and journalists.[15] Yet the links were extensive, if not widely advertised. Several Victorian newspaper editors kept that aspect of their lives in the background while continuing their professional avocations in law. This included Hardinge Giffard, later Lord Halsbury, who had helped his father edit *The Standard* while simultaneously training for the Bar (Halsbury maintained his editorial interests throughout his distinguished legal career).[16]

---

[14] Escott, *Masters of English Journalism*, p. 220.

[15] There is discussion of the lawyer–statesman on both sides of the Atlantic; see A. Kronman (1993) *The Lost Lawyer: failing ideals of the legal profession* (Harvard University Press). However, outside the growth of legal writing for professional journals and the provision of law reports and treatises, there is little acknowledgment of the lawyer–journalist or lawyer–reporter beyond such comments as those made by Duman in *English and Colonial Bars* (see above).

[16] He also (unsuccessfully) urged his father to reduce the price from five pence to a penny; see R.F.V. Heuston (1964) *Lives of the Lord Chancellors 1885–1940* (Oxford: Clarendon Press) p. 11. His career has parallels with another lawyer–journalist of this period, Sir Douglas Straight. Straight's career is interesting: he started as a journalist, became a lawyer from 1865, then an MP (continuing his

Mr Serjeant Cox, chairman of the Middlesex Sessions, 'made an enormous fortune by his marvellous newspaper ventures' even while he 'diligently discharged the duties of Chairman of the second court for many years'. Sir William Hardman combined being Recorder of Kingston and Chairman of the Surrey Quarter Sessions *and* editor of the *Morning Post*, from 1872 until his death in 1890.[17]

The 'normality' is thus represented by a range of legally trained figures who engaged seriously in journalism, yet did their best to hide this from the general public, and to downgrade its importance in their lives in the eyes of their peers. The brilliant Frederic Rogers, for instance, who was called to the Bar in 1837 (though he could never afford to practise) wrote for *The Times* between 1841 and 1844 and went on to help found the *Manchester Guardian*. However, he insisted that his links with the press remain hidden.[18] Sir William Hardman's biographer maintained that he merely engaged in a 'rather idle dalliance with law and literature' after being called to the Bar in 1852 in order to sustain his professional standing. But Hardman's enduring level of commitment to the press demonstrates that it was far from an 'idle dalliance'.[19] For such men, who valued their standing in society as well as their standing with their peers in law, journalism was (except as a 'pastime') a much less attractive descriptor of their career work, even though the law was generally less financially rewarding (commonly paying only moderate incomes of £500–700 per annum except for the most successful).[20] Frederick Conde Williams, eventually a colonial judge but, before that, editor of the provincial *Birmingham Gazette*, provides illuminating insights into this mindset in his memoirs, *From Journalist to Judge*. He made it plain that, while dependent upon it for his income initially, he consistently regarded journalism 'as a crutch', but not 'a staff'. Consequently, rather than moving up within the hierarchy of newspaper editors, he preferred the relative legal backwater of

---

journalism), before serving as a judge in India for 13 years; he then returned to take up the editorship of the *Pall Mall Magazine* from 1892 and later the *Pall Mall Gazette* from 1896.

[17] E. Purcell (1916) *Forty Years at the Criminal Bar. Experiences and Impressions* (London: T Fisher Unwin) p. 172; A Student at Law (1839) *The Fourth Estate: or the Moral Influence of the Press* (London: Ridgeway) p. 19; Ellis, *A Mid Victorian Pepys*, p. vii.

[18] Escott, *Masters of English Journalism*, p. 20.

[19] Ibid.

[20] Duman, *English and Colonial Bars*, pp. 148–149.

becoming a colonial judge, with the social and professional standing that provided for him.[21]

Some lawyers were very successful in combining journalism and legal practice, notably James Fitzjames Stephen, who had a number of personal links to the media, and acknowledged the linkage to an extent. A prolific lawyer–journalist, Stephen could expect remuneration of around three and a half guineas for each contribution in newspapers or periodicals. Like Brougham, though, Stephen was careful to focus not just on law, especially in pieces where his name was acknowledged. His first essays were published in the *Morning Chronicle* and *Christian Observer*, but he became a known regular contributor to most of the leading literary and legal journals published. His favoured journals, with which he was most closely associated, included the *Saturday Review*, edited by his brother, Lesley Stephen. According to his contemporaries, Fitzjames Stephen did not only help to make the *Saturday Review*, he *was* the *Saturday Review*.[22] Between 1865 and 1869 Stephen contributed over 850 largely anonymous articles to the *Pall Mall Gazette* alone, in addition to over 200 occasional notes and 50 items of correspondence produced during the same period. As well as a range of articles, Stephen also frequently and vociferously corresponded with the press, particularly *The Times* and the *Pall Mall Gazette*, using pen names readily identifiable by 'those in the know'.[23] All this made him, without doubt, deserve Radzinowicz's label as 'the main controversial publicist of the day'.[24]

Anonymity in action

The importance of anonymity to these men is further emphasised in the use of the correspondence columns to voice their opinions.[25] Hardman was a regular correspondent with *The Times*, and it was well known amongst literary circles that his letters were published under the pseudonym Historicus.[26] Fitzjames Stephen certainly used the

---

[21] F.C. Williams (1903) *From Journalist to Judge. An Autobiography* (London: Simpkin Marshall and Co.) p. 52.

[22] L. Radzinowicz (1957) *Sir James Fitzjames Stephen (1829–1894) and his Contribution to the development of the Criminal Law* (Seldon Society: Spottiswoode, Ballantyne and Co.) p. 9.

[23] Stephen's papers, Cambridge University ADD 7349 (C) Lytton-Stephen, 1876–1891 28 May, 24 June, 2 July 1877; 3 Dec 1877.

[24] Radzinowicz, *Fitzjames Stephen*, pp. 7–9.

[25] Brake and Demoor, *Journalism*.

[26] Ellis, *Mid-Victorian Pepys*, p. 220.

correspondence columns of the press to influence opinion. In 1877, he defended his close friend Lord Lytton, the Viceroy of India, against continued press criticism attacking his India policy on codification. This prompted Lytton to thank Stephen for the two 'masterly' but anonymous communications he had sent to *The Times* in his support.[27] The use of pseudonyms or pen names was at least partly a means of getting views published without having them formally attributed and so critiqued on the basis of interest. It suggests that such anonymity was valued by lawyer–reporters and lawyer–journalists on two key grounds: first, because it served to disguise, and so avoid, any widespread public disquiet about the implications for bias in the reportage and the delivery of impartial justice consequent on too intimate a relationship between law and press; second, because it enabled the legal profession to avoid having publicly to acknowledge the scale of its close and everyday links with such a non-professional arena.

As discussed in Chapter 1, senior figures in the legal profession were initially unhappy about the level of collaboration between lawyers and the media. Jeaffreson recalled the days when it was 'the fashion of the Bar to disdain law-students who were suspected of "writing for hire" and barristers who "reported for the papers" ', confirming that by the middle of the century it was

> almost universally held on the circuits and in Westminster Hall, that Inns-of-Court men lowered the dignity of their order by following those literary avocations by which some of the brightest orna-ments of the law supported themselves at the outset of their profes-sional careers.... [including] Such men as Serjeant Spankie and Lord Campbell, as Master Stephen and Mr. Justice Talfourd...[who were all] reporters for the press.[28]

Thus, as other later autobiographical reminiscences evidence, a better appreciation of the value to lawyers of controlling the reportage from the law courts became established, so long as anonymity was retained. The tradition of unattributed authorship in newspapers was identified by those within it as 'the true secret of its power, for it may be observed that the less we know of the writers of a paper, the more powerful or influential is the paper'.[29] Or, as King self-congratulatorily put it when

---

[27] Stephen's papers, 28 May, 24 June and 2 July 1877; 3 December 1877.

[28] Jeaffreson, *A Book about Lawyers*, p. 370.

[29] Dawson, *Practical Journalism*, p. 41.

discussing the lawyer–reporter, 'Very few persons have any idea of the important role' performed by such men, because they were normally 'so unobtrusive' that they were seldom visible to the general public. However, without them 'there would be no interesting "police news", opening up a hundred strange phases of life, and putting us upon our guard against a thousand modes of imposition'.[30]

A symbiotic relationship?

Frank Taylor, when reflecting back on the mid-Victorian era, commented on the legal profession's consciously felt need to invoke the press to expand popular support for the criminal justice reformation process, especially the move to rely more and more on summary justice to conclude cases.[31] For Fitzjames Stephen, one important theme in his journalism was the promotion of a positive image of law professionals, even though, as a law reformer in outlook, he regularly criticised aspects of the current English legal process. Writing in the *Cornhill Magazine* in 1861 in an interesting echo of current charges against lawyers, he challenged the publication of satirical images and stereotypifications of the men of the law, arguing that such caricatures not only promoted false public assumptions about lawyers but encouraged the public to believe, wrongly, that lawyers had more regard for their bank accounts than truth and justice.[32] That such arguments had some effect in establishing a more positive popular perspective on lawyers is suggested by the enhanced publicity given to individuals. Well-known practitioners such as Serjeant Ballantine or Henry Hawkins developed high public profiles, boosted by appearing regularly in a positive light in press reports. Their pictures appeared in the press and in periodicals quite regularly, and some, like Ballantine, were even the focus for cartoons. In Ballantine's case, his love for check trousers and for fees, along with his distinctive mutton chop whiskers, were readily combined into cartoon format. Not only were their professional lives and activities presented

---

[30] H.S. King (1872) *Two Idle Apprentices, Briefs and Papers, Sketches of the Bar and the Press* (London: King) pp. 186–188.

[31] F. Taylor (1898) *The Newspaper Press as a Power both in the Expression and Formation of Public Opinion. The Chancellor's Essay* (Oxford: B.H. Blackwell) pp. 13–14.

[32] J.F. Stephen (1861) 'The Morality of Advocacy', *Cornhill Magazine*, 3, 447–459. (In the *Fortnightly Review* and *Contemporary Review* he also prominently called for the state to actively interfere with the regulation of religion: see also *Illustrated London News*, 7 June 1873).

for public admiration or some (largely affectionate) mockery, but, much as today, those regarded as part of the social elite became celebrities in their own right. Lawyers, judges and journalists regularly mixed and met in the social milieu of the London clubs, forming close relationships and developing their networks.[33]

Some qualms still remained, witness the comment aimed at fellow professionals in the *Law Times* in 1861, which warned the profession that the proclivity of newspapers to intervene in the judicial process risked undermining it (in a Victorian version of 'trial by media').[34] The reality by that time was that both the criminal justice system and the newspaper industry were reliant upon each other in the wider interests of the public:

> The courts need a means of communication with the public, for they have developed none of their own; and this the media freely provide. The media in their turn have an insistent need for news material of the kind constantly available in the criminal courts: stories about crime and punishment, criminals and their exploits, virtuous citizens suddenly accused of offences and the like.[35]

A small incident from *Lloyds Weekly* in 1862 reveals the extent of both the hold that legal professionals exerted upon the courts, and the detailed knowledge they acquired, in the course of an attempt by Mr Worth, the owner and reporter for the *Hampstead Express*, to sue Mr Lavie, a lawyer– reporter, for discussing publicly a letter of complaint that he had sent to the Hampstead Bench. It becomes clear that Worth's key complaint was that he (and his son) were not allowed to look at or copy the contents of the deposition book. Men like Lavie were so privileged, because Lavie was a qualified legal professional while Worth was not.[36]

The concern that some senior legal professionals felt about barristers acting as reporters was not an issue that ever entirely went away. As late

---

[33] Strahan, *The Bench and Bar of England*, pp. 220–21: 'We Templars were then such clubbable fellows that most of us had at least two clubs...My home club was the Savage then housed in the Savoy. It was composed of journalists, most of whom were also barristers, actors, artists and entertainers.'

[34] *County Courts Chronicle*, 1 August 1861, pp. 210–211.

[35] M. Jones (1981) 'The Relationship between the Criminal Courts and the Mass Media', in C. Sumner (ed.) *Crime Justice and the Mass Media*, Papers Presented to the 14th Cropwood Round Table Conference (University of Cambridge, Institute of Criminology) p. 55.

[36] 'Police Intelligence', *Lloyds Weekly*, 28 September 1862.

as 1888, Plowden yielded his reporting for *The Times* partly because of representations that it was not a suitable role for one in his new position as a London stipendiary magistrate.[37] Generally, though, the involvement of legal professionals as journalists worked to provide opportunities for the rehabilitation of both the criminal justice system and the profession after the criticisms of the legal process in the first half of the century. It was an undoubted asset in this exercise that the traditional anonymity of writing for press and journals disguised the self-interested nature of this promotion.

The popularity of legal news (particularly crime news) also helped to shape the expansion of the press. New titles in this period, besides the *Pall Mall Gazette*, included the *Illustrated Police News*, a weekly with a target working-class audience. It was essentially the first title primarily dedicated to crime reportage, much of it from the courts, enhanced, or sensationalised, by appropriate line drawings. There was, in all the national newspapers at least, a desire to publicise legal reforms, changes to existing legislation and new procedures as characteristics of their crime reportage. This ensured that the more emotionally appealing aspects of crime narratives were tempered and focused through legally accurate messages that explained new rules and justified the impact of new legislation. Under headings such as Police News or Police Intelligence, reportage from the magistrates' courts provided the bulk of the daily content for crime news for all national titles. This provided insights into the management of criminal incidents as diverse as juvenile gangs, white collar fraud or domestic violence. As well as such mundane matters, Police News would contain the origins of the most sensational indictable cases, alerting readers to subsequent juicy narratives which could further boost sales of a title to enable readers to pore over the details of how a murderer, say, perpetrated his or her crime. This provides a picture of the profitable and positive aspects of the relationship between the press and the legal profession.

Inevitably, it could be said, the main content emphasis in reporting crime was derived from urban areas, particularly London. In London, both the population and the sheer number of police courts, as well as the proximity of so many Inns of Court and Chambers to Fleet Street, gave maximum opportunity for immediate coverage. This privileged a concentration on London in crime reportage which did act to distort, to some extent, the media presentation of the realities of crime. However, London was undoubtedly, in terms of the crime figures based

---

[37] Plowden, *Grain or Chaff*, pp. 107–108.

on prosecutions, the 'crime capital' of the country. In addition, reports of crime from other metropolitan areas such as Liverpool, Manchester and Birmingham were regularly included, as were reports from other less prominent locations where these raised significant points of law or provided interesting, amusing or sensational narratives of crime. The former point is crucial. Generally, a survey of the day's cases, in the London courts at least, indicates that the cases printed in the next day's newspapers reflected the most interesting of the typical cases submitted to the editors by the lawyer–reporters. Interestingly, what editors were also at pains to include, from anywhere in the country, were those first instance cases which suggested how magistrates were using a new or amending piece of legislation for the first time. Implicitly, and explicitly, therefore, legal professionals took an active role in seeking to educate the public about the 'science' of law, promoting an understanding of the legal process and its value from a legal perspective.[38]

By detailing the comments of individual judges, magistrates and barristers, public attention was drawn to an array of legal issues and topics through the reportage of cases, especially in the lower courts.[39] For instance, in February 1870, the much-reported stipendiary magistrate of Lambeth, Austin Woolrych, informed the public about the 'new cab regulations' through the arrest of James Morgan, who had misappropriated a sovereign given to him in mistake for a shilling. Woolrych explained the new responsibility of the cabdriver for ensuring he was given the correct money, and because it was such a 'gross attempt to appropriate the sovereign to his own use' he would 'mark his opinion of such conduct' by giving him six weeks' imprisonment with hard labour.[40] Interestingly, the prosecutor was a tradesman, not a gentleman, underlining the extent to which this reportage used popular fascination with real crimes to engage actively with the man (and woman) on the street about situations that might affect them in daily life, advising on how to behave and react towards the law, and what to expect from it.[41]

Crime intelligence

Reportage from the courts maintained the presentation of criminal justice narratives, which, despite some occasional diversity, were more

---

[38] Rowbotham and Stevenson, 'Causing a Sensation'.

[39] For example, Anon, 'Trial by Judge, and Trial by Jury'.

[40] 'The Cab Law', *Daily Telegraph*, 11 February 1870.

[41] Inevitably, the majority of cases do feature men as both prosecutors and defendants.

characterised by commonalities of attitude towards crime across class boundaries or political difference. Thus, it is commonplace to find that cases reported in, say, *The Times* would also be covered in the *Daily Telegraph* and summarised in that week's Sunday titles. Newspapers generally adopted a 'respectable' attitude towards crime reportage, packaging their narratives with varying degrees of sensationalism according to their projected audiences. Even the journalism, in the shape of opinion pieces or leader columns, was indistinguishable and rarely differentiated according to the political colouring or anticipated class of the readership of any title. There were exceptions. Trades union related prosecutions would be treated differently. Titles such as *Reynolds News* or even the *News of the World* were markedly more sympathetic to the men involved in such prosecutions than were titles such as *The Times* or the *Pall Mall Gazette*, and typically contained a clear radical edge to the reportage. Otherwise, it was not until the end of the century, accompanying the rise of the Labour Party, that such prosecutions acquired a party political dimension which influenced newspaper coverage. On the whole, the style of crime reportage produced for the national titles by lawyer–reporters, allied to the comment made by lawyer–journalists, was seen as achieving an effective balance between sensationalism and appropriate information.

This general air of collusion is further highlighted by the alarm over the less legally informed, but clearly emotional as well as politically radical, reportage in the newspapers specifically created to support the cause of the Tichborne Claimant in the 1870s. The Tichborne cause developed as a result of the appearance of a man claiming to be the missing Sir Roger Tichborne and so the heir to considerable estates. He was recognised by Sir Roger's mother, the Dowager Lady Tichborne, and some others, but most family and friends insisted he was an imposter. Since he had been declared dead officially, his claim had to be tested in the courts. In the civil trial to prove his identity, the Claimant lost when evidence was produced which suggested he was really Arthur Orton, a butcher born in Wapping who had lived in Wagga Wagga for some years before deciding on making his false claim. What followed was a criminal trial for perjury, presided over by Lord Chief Justice Cockburn, which resulted in the Claimant's conviction and a sentence of 14 years' penal servitude. It was the reportage of the trial for perjury which shows how the nation was divided on largely class grounds.[42] For instance, the appearance of

---

[42] See R. McWilliam (2007) *The Tichborne Claimant. A Victorian Sensation* (Continuum: London).

a special interest pro-Tichborne set of newspapers in the early 1870s had Chartist echoes for some contemporaries, but fortunately, in establishment eyes, this media phenomenon was relatively short-lived and never achieved circulation levels that threatened the dominance of the established national titles. Even within the main national titles, though, the Tichborne Case drew out differentiated journalism in terms of the opinions voiced. According to *Lloyds News*, the defence conducted for the Tichborne family by Sir John Coleridge was improperly sensational, and it queried whether 'the ends of justice' were being served by advocacy which appealed to the 'passions, the prejudices, the emotions of the jurymen' instead of to their reasoned judgment.[43] *Reynolds News* was equally indignant at the tone taken by the Attorney General, reflecting that it was not 'customary in a court of justice' to hear 'such Billingsgate epithets as those the Attorney General applied to the claimant', and concluding that the trial was consequently 'a shocking stigma on the administration of justice'.[44] By contrast, *The Times* simply reported, at length, Coleridge's case and made no comment on his presentation; while the *Pall Mall Gazette* took pains to highlight the comment of the Lord Chief Justice that Coleridge's lengthy speech was warranted and to add that the jury concurred (though the grounds for this assertion were not included).[45] With the major exception of this *cause célèbre*, the party political nuances of the period had no significant impact on crime reportage from the courts.

This is not to claim that there were no differences in the reportage, but rather to emphasise that such differences as are discernible are essentially focused on differing interpretations of the law, in terms of their potential socio-cultural impacts. The Tichborne type case, in which the law was, in essence, called in to adjudicate on key socio-cultural and economic clashes originating outside the courtroom, remained rare. One such case was heard in 1875 by Mr Justice Brett, who adopted what he described as a 'bold' approach to a trial resulting from a fight on Hackney Marshes, where one of the participants had died as a result of the encounter. In the consequent trial for manslaughter, Brett chose to ignore the illegal aspects of the incident (notably gambling on the outcome) because of what he identified as the 'manly' conduct of the key participants (who had all pleaded guilty). He gave credit to the defence explanations that

---

[43] 'Three Sensation Trials', *Lloyds Weekly*, 21 January 1872.

[44] 'The Interminable Law Suit', *Reynolds News*, 21 January 1872.

[45] 'The Tichborne Trial, *The Times*, 3 February 1872; 'Law and Police', *Pall Mall Gazette*, 24 January 1872.

the six men charged had in fact organised a 'proper' bout, according to the established rules of prize-fighting, with a referee to ensure fair play. In his judgment, Brett caused controversy by making an explicit reference to another (widely reported) case he had presided over the previous day, which had resulted in a manslaughter conviction by the jury.[46] That case had involved a street brawl and the use of knives. Brett asserted that there was a distinction between those incidents of public brawling which were characterised by 'cowardice and unfairness' and those (like this one) in which care was taken to ensure a 'fair fight', and in which (he held) the deceased bore a crucial responsibility for his own demise, since he had wilfully prolonged the bout by refusing to accept defeat.[47]

In terms of press reaction, the *Daily Telegraph* with its working-class audience was most flattering in its editorial assessments of the judge's expressions, particularly the way he had invoked English manliness as his guiding principle: 'Language more frank and manly has not often been heard on the bench.' It considered that the conclusion was likely to have 'a good effect' on those elements in society which were 'prone to violence'.[48] The paper was alone in arriving at such a positive conclusion on Brett's judgment. Commentary in other national titles, whether with higher-class readerships, such as *The Times*, or with more working-class audiences, was not flattering.[49] Such titles expressed a worry that Brett's judgment was problematic not just in terms of its law but also in terms of its broader impact; a perspective also reflected in the provincial press. The general feeling was that, because it was 'one of the functions of the law to educate the mass of men in such matters and uphold a high standard', then Brett's 'bold' course could have the opposite effect of encouraging men to solve their disputes through violence, even if governed by rules, rather than through law.[50]

Incidents such as this reveal the existence of groups and cliques with different attitudes to the practise of law and its application within lawyer–journalist circles, as well as to individual legal practitioners. In the words of one lawyer–reporter:

> 'Judges are seldom heroes to their reporter … he has daily before him tests of the character and capacity of his judges, and seated in court

---

[46] See, for instance, 'Old Court', *The Times*, 8 April 1875.
[47] The other two, as onlookers, received nominal sentences of three days.
[48] *Daily Telegraph*, 9 April 1875.
[49] Editorial, *The Times*, 10 April 1875.
[50] 'Justice Brett and the Prize Fighters', *Lancashire Gazette and General Advertiser*, 17 April 1875.

among his fellow barristers, as men come and go, he is inspired with the whispered criticisms of the Bar on the Bench, ... and the latest circuit story of Mr. Justice that.'[51]

The legal orientation of reportage ensured that events from the courts were regularly inflected by considerations of necessary reforms to the criminal law or legal processes, and how these might affect the public at large.

As highlighted in the previous chapter, the didactic legal angle to the reportage from the courts, particularly the summary courts, is particularly visible in an examination of cases featuring domestic violence. Cases brought by wives against violent husbands carefully laid out the grounds on which magistrates would and could grant separation orders, and the basis on which applications for maintenance orders could be made. Mrs Davison, for example, who was in possession of a mangle and so could 'support herself and her children', asked for a separation order to protect herself against her husband's violent and drunken demands for money. The magistrate, on that basis, granted the order, adding he was also prepared to consider a maintenance order, if applied for.[52] Local newspapers also provided such information, as when the Birmingham stipendiary, Mr Kynnersley, heard an application for separation from Mrs Giles, whose husband was (typically) regularly drunken and physically abusive. Equally typically, Mrs Giles advertised to the court her ability to support herself and her children. Mr Kynnersley commented there was 'no reason why we should not avail ourselves of the Act of Parliament that has been passed for the protection of women', and granted both a separation order and a maintenance order. Interestingly, Mrs Giles was reminded by the magistrate's clerk that she 'must not marry again' (she assured the court she had had enough of marriage).[53]

Cases from the Divorce Courts were also regularly reported, as much for the legal lessons to be learned as for the sensational narratives involved. Indeed, it would be fair to say that, as an everyday matter, the cases appearing in the Divorce Courts placed more emphasis on the legal dimensions to a case and judicial reactions to the responses made by husbands to the necessary assertions of cruelty made by their wives in seeking either separations or divorces. Mrs Kelly, for instance, sought

---

[51] Anon (1886) *A Generation of Judges by their Reporter* (London: Sampson Low and Co.) pp. v–vi.

[52] 'A Separation Order Granted', *Pall Mall Gazette*, 17 October 1878.

[53] 'Birmingham Police Court Yesterday', *Birmingham Daily Post*, 14 March 1879.

a judicial separation from Rev James Kelly on the grounds of cruelty, which he denied; claiming that he 'had done nothing except what the law permitted him in the exercise of his marital authority to do'. In his judgment, Lord Penzance pronounced that a man who conducted himself as Kelly claimed to have done 'is in danger of overstepping his rights' as well as being bound to fall short in his marital duties. Amongst other instructive comments, Penzance pointed out that her husband's actions in 'deposing her from her natural position as mistress of her husband's house' amounted to cruelty. He highlighted that there were limits in law, as well as morality, to a husband's rights to pressure his wife into conformity to his will and that he had obligations to protect his wife's interests. Because of this manifest failure, amounting to cruelty, Mrs Kelly secured her separation, and readers of this judgment received useful information about the limits of a husband's rights over their actions.[54]

Spreading 'conviction'

There were a number of important developments in this period, in terms of legislative initiatives and developments in practice, which were carefully reported for the readership. In their coverage of such shifts, newspapers adopted a 'respectable' attitude in their interpretation of the seriousness and impact of criminal events. One factor contributing to this uniformity was likely to be the developments in the franchise between the 1860s and mid-1880s. The nation's political landscape progressed first through Disraeli's 'leap in the dark' in the shape of the enfranchisement of the urban working classes through the Reform Act 1867. In practice, this made the largely respectable working-class male head of household numerically the largest category of voter in most urban constituencies. It was a development which helps to explain the increasing urgency felt by politically astute (or ambitious) lawyers to make criminal justice legislation more accessible or user-friendly to this increasingly politically active urban population. Legislation enacted during the 1850s, such as the Criminal Justice Act 1855, which extended summary jurisdiction to all cases of simple larceny (with the consent of the accused, who retained the option of choosing a higher court), and

---

[54] 'Court of Probate and Divorce: Kelly v Kelly, Important Judgment', *Illustrated Police News*, 11 December 1869. The Kelly case was widely reported in provincial papers and national titles aimed at a working-class readership, indicating a clear sense that such information was seen as relevant to its readers.

the 1860s, notably the Offences Against the Person Act 1861 (which finally passed onto the statute books, after nearly 30 years of various draft formats), were consequently discussed regularly through their application to particular cases. The newspaper reportage from the summary courts reveals that the importance of this legislation for criminal cases in these courts was huge. It effectively made cases of simple larceny, undoubtedly the most common example, as well as the various types of assault that characterised the everyday working-class landscape, easier to identify and to secure a successful prosecution.

In January 1862, for example, Elizabeth Driscoll brought her husband Alexander to court, complaining of his 'brutal treatment' and asking that he be bound over so she could have peace. The case was reported in some detail, and the sobriety and good behaviour of the wife and the extent of Driscoll's drunken physical brutality (kicking her so badly that she had to go to hospital) led the stipendiary, Mr Tyrwhitt, to send Driscoll to prison for two months, with hard labour.[55] Later that year, Susannah Jacquin charged her husband with a 'violent assault' and asked for him to be bound over. *Lloyds* was careful to report the case in detail in order to lay out the grounds on which the request was denied by Mr D'Eyncourt, as a warning to other women. It turned out that Mrs Jacquin had on her own admission 'pinched' her drunken husband for threatening to go to the Derby with 'some other "gal" ': he claimed that she had also thrown some of the shop weights at him and struck him on the chest, and it was after that he had hit her. Mr D'Eyncourt commented on the 'brutal and unmanly' conduct of Jacquin but that, 'as the complainant had commenced the assault', he could only discharge the defendant.[56] Isabella Ingram, who attempted suicide because of her husband's brutality, was told by Mr Woolrych at Worship Street that her proper course of action would have been to 'come here for a summons', as a result of which her husband 'would have been punished'.[57] By contrast, Mrs Searle was successful in her application to have her husband bound over, because, while he had abused her verbally and threatened her with a knife, he had inflicted no physical damage. As a result, Sir Robert Carden was happy to bind him over, in the sum of 20 guineas, to keep the peace with his wife for a year; partly because by then he would be dealt with for the bigamy which also came to light during the trial.[58]

[55] 'Police Intelligence', *Lloyds Weekly*, 5 January 1862.
[56] Ibid 8 June 1862.
[57] Ibid 7 September 1862.
[58] Ibid 20 September 1863.

What such reportage warned, or assured, readers was that most magistrates, whether stipendiary or lay, favoured imprisonment rather than binding over brutal husbands, even when wives or partners insisted they only wanted them bound over.

Equally, there was careful reportage of larceny cases which would enable both sides to get a better sense of where the summary courts were likely to invoke the Criminal Justice Act 1855 rather than automatically referring a case to the Quarter Sessions. Henry Bowyer, a clerk, and William Garner, a cooper, were charged with larceny, which focused on Garner's providing Bowyer with pockets-full of oranges. Bowyer claimed that he was 'not aware that he was doing wrong in having the oranges given to him'; while Garner admitted he knew he was doing wrong but that it was habitual for him and other men in his position to do so. Both men had good characters, and the Lord Mayor commented that he 'was inclined to make a distinction between this sort of pilfering and that of a regular system of robbery, by which some people got their living' (there was no hint in the detailed reportage that Bowyer was selling the fruit on). Consequently, 'instead of sending them for trial' he would treat them 'leniently' by fining each 3*l* [guineas] with 'the alternative of 21 days imprisonment'.[59] William Moore, 16, was charged by his sister with stealing 5s 3½d from her: he was an 'incorrigible' lad, who had not been previously convicted of a crime but would not settle to work. Moore was sentenced by Mr Partridge 'under the Criminal Justice Act [1855]' to three months with hard labour, in the hopes he would come out 'a wiser and a better boy'.[60] But, when Thomas Honner, 16, was convicted of stealing money from his father (£9 13 6d), he received six months' hard labour 'under the terms of the Criminal Justice Act'. The harsher term was clearly not so much because of the greater sum involved but because, though also a juvenile, he was given a 'bad character' by his father. Honner had endured a previous spell in a reformatory which had not worked, and he was also, as Mr Ingram, the stipendiary at Hammersmith pointed out, 'over the age' of being returned to one, so there was no alternative but the maximum prison sentence at his disposal.

Lawyer–reporters and lawyer–journalists also took the opportunities provided by the newspapers to spread their conviction that the penal servitude system introduced in the 1850s was a bad thing, enhancing

---

[59] 'Police', *The Times*, 9 January 1862.
[60] 'The Police Courts', *Daily News*, 3 October 1863.

serious criminality and so the security of the ordinary citizenry. In one editorial in 1864, *The Times* insisted that the habitual offender was 'a standing reproach to our criminal law', adding that there was 'something wrong' in legislation which permitted criminals to 'pursue a long career of crime with no more interruption than an occasional punishment so limited in its duration as to be absolutely inefficacious in checking his course'.[61] The *Leeds Mercury* in another editorial echoed such comments made in the national press, asserting that it had become 'notorious' that for convenience and cheapness the Criminal Justice Act 1855 was being wrongly employed: in many instances, 'old offenders' were being convicted under the Act, thereby encouraging such criminals to proceed to more serious crime.[62] The *Era* thundered in September 1862 that the 'dangerous condition of our public highways' was 'perfectly scandalous' and clearly resulted from the 'disgraceful habit of petting criminals' by letting them out early on tickets of leave.[63]

Throughout this period, opinion columns and reports from the criminal courts insisted that the system meant the English people suffered 'injustice' from this politically driven and practically misguided attempt at criminal reformation, and exhorted them to bring pressure on their elected representatives in order to bring about its abolition. Though it is possible to find, in the papers, the ripostes of men like Colonel Jebb, who sought to show that, in fact, the figures demonstrated the effectiveness of penal servitude and that there were low levels of actual convict recidivism, these had little effect on the overall coverage. Such explanations only 'irritated' a 'justly exasperated public', according to newspaper comment.[64] What this demonstrates is that, while there was, to a considerable extent, a very positive role played by the lawyer–reporters and lawyer–journalists in informing and instructing the public about how the law was likely to affect them on a daily basis, the profession was also perfectly able and willing to use the media in a less admirable way. The deliberate and negative sensationalising of the issue of how well penal servitude could work in this period has had enduring impacts on attitudes towards prison and the vexed question of whether or not prison 'works'.

---

[61] Editorial, *The Times*, 12 August 1862.

[62] 'Crime in England', *Leeds Mercury*, 18 August 1862.

[63] 'The Ticket of Leave Rascals and How Long are They to be Endured?' *Era*, 7 September 1862.

[64] 'Sir Joshua Jebb's Defence of the Ticket of Leave System', *Sheffield and Rotherham Independent*, 24 November 1862.

Conclusion

What lawyers working in and for the press managed to do very success-fully in this period was to establish the respectability and authority of the press as a channel for conveying both information and ideas. That success was to contribute significantly to the transformation of atti-tudes towards journalism as a whole, making it a respectable career for educated, middle-class young men. The following chapter will explore the period of crime reportage at the end of the century, including the first challenges to legal dominance of crime reportage from the courts.

3
Challenging the 'Golden Goose'? 1885–1900

Introduction

This 15-year period saw some of the most mature and wide-ranging legal reportage, but also the shift towards a new approach for incorporating sensationalism into crime reportage, with a renewed emphasis on investigative journalism. Starting with W.T. Stead's 'Maiden Tribute of Modern Babylon' campaign in 1885, such practices were to challenge the conventions established by lawyers as reporters and journalists for legally responsible and informed reportage with the emphasis on in-trial and post-trial journalism. In many ways, Stead's reportage in the *Pall Mall Gazette* was a harbinger of things to come, because, though his own trial for unlawful kidnapping featured heavily in the newspapers, the contextual background to that trial was Stead's own exercises in investigative journalism. The purpose behind Stead's series had been to demonstrate the ease with which he and his coadjutors (including Bramwell Booth and Josephine Butler) had procured an under-age girl for the ostensible purposes of facilitating sexual intercourse with a certified virgin. The aim was to ensure that the Criminal Law Amendment Bill currently before Parliament would be passed before the session ended, unlike its predecessors since 1881. These had failed largely due to entrenched positions in the Lords. His investigations into matters then of more moral than criminal concern, in order to promote legislative change in the shape of what became the Criminal Law Amendment Act 1885, required him and his collaborators to break the existing law. Given the high publicity he generated for his strategy and the clear indications in his own words that he and his helpers were criminally liable, the fact that he ended up in court was entirely predictable. But his trial also highlighted another important development in this period concerning the actual workings of the criminal justice system.

In the last years of the period examined in the previous chapter, there was a new spirit discernible in government towards the management of the criminal justice process. The frame within which this spirit should be viewed included an increased electorate post-1867, the growing power of the trades unions and a variety of debates about efficiency in the legal system (including that of the police forces, now firmly established across England and Wales and so a familiar feature of the criminal justice landscape). That drive for increased efficacy which had produced the Jervis Acts in 1848 and consequently an enhanced reliance on the summary courts was still visible in government nationally and locally in the late 1870s. The will to establish a more orderly and moral citizenry continued, but even liberal confidence in the ability and readiness of the everyday citizen to effectively prosecute indictable offences was diminished. By contrast, there was growing confidence in the ability of local police forces to initiate prosecutions on behalf of the communities they served, so long as the local funds permitted the initial outlay.[1] During this period, there was also a high profile public debate, led by Fitzjames Stephen, about the merits of codification of criminal and civil law in England and Wales. This revival of an earlier debate, originally brought to prominence in the 1830s by Lord Brougham, was prompted not by direct European comparisons (notably with France) but by the publicity given to models provided by various colonial codifications, particularly that of the Indian Criminal Code of 1870.[2]

Partly because of the issue of habitual criminality and the publicity given in court reportage to the issue of ticket-of-leave men (and women) during the 1860s and 1870s, the Government had already moved to a nationalisation of prisons in 1877, a sign that the state was increasingly willing to be more interventionist in the area of criminal justice policy. The expanding professionalism of civil servants within the Home Office helped promote the development in public prosecutions.[3] Under the direction of Augustus Stephenson, the Home Office was able to take on the financial burden of public prosecution in a growing number of

---

[1] When successful, the police could recoup the expense of a prosecution by claiming back their expenses.

[2] J. Rowbotham and K. Stevenson (2000) 'Societal Distopias and Legal Utopias: Reflections on Visions Past and the Enduring Ideal of Criminal Codification', *Nottingham Law Journal*, 9(1), 25–38.

[3] R. Chadwick (1991) 'Sir Augustus Stephenson and the Prosecution of Offences Act of 1884', in W.M. Gordon and I.D. Fergus (eds) *Legal History in the Making. Proceedings of the Ninth British Legal History Conference* (Hambledon: Continuum) p. 202.

indictable cases, because the centralising measures he promoted were cheaper than the old system of rewards and allowances to incentivise prosecutions by individual citizens. Because there was no obligation to prosecute when an offence had been committed, too many worrying offences in the 1860s and 1870s had gone unprosecuted, especially those involving fraud or other examples of what was later dubbed 'white collar' crime.[4] These cases were notoriously difficult to prove, and so notoriously expensive to prosecute (the Tichborne criminal prosecution is estimated to have cost over £100,000),[5] and the idea of establishing the national role of public prosecutor to ensure proper prosecution of such cases took hold from 1879. This was in the aftermath of Scotland's more successful initiative in allowing the courts to deal with the widely reported fraudulent failure of the City of Glasgow Bank the previous year. It was, in the words of James Bulwer QC to his fellow MPs, too 'onerous' a duty to expect 'private persons' to undertake it, and it was thus up to the state to take on that burden.[6] Reluctantly, the Treasury acknowledged such public spirit and the will of Parliament. Under the Prosecution of Offences Act 1884, the role of Treasury Solicitor was combined with the role of Director of Public Prosecutions, with a responsibility to prosecute not only all those offences previously in the remit of the Treasury Solicitor but those dealing with fraud, those sent to the office by Justices' clerks, the police and similar bodies, and those agreed to be too difficult for any single individual, firm or authority to handle independently.[7]

While the numbers of cases referred to the new Public Prosecutor expanded steadily in the last 15 years of the century, summary prosecutions remained largely untouched by this development. The Treasury, while accepting its new role in relation to indictable cases, ensured that the campaign for criminal law codification died in 1885 on the grounds

---

[4] Anthony Trollope, in *The Way We Live Now* (1875, published serially from 1872), inveighed against the inability of the English justice system to deal effectively with rogues and scoundrels like Melmotte before they have brought misery to many gullible (and greedy) individuals; in order to ensure that Melmotte does come to a credible sticky end, Trollope has him commit suicide. Another highly popular novelist writing on the same theme was Mrs Henry Wood, in novels such as *Oswald Cray* (1864).

[5] See McWilliam, *The Tichborne Claimant.*

[6] James R. Bulwer, *Hansard* HC Debates, 14 March 1879, cols. 968–969.

[7] The Treasury Solicitors were responsible for prosecutions such as those for murder, which involved the death penalty, but also cases such as rape, considered too difficult to be handled by private citizens and institutions.

of expense.[8] Equally, during this period, the campaign for the establishment of a Court of Criminal Appeal, to widen the restricted remit of the Court for the Consideration of Crown Cases Reserved established in 1848, was unsuccessful. Thus, for readers of newspapers, these important shifts in prosecution policy at the highest level, accompanied by a contextual inertia towards broader reforms, had little visible effect on the everyday practices in summary cases which judged over 90 per cent of all prosecutions. The dominant trope in this period remained reportage from the courtroom, especially the police courts. This domination was challenged only by high profile sensations such as that created by the killings in Whitechapel in the autumn of 1888. Here, the focus was new, though one now familiar to us today. Failing an identification of the perpetrator, the focus in this reportage was on the actual criminal event and the preliminaries to the trial, in the shape of the investigations to uncover the dimensions of the 'crime'. But it was unusual.

The Whitechapel murders and Sherlock Holmes – harbingers of things to come

Retrospectively, it is possible to see that the foundations for a downgrading of the importance of reportage and comment orientated around the courtroom narratives were being laid in this period. The journalism surrounding the Whitechapel murders of 1888 was sensational and indicated the swift impact on crime intelligence production of the key factor that was to undermine the legal monopoly on crime reportage: the British professional journalist. It is informative to survey briefly the nature of investigative journalism reporting on the Whitechapel killings.[9] The location was already notorious: the headline in *The Times* covering the killing of Mary Ann Nicholls simply announced 'Another Murder in Whitechapel', with a certain weariness of expectation.[10] Local newspapers made much of the issue, but, apart from the expected

---

[8] Rowbotham and Stevenson, 'Societal Dystopias', pp. 28–29.

[9] It is not intended to go into considerable detail, given the numbers of books dealing with the Ripper murders and the press. See L. Curtis (2001) *Jack the Ripper and the London Press* (New Haven, CT: Yale University Press), amongst others.

[10] 'Another Shocking Murder in Whitechapel', *The Times*, 1 September 1888. There were other similar headlines in the national and provincial papers underlining popular association between the crime of murder and the location of Whitechapel: 'Another Awful Murder in Whitechapel', *Lloyds Weekly* 2 September 1888; 'Another Mysterious Tragedy in Whitechapel', *Northern Echo*, 1 September 1888.

candidates such as the *Illustrated Police News*, the national press was not particularly concerned initially. One correspondent to *The Times* sighed that such murders were 'it may almost be said, bound to come', given the nature of Whitechapel, hoping that the strength of local reaction would finally result in the cleaning up (morally and physically) of the location.[11] In general, the sensational reportage was used to promote opinion journalism which reflected on other ongoing wider issues, including the capabilities of the Metropolitan Police, the failure of local government to provide proper street lighting in Whitechapel and the failure of government and charitable campaigns to redeem the wretchedness of Whitechapel.[12] In the *Pall Mall Gazette*, Stead commented that 'The Whitechapel murder is no doubt very foul, loathsome, and horrible. But when all is said and done, that is no reason why people should go stark staring mad over it.'[13] However, in the face of determined reporting from investigative journalists, the *Pall Mall Gazette* as well as other titles continued to produce and recycle information about the killings. The failure to find a culprit promoted journalism repeating theories about perpetrators and motivations, if with diminishing frequency after the end of 1888.[14] Apart from a number of comments, the killings largely disappeared from the news and comment columns from 1899 on (until renewed interest at points in the twentieth century). At the time, the crime intelligence produced during the last frenzied four months of 1888 was unusual, and crime reportage returned to the more traditional focus on events in the courtroom. However, it proved to the new breed of professional journalists and their editors that crime would still sell titles even when there were no scenes in the courtroom to cover.

Particularly from the 1890s, the cultural context in which crime reportage was understood by its audiences also shifted. Detective fiction developed as a popular genre from the mid-century, arguably taking over

---

[11] Letter to the Editor, *The Times*, 22 September 1888.

[12] See, for instance, 'The Moral of the Whitechapel Murders', *Pall Mall Gazette*, 12 September 1888; 'The Political Moral of the Murders', *Pall Mall Gazette*, 24 September 1888.

[13] Leader, *Pall Mall Gazette*, 10 September 1888.

[14] See, for instance, the suggestion passed on via Reuters that the killer could be a Malay, which appeared first in October and continued to be publicised into November. 'The East End Murders', *The Times*, 8 October 1888; 'The East End Murders', *The Standard*, 8 October 1888; 'The London Murders', *Manchester Times*, 13 October 1888; 'The Whitechapel Tragedy', *Reynolds News*, 4 November 1888; 'Is the Murderer a Malay?', *Pall Mall Gazette*, 10 November 1888; 'Is the Murderer a Malay?', *Freeman's Journal and Daily Commercial Advertiser*, 12 November 1888.

from the *Newgate Calendar* as a source of popular crime-related fiction (if only because it was less overtly moralistic). Dickens, in his articles on the detective police in *Household Words* in the 1850s, had established the idea that their methods were essentially scientific, but, despite fictional figures such as Inspector Bucket[15] and Sergeant Cuff,[16] it was not until Sherlock Holmes arrived on the landscape that the appeal of scientific detection really gripped the mass popular imagination. Conan Doyle's short stories in particular, published in the *Strand Magazine*, prepared the way for a greater respect for scientifically based expert testimony in the twentieth century. But, building on early successful detective fiction, it also carried a convincing message that the detection of crime was as interesting as the legal drama in the courtroom. Readers never read depictions of Sherlock Holmes giving testimony in the courtroom; the implication was that, where resort to the formal justice process was necessary, the police would carry out that mundane task. While an avid reader of newspapers, Holmes came in to remedy or prevent miscarriages of justice on his own terms, not to engage directly with the formal justice delivery system. In his work and his leisure avocations, he was not shown to be a *habitué* of the courts.[17] Interestingly, though, reporters and journalists also featured little in the Holmes stories, the exception being Neville St Clair, who, though a well-educated man of the middle classes, turns to begging because he can make more money that way than as a reporter.[18]

So who were the new journalists?

By the start of the 1880s, it would not have seemed unreasonable to contemporaries that a man like St Clair should turn to journalism. The increasingly widespread habit of reading newspapers at all levels of society had encouraged the development of journalism as something more than a part-time occupation for middle-class males. It was becoming a profession in its own right, by laying claim to specialist

---

[15] C. Dickens (1853), *Bleak House* (London: Bradbury and Evans).

[16] W. Collins (1868), *The Moonstone. A Romance* (London: Tinsley Brothers).

[17] For more comment on detectives and detective fiction (including its publication in newspapers), see C. Emsley and H. Shpayer Makov (eds) (2006) *Police Detectives in History 1750–1950* (Aldershot: Ashgate); LeRoy Panek (2011) *Before Sherlock Holmes. How Magazines and Newspapers Invented the Detective Story* (Jefferson, NC: Macfarland and Company).

[18] A. Conan Doyle (1891) 'The Man with the Twisted Lip', *Strand Magazine*, 2, 623–637.

knowledge and training in the presentation of news.[19] Numbers of young men who might in a previous generation have looked to the law now looked instead to enter journalism as a lucrative and a respectable career, carrying with it social status as well as financial rewards. As Arthur Lawrence commented, journalism did not just become respectable, it also became a 'fashionable avocation'; something which clearly turned it into a suitable occupation for those from good middle-class backgrounds.[20] The new professional dimension it had acquired and the upward shift in the class background of those taking it up is further underlined by Alfred Baker's comment that 'The modern journalist cannot be too highly educated for his vocation.'[21]

Journalism, essentially, had effectively reinvented itself; distancing its new persona from its unsavoury past by the 1880s.[22] With the new middle-class recruits to its ranks, journalism undertook an ongoing process of establishing itself firmly as a profession in the eyes of older professions including, above all, the law. A new generation of public school and even university-educated men came in, with ambitions to make their names in this arena, and so to glean the rewards of both financial success and a high public profile. They began, for instance, to develop that marker of the new Victorian profession, the professional association. In 1889 the Institute of Journalists was founded. The new breed of journalist was also interested in news-gathering. This had already become a more professionally organised affair in many areas of news information with, for example, the establishment of Reuters in 1858 and the Press Association in 1868. These two and various similar agencies had promoted greater accuracy and responsibility in providing information on foreign and political news in particular.[23]

News-gathering and reportage

This development also encouraged a new attitude towards the role of news or information-gathering by journalists. When researching social

---

[19] H. Perkin (2002) *The Rise of Professional Society: England Since 1880* (Abingdon: Routledge).

[20] A. Lawrence (1903) *Journalism as a Profession* (London: Hodder and Stoughton) p. 2.

[21] Baker, *Pitmans Practical Journalism*, p. 13.

[22] Escott commented that for a gentleman to admit to journalism was equivalent to admitting alcoholism. Escott, *Masters of English Journalism*, p. 49.

[23] See D. Read (1999) *The Power of News; the history of Reuters* (Oxford University Press); C. Moncrieff (2002) *Living on a Deadline: a history of the Press Association* (London: Virgin Books).

conditions, some earlier journalists like Henry Mayhew and James Greenwood had acted as their own investigative reporters, producing pieces with powerful public impact. Mayhew's *London Labour and the London Poor* (1854–1856) had started as a series of newspaper articles in the *Morning Chronicle*, and James Greenwood's *Seven Curses of London* (1869) also had its roots in articles published in the *Pall Mall Gazette* and *The Times* in 1866.[24] But, while both men were successful and achieved a degree of respect, if not total respectability, they were not considered, as journalists, to be 'professionals' in the modern sense, with all the implications that label had for both social standing and income.[25] However, by the 1880s, the use of legally trained reporters for court reportage had also transformed the status of reportage in general, establishing crime reportage as being at the pinnacle of that status.[26] This all served to emphasise to the new breed of specialist journalists that it would be both interesting and useful for journalists to take some responsibility for that dimension, bringing an educated judgment to bear on the issue of what was and what was not important or relevant to a particular theme, instead of leaving information-gathering to less qualified and less educated hacks, interested more in the size of the payment they received than in the quality of the information gleaned.[27] The consequence was, therefore, an increasing blurring, and eventually a disappearance, of the distinction between the two categories in terms of both prestige and pay from the 1880s onwards, so that by 1910 the comment could be made that the terms were effectively interchangeable, as they have remained.[28]

It was a help to the new journalist that this new approach to journalism complemented the approach to newspaper publishing taken by the newcomers to the field, such as Harold and Alfred Harmsworth. As Joel Wiener has pointed out, 'Profits replaced ideas as the motor force of the new industry of journalism.'[29] The late Victorian newspaper was thus

---

[24] Mayhew's articles appeared in the *Morning Chronicle* and formed the basis for the first three volumes of his 1861 publication. See also 'A Night in a Workhouse', *Pall Mall Gazette*, 12 January 1866; J. Greenwood (1869) *The Seven Curses of London* (London: Fields, Osgood and Company).

[25] J. Wiener (ed.) (1988) *Papers for the Millions*; M. Conboy (2004) *Journalism, A Critical History* (London: Sage).

[26] Baker, *Practical Journalism*, p. 113.

[27] Ibid p. 25.

[28] G. Binney Dibblee (1913) *The Newspaper* (London: Williams and Norgate) p. 20.

[29] Ibid p. xxii.

a much more overtly commercial operation than earlier productions, though it is not intended to claim that commercial motives were always a matter of significance. But the expanding profits of the new tabloid newsprint gave such proprietors greater leeway in funding aspects of the new papers, and this had a marked effect on their employees. More jobs were created on the papers, and the recruitment unequivocally targeted professional journalists.

These new professionals increasingly expected to be paid substantial salaries, commensurate with a professional status. The Harmsworths led the way, offering much higher salaries for those working on their newspapers, the recipients expected to be the dominant figures in their titles, and setting up the grounds for a challenge to lawyer–reporters and lawyer–journalists.[30] It has been said of the Harmsworth brothers that it was Harold's accountant instincts (he was the more commercially orientated of the two), quite as much as Alfred's journalistic instincts, which underpinned their success. Alfred, like Kipling, developed his interest in journalism while editing a school magazine, and, on leaving school, entered the world of publishing, working on an illustrated magazine for boys owned by the *Illustrated London News*, and later, in 1886, on a special interest periodical, *Bicycling News*. He looked with interest and envy at the great publishing success of the 1880s. A popular 'newsy' periodical such as *Tit-Bits* was selling around 900,000 copies per month, while the increasing appetite for news, especially that which could be sensationally packaged in some way and also illustrated, was reshaping even the more staid and established papers.[31] It is within this context that the enormous commercial and popular success of Stead's daringly innovative 'Maiden Tribute' journalism needs to be understood. It showed editors and proprietors, as well as journalists, that it was possible to sell papers with a new format for 'crime' journalism.

New ways forward for newsprint?

The success of Stead's campaign as a piece of journalism had been due, according to comment in other papers, not just to the content but also to the presentation of the story, and had resulted in the paper acquiring for a while a significantly higher circulation as well as an expansion of its

---

[30] Ibid p. 57.

[31] See K. Jackson (2001) *George Newnes and the new journalism in Britain 1880–1910: culture and profit* (Aldershot: Ashgate); P. Ferris (1972) *The House of Northcliffe: A Biography of an Empire* (Omaha: World Publishing) especially ch. 1.

readership outside its normal target audiences.[32] With 'Maiden Tribute', the *Pall Mall Gazette* had resorted to eye-catching warning headlines, to alert a potential readership to its exciting and lurid information (something which the *Illustrated Police News* took with some offence as stepping onto its own territory).[33] It also added another innovation: the interview, something which may have been condemned by *The Times* but which the reading public clearly reacted to very positively.[34] Finally, Stead made no secret of his authorship of the key parts of 'The Maiden Tribute', as well as his editorship of the paper. Stead was clearly influenced by the mass market American newspaper press, and the commercially remunerative popular appeal of this enterprise also interested the Harmsworth brothers. They too were determined to make their mark in this sector of publishing, which they believed involved developing a very different kind of newspaper, as well as periodicals, from the types that (with the exception of *Tit-Bits*) dominated the British media scene in the late Victorian age. After a brief foray into periodical publishing, they decided to move into newspaper publishing, purchasing the *Evening News* in 1894 and dramatically changing the format of the paper.

Alfred was aided in his vision of changing the face of British newspaper publishing by new advances in technology, assisting the development of headlines and also, affordably, illustrations to break up the solid mass of text. It was an immediate success, and by the November of that year sales were reaching 400,000. Two years later, circulation had risen to nearly 800,000, and annual profits were around £50,000. This gave the Harmsworth brothers the encouragement, and finance, to try to produce a British version of the American newspaper format, with the launch of the *Daily Mail* on 4 May 1896. At the cost of a halfpenny for the eight-page newspaper, it provided a shorter, more physically appealing newspaper that was undoubtedly easier to read and advertised as 'The Busy Man's Daily Newspaper'.[35] Its immediate success, with a circulation reaching 500,000 within a couple of years, forced established newspapers to consider changing their format also, at the very least to consider including some illustrations, if they were to continue to compete. Of course, the rivalry was greater with evening papers such as the *Pall Mall*

---

[32] For example, *Daily Telegraph*, 7 July 1885.
[33] *Pall Mall Gazette*, 4 July 1885, used the headline: 'Notice to Our Readers. A Frank Warning'. See also *Illustrated Police News*, 29 August 1885.
[34] *The Times*, 8 July 1885, for example.
[35] J. Wiener, 'How New Was the New Journalism?' in Wiener (ed.) *Papers for the Millions* p. 50.

Gazette, which radically changed its appearance, and the less substantial titles such as the *Daily Telegraph*, but even *The Times* was conscious of the impact of the new style of newspaper publishing.[36]

The new-fangled appearance of the print pages was something radical enough for Conan Doyle to make Sherlock Holmes comment on, comparing what he saw as the 'leaded bourgeois of a *Times* article' with the 'slovenly print of an evening halfpenny paper'; but it was the latter that was winning the circulation race.[37] Nor was this just because of the simpler and more accessible appearance of the new papers. Their actual content also changed radically, forcing the older established papers, however reluctantly, to follow suit. For one thing, there was a lessening of the concentration on crime as the only substantial and exciting alternative to parliamentary and other political news. Things previously seen as mainly the purview of periodicals, including gossip, sex and, of course, sport, now vied with crime for room in the pages of national daily newspapers, bringing together even more emphatically the craft of reportage as information-gathering and journalistic comment. Following the American example, the appetite of late Victorian British readers was for titles which conveyed news in ways that conferred rapid 'enlightenment', especially to commuters as they scanned the papers on their way to and from work. As a result, the expansion in newspaper readership already discernible at the start of the 1880s gathered pace and 'approximately quadrupled' over the next two decades.[38] It all testified to the appeal of this combination of reporting and journalism as a tactic to produce news items which were readily absorbed and popular with readers across a very wide class market.[39]

Sensational journalism and reporting

The long-established favoured target for reportage and associated journalism was crime, especially murder. For the new journalist, murder was attractive not just because of the intrinsically sensational nature of the crime but also because (unlike many other crimes in practice) there was potentially a pre-trial narrative with a strong human interest strand which could be exploited outside the formal criminal justice process, especially

---

[36] Ibid p. 51.

[37] A. Conan Doyle (1901) 'The Hound of the Baskervilles', *Strand Magazine*, vol. XXII, p. 467.

[38] Wiener, 'New Journalism', pp. 55–57.

[39] Brake et al., *Investigating Victorian Journalism*.

where there was a mystery about the perpetrator. Few events had the durability over several months as the 1888 Whitechapel murders; most could command pre-trial coverage for only a few days. It is informative to look at late November and December 1888, when the furore over the last Whitechapel victim was dying down and no further killings had occurred. Attention was given to the 'mysterious' murder of a boy at Havant near Portsmouth, and most titles (national and provincial) reported the coroner's inquest on 29 and 30 November.[40] However, the Winter Assizes were imminent, and a charge was immediately brought against a possible perpetrator, so it was in the reportage from the courtroom and not the news columns that the mystery drama was played out, ending in the acquittal of the lad accused.[41] An attempt was made, in the case of the murder and mutilation of an eight-year-old boy in Bradford, John Gills, in December 1888 to generate a link with the Whitechapel killings and so enhance the sensationalism of the case.[42] Many papers reported discovery of a card in a local dignitary's house with a message that 'Jack the Ripper' was about, but also had to add the rider that it was 'satisfactorily established' that this was a 'silly practical joke' and the police were aware of the likely perpetrators.[43] Once again, though, the swift identification of a likely defendant ensured that the main drama was played out in the courtroom.[44] It was reported from a 'densely crowded' courtroom that the police case against the milkman William Barrett was found by the Bradford magistrates to be unsustainable.[45] What is interesting about the reportage of these murders is that, even though the prosecutions collapsed, leaving these murders unsolved, there was no apparent appetite on the part of the new, non-legal, journalists to investigate them further. The *Illustrated Police News*, under the headline of 'Unavenged Murders', did seek to capitalise on the issue of unsolved murders in late 1888 and early 1889, through a series exploring unsolved killings back into the 1850s, including the Waterloo

---

[40] See 'The Havant Murder', *The Times*, 29 November 1888; 'The Havant Murder', *Daily News*, 29 November 1888; 'Mysterious Murder of a Boy', *York Herald*, 30 November 1888.

[41] 'The Havant Murder', *The Times*, 21 December. The defendant (a lad called Husband) was acquitted, to the general agreement of the court, and the widespread newspaper coverage of the case, see 'Havant Murder', *Reynolds News*, 23 December 1888. There was no further coverage of the murder.

[42] 'Terrible Murder at Bradford', *The Standard*, 31 December 1888.

[43] See 'The Bradford Murder', *Daily News*, 2 January 1889.

[44] 'The Bradford Murder', *The Times*, 3 January 1889.

[45] 'The Murder of a Boy at Bradford', *Leeds Mercury*, 12 January 1889; 'The Bradford Murder', *The Times*, 12 January 1889.

Bridge Mystery of 1857, when a dismembered body was discovered under the bridge.[46] But they provided no solutions which might have persuaded the authorities to reopen any of the cases. Other startling murders in this period were at their most sensational through the coverage of the trials, as in the cases of Florence Maybrick and Adelaide Bartlett, charged with murdering their husbands, or the serial killings of prostitutes by Dr Neill Cream. Essentially, the rapid identification and arrest of the perpetrators left little room for sensational pre-trial investigations.

The need for a human interest strand to attract the new journalist when dealing with unsolved murder is emphasised by the relative lack of journalistic interest in the Thames Torso Murders, presumed to be the work of another multiple killer operating between 1887 and 1889.[47] Dismembered body parts of at least four women were discovered along the banks of the Thames, but the bodies were never identified. This marks a crucial difference between the coverage of two sets of gruesome murders. In the case of the Whitechapel murders of 1888 (indeed, of all the Whitechapel killings of this period), there was no mystery about the victims. They were known, and so provided a good base for research by investigative journalism. As a result, the victims provided easily sensationalised human stories to accompany their killings, providing real meat for sensational journalism. Beyond being (it was and is presumed) prostitutes, nothing was known at the time of the Thames Torso victims, and so the new journalists had little interest in pursuing this particular mystery. And, since the killings remained unsolved, there was no court reportage either.

It was not inevitably murder that offered the new breed of investigative journalist opportunities of reporting 'crime' outside the courtroom. The human story in the background to Stead's 'Maiden Tribute to Modern Babylon' did lead to some enterprising sensational journalism during July and August, with *Lloyds Weekly* taking a lead. Mrs Elizabeth Armstrong, the mother of Eliza, applied to the Marylebone stipendiary for aid in recovering her daughter. *Lloyd's News*, as they reported the following week, had decided to take an interest in seeing Eliza returned and 'justice' done to the wronged parents.[48] Their reporter or 'representative', Mr Hales, kept

---

[46] 'Unavenged Murders III: The Celebrated Waterloo Bridge Mystery', *Illustrated Police News*, 1 December 1888.

[47] It is also argued that killings in 1873 and 1902 may have been the work of the same killer. See M. Gordon (2002) *The Thames Torso Murders of Victorian London* (Jefferson, NC: Macfarland and Company.

[48] 'A Mother Seeking a Lost Child', *Lloyds Weekly*, 13 July 1885; 'A Lost Daughter Traced', *Lloyds Weekly*, 19 July 1885.

the case alive in weekly instalments into August; and, when the Home Secretary (also keeping an eye on the high profile case) decided to involve the Attorney General, the paper trumpeted that it was largely as a result of their efforts that the Government decided to take up the matter.[49] A substantial spread was provided the following week, reporting Eliza's return to her home, and rehearsing a number of conflicting and contradictory statements from individuals peripherally involved.[50] However, the title's most extensive coverage of the case, from early September to its conclusion in November, focused on the court proceedings. Indeed, the efforts of Mr Hales actually became part of the defence case, with Mrs Armstrong being quizzed about how much her story had been changed as a result of Mr Hales' intervention; something reported in the crime reportage in *Lloyds Weekly* as well as other papers.[51]

The other area of potential sensation which journalists might have been able to tap into was that surrounding miscarriages of justice, or what the media perceived as such. For the media this was, essentially, the conviction of the innocent and so a failure of the trial process to uncover the 'truth' (the legal perception perceives a miscarriage as representing a breakdown of some kind in the actual rules governing the criminal justice process). There were contemporary debates about miscarriage of justice, but these fall into two camps. On the one hand were those arguments which were, essentially, legally orientated and informed, debating the correct use of the legal process and arguing over the need for a Court of Criminal Appeal. The QC and Liberal MP Charles Hopwood, for instance, was a vocal advocate, both in Parliament and in the public arena, writing regularly to the press on the topic.[52] Letters to the Editor were a common way of raising the issue of a potential miscarriage of justice in terms of providing a critique of the way that the legal process was handled. One correspondent identified himself as a lawyer–reporter, on a miscarriage of justice in a libel case, for instance.[53] But

---

[49] 'The Mother and Her Lost Child', *Lloyds Weekly*, 16 August 1885. Interestingly, they repeated the article, with the same headline, the following weekend: 'The Mother and Her Lost Child', *Lloyds Weekly*, 23 August 1885.

[50] 'The Armstrong Mystery', *Lloyds Weekly*, 30 August 1885.

[51] 'The Charge of Abduction', *The Times*, 9 September 1885; 'The Armstrong Case', *Lloyd's Weekly*, 20 September 1885.

[52] See 'Appeal in Criminal Cases', Charles Hopwood, Letter to the Editor, *The Times*, 3 January 1885; 'Imperial Parliament', *Morning Post*, 28 March 1885.

[53] 'Johnson v Helby', One of Your Law Reporters, Letter to the Editor, *The Times*, 21 February 1890. As this case underlines, many of the legally orientated discussions about miscarriages of justice had more to do with civil cases than criminal ones.

such legally inflected, almost arcane discussions were less apparent in provincial titles and in the weeklies. They were interested in the need for a Court of Criminal Appeal, but there was less popular demand for such a Court, especially as titles such as *Reynolds News* suggested it would undermine trial by jury and thus the 'democratic' element in English justice.[54]

The second camp was media-generated, with indignation bred by issues such as the fallibility of lay magistrates or expert testimony. *Reynolds News* and *Lloyds News* regularly provided critical editorial comment on the ineptitude of magistrates. Under the headline 'A Gross Miscarriage of Justice', the former inveighed in one leader against the 'great brainless and heartless' magistracy in the shape of the Trowbridge justices, who, on the information of an informant, sentenced one lad to ten days' jail for breaking a window in the town's Conservative Club when, according to the defence offered by local solicitor Mr Jones, another lad had confessed to the crime (but was not present in court).[55] In a further column in that same edition, however, it was revealed that the real culprit had in fact come forward and that the matter had been referred to the Home Secretary to ensure the release of the wrongly convicted lad, warranting no further reportage of the incident.[56] Two years later, an editorial commented on 'Another Magisterial Scandal', rehearsing ongoing complaints about the extent to which sentencing by the lay magistracy was influenced by class issues (though the paper rarely disputed the rightness of the relevant conviction). The claim of miscarriage of justice this time was the failure of the Gosport Bench to convict a young naval lieutenant for a drunken assault on the police. According to the actual court reportage, Lieutenant Brownrigg admitted the charge and apologised; the police then indicated that they were willing to see the charge dismissed, on payment of costs. This was labelled a 'scandalous and flagrant miscarriage of justice' (because an ordinary sailor, it argued, would have been severely punished), which brought 'the administration of justice into the utmost disrepute'.[57]

Even the Florence Maybrick case, though widely reported in the press, did not provide the foundation for a sensational miscarriage of justice campaign. The issue here was disputed expert testimony and

---

[54] 'The Criminal Appeal Trick', *Reynolds News*, 25 August 1889.

[55] 'A Gross Miscarriage of Justice', *Reynolds News*, 1 August 1886.

[56] 'Miscarriage of Justice', *Reynolds News*, 1 August 1886.

[57] 'Another Magisterial Scandal', *Reynolds News*, 16 December 1888.

the instructions given by Fitzjames Stephen, presiding over the trial, to the jury.[58] Yet, while the *Pall Mall Gazette*, amongst many other papers, reported on the 'Great Outburst of Popular Indignation' in Liverpool on her conviction and the immediate moves for a reprieve, the reaction locally and nationally was complex.[59] *The Times*, in its editorial, commented that it was 'useless' to try to disguise the fact that 'the public are not thoroughly convinced of the prisoner's guilt'. However, their conclusion was that, as there was uncertainty about her absolute innocence, the best outcome was that the case be given the 'earnest consideration' of the Home Secretary, in the interests of a reprieve;[60] which duly came at the end of the month and largely satisfied the popular clamour.[61] Certainly neither *Reynolds News* nor *Lloyd's News* made more than passing, usually comparative, reference to her after that date. Thus, there were no really sensational high profile domestic cases to hit the headlines in this period (though, retrospectively, it is possible to see the origins of cases of importance at the start of the twentieth century).[62]

This underlines the weakness of the position the new journalists were in when challenging the established lawyer–reporters and lawyer–journalists to take over crime reportage in this period. The reality was that it was still in the courtroom that so much of the sensationalism of crime reportage was to be found. It was far from being an everyday occurrence that there were unsolved murders or other sensational mysteries, accompanied by opportunities for investigative journalism in company with prolonged police investigation, permitting lengthy discussion of their details in news columns. Thus, new journalists who were eager for the opportunity to report crime still needed access to the courtroom; forensic science had not yet advanced sufficiently to make the

---

[58] For a fuller exploration of the trial and press reactions, see J. Knelman (1998) *Twisting in the Wind. The Murderess and the English Press* (University of Toronto Press); for contemporary perspectives, A.W. MacDougall (1891) *The Maybrick Case* (London: Ballière, Tindal and Cox).

[59] 'The Maybrick Mystery', *Pall Mall Gazette*, 8 August 1889 (fourth edition).

[60] Leader, *The Times*, 8 August 1889

[61] This was widely reported: 'The Reprieve of Mrs Maybrick', *Birmingham Daily Post*, 23 August 1889; 'Mrs Maybrick's Conviction', *Pall Mall Gazette*, 24 August 1889; 'The Maybrick Decision', *Reynolds News*, 26 August 1889.

[62] Miscarriages of justice in the colonies could also make headlines in Britain; however, there were none in this period as sensational as the trial of the Gaekwar of Baroda in 1875. See J. Rowbotham (2007) 'Miscarriage of Justice? Post-colonial Reflections on the "Trial" of the Maharajah of Baroda, 1875', *Liverpool Law Review*, 28(3), 377–403.

investigative preliminaries regularly sensational, and, while such expert testimony as there was might be given in the coroner's court, it was always vulnerable to being trumped in actual court proceedings.

Crime news from the courtroom

Thus, for all the physical differences in the appearance of some papers, and the occasional sensation identified at the start of the chapter, it was still lawyers who controlled the output of reportage from the courtroom. Therefore, apart from the exceptions already discussed, the nature of the drama in crime reportage was restrained by the need to maintain the precision of legality, which acted as a limit on the sensationalism. Interestingly, there was an early alarm about the potential for improper reportage which might result from too great a collusion between journalists and police during the autumn of 1888, in connection with the Whitechapel murders. The *Birmingham Post* commented that while detectives were doing their work they were 'pursued and ... hunted down by another class of detectives', that is, journalists: 'Better educated, better paid and more unscrupulous than' the police, they were sent out to 'observe, to cross-question and we fear, sometimes to fee the police'. In response to the charge that, in so doing, reporters did 'little harm', it added that there was 'a great body of facts to prove the contrary', in the shape of damaging defence and prosecution cases for murder.[63] The acceptance of the legal profession as important in disseminating information via the press about the operation of the criminal justice system, and those who were involved in it, ensured that judges and magistrates, as well as barristers and solicitors, and court officials were accustomed to the presence of lawyer–reporters. The range of provincial as well as metropolitan crime coverage was thus at its most sophisticated (in legal terms) in this period, though always inflected by the issues of the day in which the public could be expected to take an interest.

As already discussed, it is unsurprising, given the furore surrounding the 'Maiden Tribute' campaign, that when Stead himself appeared in the summary courts to face charges for taking Eliza Armstrong from her parents without paternal consent, as well as indecent assault, it should attract a considerable amount of coverage. This coverage is significant to those interested in the history of crime news in terms not just of the sensationalism but also the attention paid to the fact that it was

---

[63] 'Detectives and Reporters', *Birmingham Daily Post*, 22 October 1888.

the first high profile prosecution under the remit of the Prosecution of Offences Act 1884, whereby the Treasury took responsibility for a prosecution on the grounds of public interest. It also featured an established (but legally unqualified) journalist defending himself in court and expecting to use the columns of his own paper to publicise court proceedings and their ability to provide 'justice'. With the exception of the *Pall Mall Gazette*, one theme in the coverage of Stead's appearances in both the summary and Assize courts was the highlighting of his inability to defend himself. A certain glee is apparent in the recording of his exchanges with Mr Vaughan, the stipendiary at Bow Street. Stead had a statement he wished to read: Vaughan's response was that he wished to hear only such comment as was relevant to 'the law in the case'. When Stead asked if he was to be denied the chance to air his motives, Vaughan's response was that, since he was not addressing a jury, the issue of motive was 'immaterial' to his decision on whether to commit Stead for trial. Stead must confine himself to comment on 'the facts and the law'. After a further debate in court, the first 14 'folios' of Stead's speech were rejected (apparently to laughter in the court) as irrelevant to the facts and the law. Stead was permitted to read parts of his 15th 'folio', as it dealt with the 'facts' of the case, being a narrative of the events surrounding his involvement with Eliza Armstrong (though he was stopped from reading his critical comments on Scotland Yard).[64] However, the provincial press in particular also included coverage of commentary on the legal proceedings by figures such as Ellice Hopkins on the 'justice' of bringing 'the whole power of a Government prosecution' (and so taxpayer-funded) against a man who had acted out of the highest motives (if not necessarily the best methods) in acting to alert the nation to the 'real criminals' besetting innocent young girls.[65] Was it right or appropriate so to do? enquired a number of correspondents to the press.[66]

All this ensured continuing coverage of the case when it came to trial before Mr Justice Lopes, at the Central Criminal Court, over a period

---

[64] See 'The Charge of Abduction', *The Times*, 28 September 1885; 'The Armstrong Case', *Lloyds Illustrated Paper*, 4 October 1885; 'The Abduction of Eliza Armstrong', *The Lancaster Gazette*, 30 September 1885.

[65] See 'Miss Ellice Hopkins on Social Purity', *Freeman Journal and Daily Commercial Advertiser*, 3 October 1885; 'The Purity Crusade', *Northern Echo*, 5 October 1885.

[66] See for instance 'The Armstrong Trial', Josephine Butler, *The Christian*, 1 October 1885; reprinted in *Northern Echo*, 1 October 1885.

of 12 days. Summing up, the judge explained the length of the trial by commenting that this was because of the 'large interest' the case had created, and because it was the 'first case ... of any importance tried under a new Act of Parliament, called the Criminal Law Amendment Act', which had 'introduced a great change into the criminal law' (including permitting accused parties to 'give evidence in their own defence'). He answered charges that it had been inappropriate for the Attorney General to bring a prosecution by saying he had 'wisely elected' to do so, as it enabled 'every fact and circumstance' which could exonerate them to be heard. He applauded the restraint of the Attorney General in allowing evidence which, in his opinion, would have been inadmissible if challenged (and carefully identified these). He commented on the able defence provided by the Bar to all the defendants but Stead himself, adding that he thought Stead's speech 'impressive' (while he was 'unable to agree with many of the observations he made'). He then advised the jury against finding a verdict 'consonant with your sympathies' but 'contrary to the law and contrary to the evidence', as they had been asked to do by Stead. After three hours, the jury convicted Stead on charges of abduction without the consent of the father.[67] But, though Stead was given a prison sentence, there was no cry of miscarriage of justice. There seems to have been an agreement that, in law, he was correctly convicted, though there remained amongst many a sympathy and a belief that it had been an inappropriate prosecution. For instance, 21 Oxford undergraduates published a memorial of sympathy regretting the use of 'public money and authority' to punish what they termed a 'legal irregularity'.[68]

Stead had succeeded in creating an atmosphere in which the Criminal Law Amendment Act 1885 had been rushed through Parliament and into force, and, ironically, he was one of its first targets. Given the high profile coverage of Stead's trial, it is not surprising that in the summer and autumn of 1885 this sparked off a greater will to highlight dealing with age of consent, seduction and abduction issues (including indecent assault, rape or child prostitution). But, while reportage soared, in the courtroom the difficulties of making an accusation that would be accepted by the court remained. The importance of providing sustainable

---

[67] 'Central Criminal Court: The Charge of Abduction', *The Times*, 9 November 1885; also 'The Armstrong Case', *Birmingham Post*, 9 November 1885; 'The Armstrong Abduction Case', *Ipswich Journal*, 10 November 1885.

[68] 'Mr Stead in Prison', *Northern Echo*, 14 November 1885. Stead received a three month sentence.

evidence to support any female complainant's case continued to be crucial. When 15-year-old Harriett Allen charged hairdresser Isadore Beconsfield with indecent assault, the reportage made the weaknesses in her case very plain. She had not resisted or cried out during the assault, as there was 'nobody else in the house'; she delayed reporting the case until she saw her mother, several hours later, even though she had encountered the defendant's wife on her way home (Harriett claimed that 'she did not like' to make the complaint to her). Consequently the stipendiary, Mr Saunders, 'did not think the case was made out'.[69] By contrast, on the same day Emily Scheitzer's charge saw Arthur Walker committed for trial at the Surrey sessions, because, even though she had been walking down a road 'infested with prostitutes', she had had a respectable reason to be there (meeting her husband after work); she had resisted and could show the marks of that resistance in the shape of a blow to her face, *and* she had immediately reported the assault to a nearby police constable. On those grounds, the stipendiary, Mr Chance, argued that 'nothing had been shown against the character of the prosecutrix' and so she made her case.[70]

That Stead's campaign and the resulting legislation did have some impact on the courts, however, is also plain from the reportage. There was, immediately, a greater concern over girls under 14. In the summer of 1885, the *Illustrated Police News* informed readers that, in the case of John Coulbertt, described as a 'physician's assistant', charged with 'abducting' such a girl 'without her mother's consent', Alderman Cowan made full use of the 'discretion' allowed him under the Act. Cowan was urged by Coulbertt's solicitor to release his client on bail since the charges of abduction and 'the other offence' (clearly having intercourse with the girl) were 'only misdemeanours'. However, Cowan stated that he had 'made up his mind' to 'commit the prisoner for trial' and to refuse him bail in the light of the Act.[71]

A string of prosecutions, featuring the Public Prosecutor acting on information received (especially from the police), highlighted cases for procuration of under-age girls for immoral purposes; brothel keeping and 'abduction'. One such scandal unfolded in the first part of 1886, when

---

[69] 'Yesterday's Law, Police, etc. Thames. Alleged Indecent Assault'.
[70] 'Yesterday's Law and Police etc. Lambeth: Alleged Indecent Assault on a Married Woman', *Reynolds News*, 1 July 1888.
[71] 'The Criminal Law Amendment Act', *Illustrated Police News*, 29 August 1885. The implication in the reportage of this case is that the girl was not the complainant, but the mother was.

Mr Mead 'acting on behalf of the Treasury' opened proceedings against Mrs Louisa Hart on a charge of 'having procured Florence Richardson, 12, and Rosie Shires, 13, for immoral purposes' under the terms (as readers were reminded) of the Criminal Law Amendment Act.[72] When the prosecution concluded in the Old Bailey, Mr Justice Willes was careful to lay out that, though, in many ways, she could be regarded as a victim herself (of her mother-in-law and husband), 'if a person concerted a crime with another, prepared the way for the commission of the crime by the actual perpetrator, helped him up to the actual moment of the crime', then (especially as she had subsequently 'helped him to escape undetected') that person was 'a principal aider and abetter'. In so doing, he explicitly contradicted the comment given earlier by Mrs Hart that her husband had told her that if there was trouble, he – not she – would be held responsible, and explained why he did so.[73] In other words, one of the most obvious features of everyday crime reportage in the post-Criminal Law Amendment Act period were state-funded prosecutions (summary or more serious) under that legislation.

Otherwise, the usual staples of crime reportage continued. There was, in this period, less concern about younger juveniles, with more cases featuring gangs of older youths than had been the case in the 1860s, for instance. Violence remained an issue, including domestic violence, but there was no high profile legislation in this period that significantly affected the tone of the coverage, which remained largely as it had been pre-1885. Equally, the police courts remained places where the poor went to get advice, even if they were not always happy with the outcome, as in the case of one applicant to Mr Biron, the Lambeth stipendiary. He asked for advice on a legal remedy to deal with his wife, who 'pawned everything she could get hold of for drink'. Mr Biron pointed out that he had married her 'for better or worse' and his only recourse was to make 'some arrangement' (clearly maintenance) for a separation.[74]

Cases of petty fraud, embezzlement and deceit also continued to be reported regularly, but there was one key development. In previous periods, reportage of such cases was often not followed up by prosecutions

---

[72] 'Police', *The Times*, 3 March 1886; 'Occasional Notes', *Pall Mall Gazette*, 3 March 1886; 'Committal of an Alleged Procuress', *Reynolds News*, 14 March 1886.

[73] 'The Sentence on Louisa Hart', *Pall Mall Gazette*, 10 April 1886. Equally explicit comment was provided in other papers, for instance, 'The Fashionable Procuress at the Old Bailey', *Reynolds News*, 11 April 1886.

[74] 'Lambeth: For Better or Worse', *Lloyds Weekly*, 15 February 1885.

at the Quarter Sessions or Assizes if a decision was reached by magistrates that the case was too serious to be concluded in the summary courts. In this period, an extra dimension was added to the reportage, with the new office of Public Prosecutor, who could make the decision to prosecute even small frauds if it was held by him to be in the national interest, as in the case of William Pierce. Falsely claiming university degrees, he was brought up before Mr Chance at Lambeth, charged with obtaining money (£7.10s) with 'the intent to cheat and defraud' (he was offering examination tuition for civil service posts at home and abroad). Informed by the police that there was evidence of a possible nationwide dimension to the fraud, Mr Chance directed that he be remanded and 'also directed that the matter be brought under the notice of the Public Prosecutor'.

One type of case appearing more frequently in the summary courts was prosecutions for cruelty to animals. While such prosecutions were not unfamiliar in previous periods, the majority of cases had featured cruelty by working men to their animals or by juveniles towards dogs and cats. Prosecutions of this nature continued and increased in number.[75] But, in addition, the last decades of the century saw a growing number of prosecutions aimed at middle-class men and women in an age which saw the beginning of the dog show and breeding for fashionable appearance alone. For example, William Clements, a 'dog fancier', was charged with 'causing or procuring the torture of an animal' by having the ears of a boarhound clipped (there being no direct evidence he was the actual perpetrator). The defendant's plea that it was 'fashionable' for this to be done was rejected by Mr D'Eyncourt, who commended the RSPCA for very properly taking up this case, and convicted Clements.[76] Conditions at dog shows became a cause for concern, as the *Pall Mall Gazette* commented, arguing for the RSPCA to be even more vigorous in enforcing the law in these contexts. It pointed out that it was 'rare' for a show to be held without some of the dogs being found dead in the boxes used to convey them to the shows, under the care of inappropriately trained railway men.[77] The reportage, in line with that for other prosecutions, sought to inform or warn of how the law was being applied, as in the widely reported case from a Liverpool dog show. One

---

[75] 'Gross Cruelty to a Horse', *North-Eastern Daily Gazette*, 16 March 1886; 'Liverpool Police Court: Before Messrs Joshua Sing and John Bateson – Cruelty', *Liverpool Mercury*, 3 June 1887; 'Police. At Lambeth', *The Times* 28 March 1894; 'Bristol Police Court', *The Bristol Mercury and Daily Post*, 18 July 1896.

[76] 'Police. At Westminster', *The Times*, 14 July 1886; 21 July 1886.

[77] 'Occasional Notes', *Pall Mall Gazette*, 11 August 1891.

dog owner had acquired a 'tame rabbit' for the purpose of 'brightening up his dogs': the instruction he had given to his kennelman was that, when the dogs were shown, the rabbit (with a string tied around its leg) should be thrown before them and then pulled back. The issue was whether or not this constituted cruelty to the rabbit (in terms of both the physical pain caused by the tight string around its leg and the alarm caused to it), and whether a rabbit was 'a domestic animal within the meaning of the Act'. After hearing evidence and opinion, 'the stipendiary, in giving his decision, said he was of the opinion that this was an act of cruelty'. Once again, he endorsed the prosecution brought by the RSPCA as being a 'proper case for the Society to investigate'.[78]

Conclusion

While it is during this period that the relationship between proprietors and editors and their employees changed in respect of reportage of events outside the courtroom, this had as yet little effect on the main focus of crime reportage. This remained on news from the courtroom, which sought to inform and warn as well as entertain. Apart from the opportunities offered by sensational murder cases with a human interest dimension, the dramatic revelations were most commonly those made in front of magistrates, or judges and juries. Yet, retrospectively, it is plain that the change in the broader context of newsprint meant that it was only a matter of time, and development in both investigative techniques and forensic science, before the new journalist could challenge the lawyer–reporter and lawyer–journalist to hold the public interest when it came to reporting crime. The professionalism associated with the new journalist ensured that the challenge would be made. Where did this leave the part-time reporter/journalist and professional lawyer? The comment of J.A. Strahan is telling in confirming the amateurism that characterised most of their public attitudes towards this remunerative work. Though for many it was their main source of income, at least at the start of their careers, it was not to their advantage to acknowledge this. Instead, despite the clear professionalism of the reportage and journalism produced by them, it was publicly advertised by such men as 'occasional journalism', not a full-time professional commitment; something which merely brought in extra earnings to 'provide for our pleasures'.[79] It was

---

[78] See 'Extraordinary Proceedings at a Dog Show. President of A Club Fined. Important to Exhibitors', *Belfast News Letter*, 16 September 1897.

[79] J.A. Strahan, *The Bench and Bar of England*, p. 210.

to be the challenge to anonymity in the press, and the rise of the by-line, that convinced many lawyer–reporters that maintaining their grip on the courtroom was not worthwhile, as the next chapter will discuss. Lawyers desired neither the publicity that the new journalists craved, nor the full-time commitment to a profession they saw as a lesser one, in terms of overall standing in the professional hierarchy, than that of law.

4
New Journalism Triumphant: 1900–1914

Introduction

At the start of the twentieth century, newspaper readers were still fascinated by crime, but other types of event and interests were also now being identified as news, competing for space with coverage of law-breaking in its various forms. The inexorable rise of the modern tabloid in the first decades of the twentieth century signalled the sustained market for this more commercialised and lucrative format for the popular press, relying on a compressed physical presence matched by a more succinct reportage. This contextualises a shift in attitudes towards the production of crime intelligence. From 1896 when Alfred Harmsworth launched the halfpenny *Daily Mail* with 'the explicit object of entertaining as well as informing its readers'[1] until the eve of war in 1914, there was a 'rapid acceleration of newspaper chains'.[2] The monopolies over the 'new' papers, showcasing the particular talents of the 'new' journalist, were established in the hands not of a range of regional and national proprietors, as before, but of only three dominant press barons. The original pioneers of the modern British tabloid came in the shape of the Harmsworth brothers (later Barons Northcliffe and Rothermere) with their Amalgamated Press, and Arthur Pearson, the creator of Pearson Publishing, who established the halfpenny *Daily Express* in 1900 as a direct competitor to the *Daily Mail*.[3] The

---

[1] A. Briggs and P. Burke (2009) *A Social History of the Media: from Gutenberg to the Internet* (Cambridge: Polity Press), p. 181.

[2] J. Eldridge, J. Kitzinger and K. Williams (2005) *The Mass Media and Power in Modern Britain* (Oxford University Press).

[3] The *Daily Express* was sold by Pearson to the Canadian newspaper magnate and politician Max Aitken, later Lord Beaverbrook, in 1916, forming the core of the Express Group.

Harmsworth empire, due in particular to Northcliffe's understanding of the intrinsic relationship between circulation and advertising, led the way in changing the media context. It was to have a profound effect on crime reportage, even if this was not immediately visible to contemporaries.

This new generation of newspaper moguls were, like their predecessors, considerable personalities with a firm belief in their mission manifested through the papers they pioneered or reshaped. But, as Joel Wiener has commented, these 'great newspaper personalities' bore little resemblance to their mid-Victorian equivalents, who had been driven by a will to inform and a belief in the moral responsibilities of the press as the Fourth Estate.[4] For the modern newspaper baron, 'profits replaced ideas as the motor force of the new industry of journalism'.[5] While coverage of crime remained a source of profit, it was no longer identified as the key guarantor of regular sales for all titles and all classes. The claim of these twentieth-century moguls was still to 'represent the public'; now using the analogy of representing their readership much as politicians represented their constituencies. However, their rhetoric lacked the moral force of their Victorian predecessors. This was not the whole story of the newspaper press during this period; there were titles founded which were ideas-driven, but these were much narrower and more overtly political than, say, *Reynolds News* had been in that they were primarily socialist. For example, in 1912 George Lansbury founded the Labour strike paper, the *Daily Herald*, later purchased by the TUC in 1922 in a testament to its importance to the developing socialist profile of the unions and the post-war Labour Party.[6] Yet it was not these titles that the masses responded to enthusiastically at the news-stands. In the same year as the *Daily Mail* launched, with its strapline of 'the first truly national newspaper', *Lloyds Weekly* finally broke through the magical one million circulation barrier. The *Daily Mail* achieved this a mere four years later. From 1880 to 1914 the number of purchasers of daily newspapers roughly quadrupled, and what they bought in increasing numbers were the tabloid titles, both newly established and converted.[7] For most

---

[4] Wiener, *Papers for the Millions*, p. xi.

[5] Ibid p. xii.

[6] When acquired by Odhams Press in 1929, it developed into a profits-driven mass circulation newspaper and lost its political edge (it later transmogrified into *The Sun* in 1964).

[7] Wiener, *Papers for the Millions*, p. 57. An increasingly tabloid-style *News of the World* continued to be the most widely read title, achieving a circulation of circa1.5 million by 1910.

readers, as Conboy points out, the 'entertainment and consumerism' provided by this approach 'offered a temporary and vicarious way out of...the relatively helpless position of ordinary people'.[8] But a major part of that entertainment was still provided by crime news.

Reshaping crime intelligence

This signalled a development which actually provided a more distinct difference in the type of news available than had previously existed, in that broadsheets aimed at different audiences had tailored their content to particular class or political interests but had shared the same predilection for similar presentations of solid, serious and substantial reportage, backed up by visibly informed journalism. Despite its sensational front page, even the *Illustrated Police News* had shared that presentational approach. Now, readers could choose to read a broadsheet or a tabloid, knowing that the former format continued to provide what it had always done, while the latter format provided something whereby, thanks to a combination of reportage and journalism, the headlines and suggested interpretations of those headlines could be rapidly consumed. If the tabloid format did not inform to the same degree, it enabled, arguably, a speedier absorption of the main issues ahead of or at the end of a day's work. The appeal thus transcended class as the main governor of choice of title. As Wiener comments, 'classlessness edged past class as the circulation of newspapers soared into the millions'.[9] If it created a new audience (the 'mobocracy', as readers of the *Daily Mail* were sometimes labelled), that audience still wanted to read about crime, but apparently preferred it packaged in ways that simply emphasised its sensationalism, not the carefully selected legal detail that had characterised the reportage of the last half century.[10] The summary approach of the tabloid thus created a novel context for the dissemination of crime news, but one which did a great disservice to the quality and amount of legal information available to the ordinary citizen reader.

That reader was now presented with expanded opportunities to read gossip, as well as sport, partly because of the new internal arrangements of the tabloid. Newspapers had long been sub-divided into various sections, political, legal (including criminal), news, and so on; initially the *Daily Mail* had followed suit with crime news presented under

---

[8] Conboy, *The Press and Popular Culture*, p. 89.

[9] Wiener, *Papers for the Millions*, p. xii.

[10] Eldridge et al., *The Mass Media and Power in Modern Britain*, p. 29.

similar headlines to its competitors, 'Law Courts' and 'Police'.[11] But twentieth-century tabloid papers like the *Daily Mirror* preferred a less serious emphasis in their content sub-division to highlight the human interest story dimension, providing sections under headlines such as Today's Reflections, Court Circular, Latest Intelligence, Today's News at a Glance, each listing perhaps some 20 two- or three-line national and international items, heterogeneously arranged and usually with a brief reference to a crime case, often humorous in content. Change to crime reportage manifested itself not just in terms of context but also in presentation. The popular press experimented with layout, typography and visual imagery to widen circulation and appeal as well as introducing a more 'journalistic subjectivity' in the writing, drawing the reader into the story through the use of more 'emotive strategies'.[12] As this change to physical context underlines, the populist press thus enthusiastically embraced the New Journalism on the American model of condensed and rapidly absorbed writing that combined both information and opinion.[13] This required a conflation of the role of the reporter and the journalist, something already an increasing characteristic of the New Journalism and driven by leading professional journalists. The result, when it came to crime reportage, was the continued promotion of sensationalism without the inherent reliance on a substantial underpinning of legally informed comment that had characterised the earlier forms of modern reportage and journalism.[14] Thus, the tabloid demand for condensed but appealingly sensational news was well met.

Professionalising Journalism

This was the period when the claim of the modern journalist to be a 'professional' was successfully promoted, establishing the new journalist as the key figure in the production of newsprint. Encouraged by the new breed of proprietor, they challenged lawyer–journalists in identifying themes and topics for leader columns, and gradually took over responsibility for crime stories, including reportage from the courts. The reality was that, in the 14 years before the start of the First World War, the

---

[11] See, for instance, *Daily Mail*, 4 May 1896.
[12] Conboy, *Press and Popular Culture*, p.104.
[13] See G. Muhlmann (2008) *A Political History of Journalism* (London: Polity Press); Wiener, *Papers for the Millions*; Wiener, *The Americanization of the British Press*.
[14] Wiener, *Americanization of the British Press*.

lawyer–reporter became a rarity and the lawyer–journalist a declining breed. A problem for the legal profession was that the new media approach to news meant that the more traditional forms of coverage of crime intelligence would not survive because commercial realities dictated they could not. The halcyon days of the lawyer–reporter meticulously 'replicating' the trial dialogue, even if condensed down, to form the core of the media crime narrative, and of lawyer–journalists then offering expert commentary on aspects of court proceedings through leaders and other opinion pieces, were clearly numbered.

There was a further dilemma for barristers seeking to continue a role as reporter or journalist. Given the increasingly commercial nature of the early twentieth-century newspaper enterprise, it had, as one editor reflected in 1915, become 'impossible to serve two masters', in the shape of marketplace realities and public duty. In practice, 'Either a newspaper...put before its readers the truth, as it sees it, or it must deceive them.' The editor added that it was 'impossible to combine honesty of thought and personal ambitions' (the latter reflected in the demand for by-lines) given the need to promote a title's circulation above all.[15] The issue was how far that impinged on the claims to professional status of the modern journalist, and how far it shaped attitudes towards the need for accuracy as a matter of public responsibility when it came to investigative reporting. In the light of recent events and the revelations of the Leveson Inquiry, this turning point in crime reportage assumes a new significance.

Initially, dispensing with legal professionals was not straightforward and easy. The new editors were well aware that crime sold newspapers, and that it was still in the courtroom that sensational testimony was most usually revealed in high profile cases including murders, rapes and burglaries. How could the new professional journalists regularly exploit crime stories in ways that would compete with the reportage produced from the trials? In terms of delivering responsible and accurate crime coverage, the professional journalist would never be as legally sensitive to the nuances as a professionally trained lawyer acting as reporter in the courts. On 4 November 1903 at the King's Bench Division, Mr Justice Kennedy and Mr Justice Channell dealt with a possible contempt of court charge against Thomas Catling, the editor of *Lloyds News*. That paper had published an article on 11 October commenting on the case

[15] H. Gwynne (1915) *Newspaper Editor Files* (St Bride Printing Library) cited in G. Boyce et al. (1978) *Newspaper History from the Seventeenth Century to the Present Day* (Press Group, Acton Society) p. 159.

of W. James, formerly a senior Metropolitan Police officer, who was charged with the murder of Dorcas Pizer and a further attempted murder. It suggested not only that James's defence would be that of insanity but also that his prosecution was being delayed because of his involvement with the investigation of 'certain long-term frauds', which was information from the inquest 'brought to *Lloyds* newspaper by a reporter who had supplied them with news for some years and whom they had always found reliable'. When James appeared to answer the charge of murder on 15 October, the magistrate required *Lloyds* to deny the report, which it had done on 18 October. Kennedy and Channell, however, remained concerned because it was now the case that 'newspapers give accounts of other matters which would not be admissible in evidence on his trial' and it was 'prejudicial to justice that a man's antecedents should be discussed when he was awaiting trial'. Giving judgment, Kennedy stressed that 'it was obvious that comments contained in a newspaper of reputation and large circulation was more likely to do serious mischief than comments contained in a newspaper of less credit'. Editors needed to understand that they were doing a 'great public mischief' in publishing comments on 'the special circumstances of a case where a man was awaiting trial'. A trial the previous year which had addressed the same issue should have settled the matter, but Kennedy and Channell understood it was 'difficult for men not trained as Judges or barristers' to know what it was safe to publish. Interestingly, it was agreed that it was the first time that the paper had so transgressed, underlining the consequences of its new reliance mainly on professional journalists.[16] Catling paid the required £50 fine, but, considering the continued coverage of murder cases, the question was clearly beginning to be whether such rebukes mattered, given that the buying public for such titles was clearly not concerned.

What truly spelled the end for the lawyer–reporter in particular, but even for the lawyer–journalist, was not a surrender to the direct challenge of the new journalist for seats in the courtroom or even a diminution in the popular respect for lawyers. It was the arrival of the by-line identifying the professional journalist. As seen in the three previous chapters, what had made the presence of the lawyer–reporter in the courts acceptable, and had encouraged the growth of lawyer-authored journalism about crime and the criminal justice process, had been its anonymity. For the lawyers writing in the press, their professional identities rested on their credentials as lawyers. They neither sought nor

---

[16] 'Kings Bench Division', *The Times*, 4 November 1903. The previous case referred to was *K v Tibbits and Windust* [1902] 1 KB 77.

craved an acknowledgement of their reportage from the courts in the media. Even the lawyer–journalist was more likely to eschew anonymity for some productions at least, but, as in the case of the many opinion pieces and editorials that were authored by them, anonymity was their default position. After all, as the largely anonymous memoirs that initially led to the uncovering of this dimension underline, an amusement was to be had from reading one's opinions in print without the potential embarrassment of its being known to a wider public who was the author responsible for such views. The full-time journalist could attain a professional identity only when, and if, so identified in the media, which meant use of American style by-lines. It was a move that made sense to the new brand of newspaper proprietor, but not to the Bar, which had, let it be remembered, only supported lawyer–reporters on the basis of their anonymity.

New relationships

This shift did not happen overnight, nor did it signal an end to the links between the legal profession and the media. At the start of the century, the monopoly maintained by lawyer–reporters over reportage from the criminal courts, rooted in their relationship with their fellow professionals, meant that those few professional journalists who gained access to one of the highly sought after designated press seats in the lower and higher courts were still at a disadvantage. They had no easy access to the authority provided by the intimacy of personal legal contacts enjoyed by the lawyer–reporters, which enabled the profiling of personalities of a case that was so appealing to the readership. Even reputed professional journalists, with high standing earned in other areas of reportage, such as the *Daily Telegraph*'s J. Hall Richardson, could only take advantage of a press seat in Old Court when one of *The Times*' resident lawyer–reporters vacated it on joining the Bar. Even then, the good will of the vacatee was required to secure it for him.[17]

If lawyers were no longer directly responsible for reportage from the courts, there are clear indications in various sources, including memoirs, of a linkage between the journalists who became responsible for crime reportage and criminal barristers and solicitors. When the American

---

[17] J. Hall Richardson (1927) *From the City to Fleet Street* (London: Stanley Paul) p. 205. The representatives of the new tabloids were further down the pecking order, often lacking the requisite legal knowledge to decipher and so report court proceedings effectively.

journalist R.D. Blumenfeld moved to London to establish himself as a key figure in journalism at the end of the nineteenth century, his diary records his early efforts to meet and get on good terms with leading barristers like Montague Williams QC and Alfred Cock QC, and solicitors such as George Lewis.[18] Equally, J. Hall Richardson's memoirs recount his close association with such figures as Lord Alverstone and Edward Abinger.[19] Public acknowledgment of this new dimension to the relationship came in 1911, when reputed barrister Edward Abinger agreed to talk on record to the leading crime reporter for the *Daily Express*, which promptly and proudly trumpeted the fact. Under banner headlines,

JUSTICE FOR PRISONERS
HARDSHIPS OF THE LAW OF EVIDENCE
NEED FOR CHANGE

it informed its readers that the QC had 'repeated to the "Express" representative what he told the Court of Appeal' and his opinion that 'The law...needs such amendment as will allow the defence in capital cases to cross-examine thoroughly witnesses called by the Crown without the prisoner being exposed to the penalty of being cross-examined regarding his own conduct.'[20]

The substance and shape of the comments differed little from the anonymous leader comment that was to be found in earlier reportage. The significance was that one of the leading barristers of the day had shown himself willing to be quoted, and in a tabloid. In so doing he became linked directly and publicly with the expression of a substantial legal opinion, rather than remaining an anonymous informant. Such developments depended on the increasing recognition by barristers of journalists as fellow professionals with whom they could appropriately discuss matters of mutual concern and interest. In this development, the tactics of the Harmsworths, along with Arthur Pearson, were crucial, as it was in their interests to promote an acceptance of journalists as professionals in their own right to enhance the status of their titles. A part of the claim was that journalists were at least quasi-professional because they had been trained to respond appropriately to the expanding constant public demand for access to 'verified' facts (or at least double-checked ones). As Allen comments,

---

[18] R.D. Blumenfeld (1930) *R.D.B.'s Diary* (London: William Heinemann) pp. 37–38; 43.
[19] Hall Richardson, *Fleet Street*.
[20] *Daily Express*, 4 April 1911.

journalists sought to legitimise their claim to professional status with reference to a larger sense of 'public responsibility'... A commitment to exposing the 'truth' about public affairs, regardless of the consequences, and no matter how unpalatable.[21]

At the turn of the century, it began to seem as if those claims were being accepted officially. It is a measure of how rapidly official attitudes to the tabloid style of new journalism were changing at the turn of the century that in December 1900, before the full impact of the tabloid explosion on the media landscape, the Home Office relaxed its previous opposition to the establishment of journalism as an independent and discrete profession in its own right. In that month, the Home Office indicated that it would permit the Institute of Journalists to resubmit its application for formal acknowledgement via the conferring of the Royal title that it had only recently rejected. This time, it acknowledged that 'The English press starts high as regards dignity, enterprise for an honourable sort and freedom from corruption', an aid to its claim to competence when it came to taking on responsibility for crime reportage.[22]

This rise in the status of journalism came at a time when the status and respect accorded to the criminal justice process was under a level of critical scrutiny it had not known since the revelations surrounding the defence of Courvoisier, discussed in the first chapter. The arrival of the new professional journalist enabled the press in the first years of the century to develop news stories which, in different titles, revealed to various readerships across all classes a number of actual, unassailably proven, miscarriages of justice which had clearly resulted from the workings of the criminal justice process. Before the mid-1880s, if there had always been some popular debate about the length of sentences awarded to particular individuals for their crimes, there were (with the exception of the Tichborne Claimant) no high profile individual cases where there was, in the aftermath of the trial, any serious popular doubt about the accuracy of the actual conviction as the basis for any miscarriage of justice.[23] One widely publicised case discussed in the previous chapter

---

[21] S. Allen (2004) *News Culture* 2nd edn (Oxford University Press) p. 21.

[22] TNA HO144/589/B7902.

[23] It is, of course, true that there was debate over whether or not particular types of conduct should be criminalised, such as trades union activity or imprisonment for default in the case of conscientious objection to smallpox vaccination. However, there was no real argument that those convicted of such were wrongly convicted in that they were innocent of the actual offence as it was currently constituted in law.

raised widespread popular concern about the ability of the system to avoid such wrongful conviction: the questionable conviction of Florence Maybrick on the basis of what many then (and subsequently) have felt to be judicial misdirection on points of law to the jury.[24] Legally, the only option available to those who, after conviction, maintained their innocence, or claimed their court proceedings to be unfair, was to petition the Home Secretary. However, as one legal commentator asserted, it was no longer tenable to claim that such 'appeals' guaranteed the imposition of 'justice', because the Home Secretary could only grant a pardon resulting in the remission of sentence; he had no power to quash a conviction even on receipt of genuinely new evidence which made the original conviction unsustainable.[25] Early twentieth-century crime journalism now reminded readers of cases where there had been unease about trial outcomes because they were able to focus on what was becoming identified as a 'flaw' in the current criminal justice process: its inability to take account of new evidence produced by advances in forensic science.

New realities in the courtroom: the return of miscarriages of justice as news

Such advances had already signalled a new reality in the adversary trial: where prosecution or defence rested upon scientific evidence of some kind, the only response for the opposing side was to find an expert witness of their own in order to mount a challenge. For example, fingerprints, when scientifically analysed, were presented as providing 'one of the most seemingly powerful and unshakeable forms of truth around'.[26] From the first tentative mentions in the press in the 1890s, fingerprints rapidly became a regular feature in the evidence presented in the courtroom. It was only in the early period that magistrates or juries showed themselves occasionally reluctant to accept fingerprint

---

[24] See J.H. Levy (1899) *The Necessity for Criminal Appeal as illustrated by the Maybrick Case and the jurisprudence of various countries* (London: P.S. King and Co); J. Knelman (2003) 'Why Can't a Woman be More Like a Man: Attitudes to Husband Murder 1889–1989' in J. Rowbotham and K. Stevenson (eds) *Behaving Badly. Visible Crime, Social Panics and Legal Responses* (Ashgate, Aldershot).

[25] See A. Forster Boulton (1908) *Criminal Appeals under the Criminal Appeal Act 1907* (London: Butterworth and Co.).

[26] S. Cole (2001) *Suspect Identities. A History of Finger-printing and Criminal Identification* (Harvard University Press) p. 4.

evidence; the common reaction was acceptance.[27] *The Times* could note in 1904 that 'the system was now thoroughly established in England', and that there were 60,000 sets of prints registered by the police.[28] Under the headline TELL TALE FINGERPRINTS, the *Daily Mirror* acknowledged 'the important part which fingerprints play nowadays' by reporting the identification of George Young as the culprit in the theft of jewellery and banknotes from the Great Western Hotel, Paddington. The implication in the coverage was that the subsequent trial would be a formality, since 'Marks had been found on the white paint of a bedroom window' which the police had clearly linked to Young and, indeed, that event was not reported in any detail.[29] This indicates a growing trend whereby science was replacing religion as the ultimate source of 'truth' in popular minds. The term 'forensic', meaning detailed, began to be applied solely to medical or other scientific testimony. With the public increasingly interested in the scientific proof of criminality (as a new readiness by juries to convict on such expert testimony underlines)[30] to reveal the dimensions not just of the *actus reas* but also the *mens rea* involved in any crime, there was a growing readiness to believe in the possibilities for 'truth' to be uncovered by science rather than law.

Journalists were able to capitalise on this because they were no longer mainly dependent upon legal expertise for their authority when presenting these miscarriages of justice to public scrutiny. The introduction of fingerprint technology had been crucial, because it put an emphasis on the effectiveness and 'professionalism' of pre-trial investigation by the police, rather than on the predominantly legally constructed prosecutions or defences in the courtroom, as being key to the outcome of a trial. Equally, the new respect accorded to scientific testimony enabled them to look to doctors and scientists to explore the context of a crime. They also, increasingly, used their critical commentaries to reflect on the flaws of the current criminal justice system. The fact that one such expert was Conan Doyle, the creator of Sherlock Holmes, and that he was instrumental, using the powers of the press to do so, in

---

[27] See, for instance, 'Police', *The Times*, 2 December 1903; 'Central Criminal Court', *The Times*, 8 February 1905; 'The Editor to His Friends', *Penny Illustrated Paper and Illustrated Times*, 1 July 1905.

[28] 'Identifying Criminals', *The Standard*, 22 March 1894; *The Times*, 8 October 1904.

[29] *Daily Mirror*, 19 August 1904.

[30] For a history of changing attitudes to scientific expert testimony, see T. Golan (2007) *Laws of Men and Laws of Nature. The History of Scientific Expert Testimony in England and America* (Harvard University Press).

uncovering the dimensions of one miscarriage of justice by using the forensic approach espoused by his fictional creation, was a significant boost to the standing of scientific testimony in the minds of readers. It helped that they were already predisposed to accept such testimony in a way that they had not been in the pre-1890s period, because of the popularity of stories of scientifically based detection in the 1890s.

Conan Doyle's involvement in the Edalji case offered a substantial challenge to the established process and to an exclusion of professional journalism from the area of crime reportage. The case enabled sensational but fact-based crime journalism which echoed and so made seem more 'realistic' the popular crime fiction of the day, further heightening public expectations of scientific investigation as providing a sure path to justice. George Edalji, an Anglo-Indian solicitor, was convicted in 1903 of a series of brutal cattle and horse-maiming offences, labelled in the press as the 'Great Wyrley Outrages'. His protestations of innocence attracted the support of not only the *Daily Telegraph* with its mass popular readership but also Sir Arthur Conan Doyle.[31] After he had served three years of a seven-year sentence, a petition with 10,000 signatures secured his release, but without exoneration. Edalji needed to clear his name as the conviction barred him from practising as a lawyer. The paper set up the 'EDALJI fund', appealing to its readership to send cheques to the newspaper to obtain the 'best legal assistance'. In just three days the paper had received £140 6s 6d.[32] Conan Doyle's involvement caught the popular imagination as he deployed scientifically based forensic skills in proving Edalji's innocence, publicised through a supportive *Daily Telegraph*, which promoted a serialisation of the bizarre case in *Pearson's Weekly*:

'MY OWN STORY
The narrative of eighteen years' persecution By GEORGE EDALJI Starts in Pearson's Weekly. In 1903 I was arrested' etc.[33]

Such interventions (witness the Tichborne Claimant) were not unknown. Conan Doyle's scientific investigations uncovered Edalji's myopia, which proved Edalji could not have committed the crimes alleged. Conan Doyle's actions effectively forced the establishment of

---

[31] For a detailed narrative see G. Weaver (2006) *Conan Doyle and the Parson's Son* (Cambridge: Vanguard Press).

[32] *Daily Telegraph*, 13 February 1907; 16 February 1907

[33] *Daily Telegraph*, 1 February 1907.

a Parliamentary Inquiry, which included himself and Jerome K. Jerome, ensuring continuing newspaper coverage of, and public attention to, the case and its implications. The Home Secretary finally granted a pardon absolving Edalji of the cattle-maiming but confirmed his guilt concerning the writing of a number of defamatory letters received by the local Chief Constable, Captain Anson.[34]

The Edalji case is important for two key reasons. First, it finally prompted the Government to revisit the issue of a Court of Criminal Appeal, dismissed in the 1880s amidst Treasury concerns and lack of public support. Public support was now present, and this overrode continuing Treasury resistance. The Criminal Appeal Act 1907 abolished the Court for Crown Cases Reserved (established in 1848) and replaced it with a new Court of Criminal Appeal. Section 3 provided those convicted on indictment with grounds for appeal on a question of law, and with leave, on a question of fact, mixed fact and law, or sentence. Second, it 'proved' that what Sherlock Holmes did in investigating crime was not simply enjoyable fiction, but had a real application in the criminal justice process. Coming at a time when finger-printing was also being ever more widely used to identify the 'real' culprits in a case, the scientific proof that Edalji could not have been guilty finally established in the popular mind that there was a mysterious, almost arcane, dimension to scientific investigation and subsequent testimony in criminal trials. For the first time, it showed in a high profile case with substantial media coverage that scientific expert testimony was a better path to justice than the legal debates hitherto favoured by English and Welsh juries.

The Edalji case was not the only example of a miscarriage of justice revealed to a concerned public through the press. Consider also the conviction for fraud, in 1896, of Adolph Beck, on the basis of what was subsequently demonstrated to be unreliable identification witness testimony resulting in the admission of misdirected evidence to the case. Beck's case had been taken up as a popular cause by the press. As a result of their efforts, supported by numerous petitions encouraged by

---

[34] Given racist undertones within the local community, Anson was convinced Edalji had authored them. Anson was also embarrassed about the negative publicity concerning the police investigation, and there was a real conflict of interest as his second cousin, the Chief Metropolitan Magistrate, was one of the three Commissioners on the Inquiry. Years later, labourer Enoch Knowles admitted to sending some of the letters. See Weaver, *Conan Doyle and the Parson's Son*.

the high media profile Beck acquired, his release had been secured in 1901. It was a further blow to confidence in the validity of the criminal justice process that he was *again* arrested, as a result of entrapment by the police, in 1904 and again initially convicted on the basis of yet more unreliable witness testimony to a further prison term. It is unlikely to have been coincidental that the *Daily Mirror*'s 1904 coverage of the Beck case coincided with its decision to revisit the 1889 conviction of Florence Maybrick, presenting the evidence to let its readership decide on her guilt or innocence.[35] While Beck did secure a pardon for both convictions (and £5,000 compensation), many felt that this was a miscarriage of justice which highlighted flaws not just in the trial process but also in the way the state managed post-conviction challenges to that process.[36]

This perception was also crucial in one of the most controversial appeals against sentence heard by the new Court of Appeal: that against the conviction of Stinie (Steinie) Morrison, a Ukrainian 'alien' and convicted burglar. When he was sentenced to death in March 1911 for the murder of Leon Berham (a Jew thought to be a police informant), there was widespread public unease about the conviction because of the way that prosecuting counsel, Sir Richard Muir, had manipulated an unsolicited comment by Morrison on his arrest.[37] Muir ensured that the jury was aware of Morrison's five previous convictions and, by implication, his established burglarious character.[38] The result of

[35] 'Confessions of Credulity', *Daily Mirror*, 2 May 1904; 'Today's News at a Glance: Law and Crime', *Daily Mirror*, 13 July 1904; 'The Double Case'; 'Re-Trying the Maybrick Case. "Mirror" Readers Will Be the Jury and Have the Case Impartially Put Before Them', *Daily Mirror*, 15 July 1904. For further details of the Maybrick case and the ongoing concerns about the conduct of the trial, see J. Knelman (2003) 'Why Can't a Woman Be More Like a Man? Attitudes to Husband Murder 1889–1989' in J. Rowbotham and K. Stevenson (eds) *Behaving Badly. Social Panic and Moral Outrage – Victorian and Modern Parallels*, pp. 193–205.

[36] See 'The Police Courts. Charge of Fraud – Miscarriage of Justice', *The Times*, 8 August 1904, when the real culprit, William Thomas (described as a journalist), was identified and Beck publicly cleared. However, Beck was to die in poverty in 1907, to the indignation of many commentators.

[37] Muir is best known as the prosecutor of Crippen. Given his involvement in the Beck miscarriage of justice, there is, of course, a current irony in that subsequent DNA-based forensic tests on the body assumed to be Crippen's wife have indicated that it was not her. Thus, did Crippen murder someone else, or was he genuinely innocent of any murder? See *Daily Mail*, 17 January 2011.

[38] The trial was fully covered in the press: 'The Clapham-Common Murder', *The Times*, 13 March 1911; 14 March 1911; 15 March 1911; 16 March 1911. For the expressions of unease, see 'Stinie Morrison Condemned to Death for Clapham

this was an appeal, swiftly heard by Lord Chief Justice Alverstone and two High Court judges in a test of the public acceptability of the new Court. Edward Abinger had raised the issue of jury prejudice as one of the grounds for appeal, but Muir had countered that, through his own testimony and comments during his trial, Morrison himself had created the scenario whereby the jury became aware of his previous character. The conclusion reached by Alverstone and his colleagues was that, legally, the verdict was sound and that there had been no misdirection or mistrial. *The Times* (which covered the appeal in detail) accepted this outcome with apparent content, in that there was no editorial comment at all on the appeal.[39] However, this result did not go down so well with the popular press.[40] The *Penny Illustrated Paper* reflected that the English, who had been 'wont to plume themselves on the just workings of their criminal law', had been led to believe that with 'the establishment of a Court of Criminal Appeal, miscarriages of justice might be reckoned to be next door to impossible', but unless the Home Secretary intervened a man would be hanged who should have been adjudged innocent by the system.[41] With the issue raised in Parliament, the Home Secretary commuted Morrison's sentence to life imprisonment, with many in the press arguing that he did so because of the 'fishy nature of the evidence': that the Court had not come to a similar conclusion indicated that the new system was still deeply flawed.[42] Indeed, it continued to be an issue, with a petition being submitted to the Home Office for Morrison's release in 1913.[43]

If the criminal justice system was publicly identified as flawed, a lack of revelations in the press about the quality and capability of barristers enabled them to continue to assert a place on the legal moral high ground, though solicitors continued to be revealed as dishonest or corrupt with reasonable regularity, with their misdoings duly reported

---

Common Murder', *Daily Mirror*, 16 March 1911; 'Should Prisoners Give Evidence? Legal Privilege That Has a Double Edge', *Daily Express*, 16 March 1911; 'Mr Muir and Ex-Inspector Syme', *Penny Illustrated Paper*, 25 March 1911. This is the context of Abinger's comments quoted earlier in this chapter. For full details of the affair, see A. Rose (1985) *Stinie: Murder on the Common* (London: Bodley Head).

[39] 'Court of Criminal Appeal', *The Times*, 30 March 1911.

[40] Letter to the Editor, Legal Expert, *Daily Telegraph*, 1 April 1911.

[41] 'Has Stinie Morrison's Guilt Been Proved?' *Penny Illustrated Paper*, 15 April 1911. See also 'Notes for the Week', *The New Age*, 6 April 1911.

[42] 'Plain English', *Penny Illustrated Paper*, 22 April 1911; also Rose, *Stinie*, chapter 26.

[43] 'Clapham Common Murder', *The Times*, 10 July 1913.

as being successfully managed on the whole.[44] One particularly embarrassing incident involved misconduct on the part of both a newspaper editor and a solicitor. The high profile editor of *John Bull*, Horatio Bottomley, published a letter supposedly written by Dr Crippen from prison. It turned out, however, that it had been the product of collusion between Bottomley and the solicitor, Arthur Newton, regularly commented on in the press as a solicitor in high profile cases, with a role in commissioning prominent barristers such as Edward Marshall Hall to represent his clients in court. Bottomley was roundly condemned for immoral journalism by figures such as Mr Justice Darling.[45] Nonetheless, as his immoral journalism was rooted in the equally immoral actions of a legal professional, the comments had a distinct ring of hypocrisy.[46]

Re-presenting the law and the legal profession

If individual barristers escaped individual charges of professional misconduct against them in the media, their profession as a whole (including the judiciary) was open to criticism that they had no real interest in seeing the criminal justice system improve its delivery of justice in line with the expectations of the ordinary citizenry.[47] Associated with debates over miscarriages of justice and reflections on the ability of the criminal justice system to deliver justice was the highly controversial Poor Prisoners' Defence Act 1903. This came into effect on New Year's Day 1904, permitting judges and committing justices to order the services of a defence barrister or solicitor where 'necessary in the interests of justice'. It was not universally welcomed by the legal profession, as reportage of reactions to its introduction illustrate. The Chair of the Middlesex Quarter Sessions, Sir Ralph Littler KC, was 'severely' critical, claiming it was 'an unnecessary, useless and mischieving Act that only throws an additional burden on the ratepayer' and insisting that, while he had acted as Chairman, 'some 2,500 prisoners have passed through my hands and it is the unanimous opinion of the Bar that not one was wrongly convicted' – an unfortunate claim in the light of later events that year.[48]

---

[44] Financial misconduct was generally severely dealt with but other forms of misconduct were less easily managed, on the evidence of a letter to the press: 'The Law Society and Professional Misconduct', Letter to the Editor, A. Kipling Common, *The Times*, 4 October 1904.

[45] See *The Times*, 21 June 1911; 13 July 1911; *Penny Illustrated Paper*, 29 July 1911.

[46] Newton was struck off by the Law Society.

[47] Leader, *The Times*, 29 April 1901.

[48] *Daily Express*, 11 January 1904.

Equally unfortunately, it was not universally well received by those it intended to help, because legal representation could only be proffered once the accused had disclosed his/her defence, defeating the intended aim of providing effective legal advice. One of the first defendants to be offered the concession, Alfred Bevan, charged with obtaining £40 under false pretences at Hertfordshire Quarter Sessions, clearly identified the problems of this when responding, 'amidst laughter, in which both Bench and Bar joined... that he much preferred to defend himself'.[49] It is interesting that William Thomas, the real culprit in the Beck frauds, also declined a defence when brought to trial.[50] Further evidence of the limitations of the legislation came early, when an attempt was made to provide James Curry, accused of murdering his two young sons, with counsel under the terms of the Act. As the prosecution cross-examination of the defendant's brother indicated, a defence of insanity was likely, especially as the prisoner was unfit to be called, and so, when a discussion 'as to the meaning and intention of the Act' ensued, it was agreed that the application had to be refused.[51]

A survey of the media coverage of all these issues indicates that by 1905, especially in the tabloid press, comment on the legal profession and reportage of high profile cases was provided by professional journalists as well as the lawyer–journalist. The reaction of the legal profession to this development is complex, but also informative about the factors involved in promoting the shift away from crime reportage and commentary provided by lawyers. On the one hand, the legal profession was not universally welcoming of the new journalism's competence to report news from the courts. At the Institute of Journalists' annual conference in 1900 one 'honourable sort' delivered a scathing criticism on the intrusion of professional journalists acting also as reporters in the law courts:

> Has the vicarious triumph of the reporter in the law courts synchronised with a volcanic disturbance of editorial security of tenure? Will the historian of journalism in the nineteenth century regard it as a curious coincidence that a sudden elevation of the note-taker to the

[49]   *The Times*, 7 January 1904.

[50]   'The Police Courts. Charge of Fraud – Miscarriage of Justice', *The Times*, 8 August 1904. While the aggrieved individuals had brought the prosecutions against Beck in 1896 and 1904, the prosecution of William Thomas was conducted by Mr Sims 'on behalf of the Public Prosecutor'.

[51]   'The Police Courts. Alleged Murder at Bethnal Green', *The Times*, 29 January 1904.

rank of author was contemporaneous with an insidious weakening of the authority and independence of the newspaper editor?[52]

However, the reality was that, certainly when it came to serious criminal cases, the popular demand for precise legal detail had already diminished by the start of the century. It signalled the 'distance' between the ordinary citizen and the formal legal process that had begun with the establishment, back in 1885, of the office of Public Prosecutor, charged with prosecuting cases with a 'public moral interest' aspect to them. This distance widened significantly at the start of the twentieth century because a new generation was growing up who had never needed to consider whether or not they had a duty, as citizens, to bring a prosecution in the Assize court or Quarter Sessions or whether to let it lapse.

Citizens were increasingly used to letting individuals within the formal criminal justice process, in the shape of police or the public prosecution office, decide whether it was right to proceed (or not) with a prosecution. There was none of the debate or furore over whether it was right to spend taxpayers' money on initiating a particular prosecution that accompanied Stead's prosecution in 1885 on child abduction charges under the Criminal Law Amendment Act 1885. By 1900, the public accepted, largely uncritically, that the state had that duty, and there was less active concern about the finer nuances of the law and how it shaped prosecution possibilities.[53] While citizens still regularly took responsibility for prosecutions in the summary courts, making their own judgments about whether or not to pursue particular cases, there was a different perception established when it came to serious crime: it was now the responsibility of the state to make decisions to prosecute. With this development came a diminishing demand for legal accuracy and precision in reportage from the Assizes and Quarter Sessions. This fitted in well with the tabloid agenda of promoting sensationalism via the human interest aspect of such serious cases. Culturally, a key problem for such legal commentators was that, in terms of the populist coverage of crime, and as part of its advertised mandate to expose the 'truth', reader expectations increasingly demanded that journalists should 'investigate' crime rather than simply report its revelation in the courtroom.

---

[52] TNA HO144/589/B7902: H. Strong 'The Position of the Editor Today', *Proceedings of the Institute of Journalists*, 34, September 1900, p. 23.
[53] It is accepted that in some areas besides rape and murder the state had always stepped in, but mainly in areas which did not directly impinge on the responsibility of the ordinary citizen.

Inevitably, when creating a format for the reporting of crime incidents in the tabloids, the coterie of new professional journalists were inspired by British journalists like Stead, willing to highlight a difference between popular understandings of 'justice' and offering some legal perspective on what consequently amounted to a miscarriage of justice in the context of providing crime intelligence. The legal perspective had largely carried the day in the nineteenth century, but not in the twentieth. As discussed in the previous chapter, Stead had shown himself willing to manipulate (or try to) the criminal justice process for his own agenda. The modern twentieth-century professional journalists aspired to report crime (which they continued to view as representing the pinnacle of professional success), but, increasingly, they evolved a sensational form of crime 'intelligence' that was external to the formal criminal justice process contextualised within a discussion of popular 'justice', highlighting where the law 'failed' to deliver on that front. Consequently, it was only in the broadsheets that proper legal detail of a complex case, such as the Stinie Morrison appeal, was presented for mass public consumption. It was not to be found in any substantive way in titles aimed for easy and quick consumption such as the *Daily Mail*.[54]

This gave the broadsheets a continuing edge with that quantitatively smaller readership which remained interested in legally informed crime reportage as a way of keeping up to date with the law. The broadsheets, such as *The Times* and even the *News of the World*, continued to employ lawyers as reporters, but increasingly on a freelance basis, and with an emphasis now on reporting on appeal cases rather than the everyday criminal justice process. These titles, together most notably with the *Daily Telegraph* (which consequently began a move up the social scale in terms of its appeal), did continue to publish the daily round-up of police court and summary proceedings. However, the column space given to it diminished in parallel with the reduction in use of direct legal expertise in the reportage. Thus, even in these titles the tradition of extensive, legally informed court reportage of the nineteenth century was marginalised. By early 1913, even *The Times* had abandoned regular in-depth daily coverage from the London police courts in favour of a short selection of cases. The regular provision of intelligible and exacting information about the practical impact of legislative reforms for lawyers and lay

---

[54] See 'The Clapham Common Murder', *The Times*, 27 March 1911; 28 March 1911.

persons alike, particularly in the summary courts, started to fade away and has never featured so substantially since – even in the comments provided by *The Guardian* or *The Times*.

'Get me a murder a day'

In terms of how this shaped the content of newspapers, outside politics it was crime (in the shape of murder) that remained the most likely topic to provide journalists with extensive (in column terms) and long-running (over several issues) stories; partly because it gave an opportunity to combine gossip and crime into a single narrative presentation by prioritising the human interest angle to their investigations into the context of the killing without waiting for the more sober legal details. Northcliffe's famous motto of 'Get me a murder a day!' underlines the new journalism's consciousness of the commercial 'pull' of a good murder story.[55] By 1900, professional journalists were accustomed to seeking out information on suspicious deaths, and developing good contacts with the police in order to get early news of such so that they could attend coroners' court proceedings and hope to pick up information which could be packaged sensationally. It was, for instance, acknowledged in the inquiry into the conduct of the police following the Stinie Morrison appeal that news of what the papers dubbed the Clapham Common Murder and Morrison's late night arrest was 'published in Fleet Street at 1.45am', the day before he actually appeared in the summary courts, indicating a clear acceptance of a reality that the police were acting as informers (paid or unpaid) to a number of the new professional journalists.[56] Coroners' courts were also identified as a fruitful source of information.[57] Developments in the nature of scientific or medical expert testimony given in those courts, to decide the cause of death and so whether or not a death was suspicious, could be usefully sensational.[58] Professional journalists had a free rein; there was no competition in these courts from lawyer–reporters, because they were outside the formal legal process. Lawyers did not,

---

[55] K. Williams (1997) *Get Me A Murder a Day.! A History of Media and Communication in Britain* (London: Hodder).

[56] 'The Clapham Common Murder Trial', *The Times*, 5 April 1911.

[57] The numbers of inquests had risen steadily since 1877, after which coroners were required to enquire not just when there was reasonable cause to suspect a violent or suspicious death but also when the cause of death was unknown.

[58] The extent to which this could prove problematic, even prejudicial, to a later trial was highlighted by defence lawyers in many cases, such as Crippen, discussed later in this chapter, and the Brides in the Bath, discussed in the next chapter.

as a matter of course, attend such courts unless acting as coroner. Up to the turn of the century, it had mainly been deaths potentially by poisoning or unsolved murders which had given opportunity to the full-time journalists for sensational pre-trial narratives. The demise of James Maybrick in 1889 and the charge against his wife Florence Maybrick were a good example of the former; the 1888 Whitechapel killings of the latter. Foreshadowing future developments, audiences were engaged in these crime narratives through a profiling of any underlying human story in ways which enabled a journalist to emphasise aspects having, potentially, the greatest impact on an individual reader. As pointed out in the previous chapter, though, these were not regular occurrences and had always been likely to be 'trumped' by the details given in the court-room at the actual trials. However, advances in science generally and forensic medicine in particular gave a new human interest dimension and authority to evidence in the coroners' courts at a time when the space for authoritative reportage from the formal criminal justice procedures was diminishing.

There were a number of high profile murders to engage the public interest during this period, such as the Camden Town Murder in 1907, which first brought Edward Marshall Hall to public prominence as a defence barrister when he defended Robert Wood on a charge of murdering Emily Dimmock.[59] The eloquence displayed by Marshall Hall was commented on in the tabloids, but not, as would have been the case in the previous century, his detailed legal arguments. As the broadsheets reveal, Marshall Hall sought, meticulously, to challenge what he saw as a flawed prosecution case through cross-examination of their key witnesses, including the police.[60] Mr Justice Grantham described it as a 'remarkable' case, but even coverage in the *Daily Telegraph* remained sober by comparison with the tabloids.[61] For the tabloids, the key drama lay in Wood's behaviour in court, summed up in Marshall Hall's question to his client: had he murdered Emily Dimmock? To which Wood gave the strange response that it was

---

[59]   Marshall Hall was not unknown to the press in 1907, thanks to coverage of cases such as his unsuccessful defence of Herbert Bennett in the Yarmouth Beach case in 1901. But the 1907 Camden Town Murder elevated him to a new level of legal oratory in the eyes of professional journalists. See E. Marjoribanks (1929) *The Life of Sir Edward Marshall Hall* (London: Victor Gollancz).

[60]   'Central Criminal Court. The Camden-town Murder', *The Times*, 13 December 1907; 14 December 1907.

[61]   'Central Criminal Court. The Camden-town Murder: Verdict', *The Times*, 19 December 1907; 'Camden Town Murder', *Daily Telegraph*, 19 December 1907.

'ridiculous'. The lavishly illustrated *Daily Mirror* coverage built on their pre-trial reportage of the case, up to the final full page illustration of the acquittal, with a caption commenting on Marshall Hall's 'masterly' speech.[62]

The murder case which gave the greatest scope to journalism, in terms of pre-trial build-up, was undoubtedly the Crippen case, starting with the discovery of a dead body in the cellar of the house shared by Mr and Mrs Crippen after an exhaustive search when it was discovered by the police that Crippen and his lover Ethel le Neve had fled London, apparently out of guilty panic.[63] When Captain Kendall on the SS Montrose revealed their presence on board his ship, Chief Inspector Drew set out for Quebec on a faster steamer; he was either accompanied or met by professional journalists working for British national titles including the broadsheets and the tabloids. A comparison of coverage in *The Times* and the *Daily Mirror* of Crippen's detention and his despatch back to Britain is particularly illuminating about the difference between the two styles of reportage. *The Times* reported the 'Arrest of "Dr" Crippen. Scene in the Montrose' provided by 'Our Special Correspondent'; who noted that, after Drew and his accompanying constables had gone on board and arrested Crippen, a signal was blown 'to permit the Press representatives and Press photographers' to come on board. This was announced as pre-arranged between Drew and the Press, indicating the close relationship that existed between the key figures involved in the case at this time.[64] The following day, the Special Correspondent carefully explained the legal process through which Crippen and his lover would be returned to Britain under the terms of the Fugitive Offenders Act 1881, which 'applies to fugitives from British justice to other parts of the Empire or to countries to which the Foreign Jurisdiction Acts have been applied' as 'the Act empowers the arrest on an endorsed warrant or a provisional warrant' of persons accused of a crime 'punishable by

---

[62] 'Robert Wood Acquitted', *Daily Mirror*, 19 December 1907. See also 'Camden Town Murder. Fighting for Wood's Life at the New Bailey. His Demeanour in Court', *Daily Mail*, 13 December 1907; 'Wood Tells His Story. Dramatic Scenes at the Great Murder Trial', *Daily Express*, 18 December 1907.

[63] 'London Crime Mystery. Woman's Dead Body Found in Cellar. Silent House. Police Search for Husband', *Daily Express*, 14 July 1910; *Daily Mail*, 16 August 1910; and the considerably more restrained broadsheet coverage. Broadsheet coverage was mainly a day later: 'The North London Murder', *The Times*, 15 July 1910.

[64] 'Arrest of "Dr" Crippen. Scene in the Montrose', Our Special Correspondent, *The Times*, 1 August 1910.

imprisonment for twelve months or more with hard labour or by any severer penalty'.[65]

The *Daily Mirror* on 1 August devoted much of its fourth page to coverage of a series of stories about the arrest of Crippen and Le Neve, including the comments of Captain Kendall on how the couple had behaved on board the SS Montrose during the journey.[66] Providing a picture of Ethel Le Neve's mother and her message to her daughter on the front page, the *Daily Mirror* went on, the following day, to use its second page to provide further human interest details, including Le Neve's failure to respond to pleas from her parents (conveyed telegraphically to her via the Canadian examining magistrate) to tell all she knew. Interviews with other passengers and the conversations of the couple on the ship about literature, art and music sated further curiosity. The sole comment relating to the legal niceties was confined to the information that the necessary extradition papers were being sent to Quebec in charge of another policeman who would assist in bringing Crippen back to Britain.[67]

The focus established here continued to shape coverage of the return of the couple to Britain, the conclusion of the inquest and the subsequent progress of Crippen through the formal criminal justice process. *The Times* in particular kept its pre-trial coverage relatively brief and sober; the tabloids revelled in every possible human interest detail, usually of little relevance to the actual legal conduct of the case against Crippen. Coverage was almost daily in August, continuing with fair regularity into September and October, until the trial started on 18 October 1910, even though there was little of any substance to report and the coverage was largely speculative about the characters of the couple and their motives. Once the trial opened, both tabloids and broadsheets covered it in significant detail, but the emphasis in the broadsheets was on how the trial process was managed by the Lord Chief Justice and counsel for the defence and prosecution.[68] The focus for the tabloids was the demeanour and appearance of Crippen, Ethel Le Neve and the various witnesses giving evidence. The coverage in the *Daily Mirror* started with a full page illustration of Crippen's arrival at the Old

---

[65] 'The Arrest of Crippen', Our Special Correspondent, *The Times*, 2 August 1910.

[66] 'Captain Kendall's Graphic Description of the Suspected Couple on the Montrose', *Daily Mirror*, 1 August 1910.

[67] 'Miss Le Neve Refuses So Far to Give Information that Would Harm Crippen', *Daily Mirror*, 2 August 1910.

[68] 'The Crippen Case', *The Times*, 19 October 1910.

Bailey, and continued with coverage of the trial on the second page, continuing onto the third and fourth pages of the issue, a pattern that was to continue for the remainder of the trial.[69] As the highest profile solved (or unsolved) murder of this period, the Crippen case was iconic; the extensive coverage undeniably reveals, how, by 1910, the divergent approaches of the tabloids and broadsheets to crime coverage had become established.

Everyday crime reportage

With crimes other than murder, the combination of the new popular drive for a less specialist prose style generally in the tabloids, and the relative legal ignorance of non-lawyer journalists and witnesses who were ready to talk independently to those journalists (including, quite frequently, the expert witnesses) outside the courtroom, made for exciting, but less substantial and accurate, tabloid reportage, both pre-trial and trial-based. The lack of substance, however, was less apparent than it would have been even in the last decade of the nineteenth century because of the curtailing in those same titles of crime reportage from the actual criminal courts. Whether from the Assizes or the summary courts, the 'pithier' entries contained significantly less legal detail and precision. Reportage of certain categories of law-breaking reduced significantly in this period, notably domestic violence. There are some examples of reportage in which the broadsheets provided the most consistent coverage of the offence involved, such as motoring offences. These first made their appearance in the columns of *The Times* in 1896 and continued to appear in relation to meticulous comments on the state of motoring law and what its implications were for motorists seeking to avoid criminal convictions for violating it. Such law was, on the whole, of more interest to the more moneyed or leisured readers likely to rely on the broadsheet rather than the tabloid for sound crime intelligence. On 3 July 1901, Sir Edgar Vincent was summoned to respond to a charge of driving at over 12 mph, according to police evidence. The stipendiary, Mr Lane KC, accepted that the car had been driven with skill and care but pointed out that the regulations prohibited greater speed. On that basis he imposed a £5 fine with three shillings' costs, 'which would not be serious to the defendant but would be useful to other drivers of motor-cars'.[70] However,

---

[69] *Daily Mirror*, 19 October 1910; *Daily Express*, 19 October 1910.
[70] 'Police', *The Times*, 26 August 1896; 3 July 1901.

so long as a motoring offence did not involve either injury to others caused by dangerous driving or driving when drunk, reportage under-lined the perspective that this type of offence carried 'no moral stigma', even if the law-breakers were regularly fined.[71] The numbers of cases in the summary courts and the broadsheets expanded steadily up to the outbreak of war, and, in sensational cases where death or injury (espe-cially to a child) were involved, also appeared in the tabloids, but not regularly, as in the broadsheets.[72]

It is informative to compare the presentation of news in the broad-sheets and the tabloids from the start of the century. A typical example from the *Daily Mirror*, 2 November 1903, provided crime news under the succinct but vague headline of 'Today's News at a Glance' and included items on the suicide in a Euston Hotel of a Yorkshire man, the remand of three boys for stealing telegraph wires (the ages were not given, nor any further details), and the subhead of a STRANGE 'MARRIAGE' STORY, amplified only as 'Charge of false marriage certificate'. By contrast, *The Times* on the same date provided a more traditional format for its crime reportage. Included in reports for 3 August 1903, a time when popular feelings over vaccination legislation were still running high, was an item from the Greenwich court which informed readers that 'Mr Baggallay had given his decision in the case of JOHN PERCY STEVENS, of Ermine-road, Lewisham, summoned for neglecting to have his child vaccinated.' A brief summary of a previous hearing and defence case was provided, and the details of the stipendiary's decision: 'Mr Baggallay held that the defendant had shown reasonable excuse for not having his child vacci-nated, and he therefore dismissed the summons.' The report further added that prosecuting counsel, Mr Coote, 'asked that a case might be stated, as the point was an important one. Mr Baggallay agreed to state a case'.[73] While *The Times* did not include the false marriage certificate

---

[71] For example, 'Lights on a Motor Car', *The Times*, 9 December 1904; also 'The Police Courts', *The Times*, 16 October 1906, reporting stipendiary Mr Fenwick at Bow Street sending Mr George Mitchell to prison for a month with hard labour and no option of a fine, for driving while drunk in Long-acre.

[72] 'Central Criminal Court', *The Times*, 10 January 1908; 'Motor Car Driver Sentenced', *Daily Express*, 10 January 1908. The case involved the manslaughter of Mrs Munday, knocked down by Harry Davis who was, according to witnesses, driving 'recklessly'; Davis was sentenced to six months with hard labour.

[73] *The Times*, 3 August 1903. For a discussion of the vaccination controversy and its reportage, see J. Rowbotham (2009) 'Legislating for Your Own Good: the Lessons of the Victorian Vaccination Acts', *Liverpool Law Review*, 30 (1), 13–34.

case in its coverage on 3 November, it did cover the remanded case in considerable legal (if with less human) detail, providing a marked contrast to the paucity of the tabloid reportage.

This appeared on the following Monday, 9 November 1903, and constituted a nicely sensational case. Mr Fenwick, the Bow Street stipendiary, heard the details of a claim to bigamous marriage accompanied by domestic violence, featuring Miss Nellie Buss, 23, and Frank Collet, 40, a schoolmaster. He, according to the prosecution, had enticed Nellie into living with him as his wife by arranging a false marriage ceremony and certificate (a process which also implicated two of his friends). The local Registrar attended to testify that the certificate was a 'complete forgery', details of counsel for the defence and prosecution were given, and the prisoner was remanded for trial at the Assizes.[74] Such a trial would also have been enthusiastically reported by the more popular papers in the nineteenth century. There was, however, no mention of it in the *Daily Express* or *Daily Mirror* on 9 November. A search of their crime news for the day reveals, instead, some amusing snippets such as the information that defendant Alfred Gaunt agreed with the Stratford stipendiary that the policeman who had captured him was 'smart'. The report then informed readers that Alfred was sentenced to 'two months hard labour for robbery', but without any further detail of the nature of the charge, the evidence against him, and so forth.[75] The day's crime news, as in much of the tabloid crime reportage in these years, included foreign crime, especially from the USA and British colonies, though, again, with few legal details to accompany the human details. During November 1907, the British tabloids enjoyed publishing news and even pictures of Mrs Annie Bradley, the mistress of Senator Arthur Brown of Utah, on trial for his murder, and whose defence was 'temporary insanity' on hearing of his intended marriage to Mrs Kiskadden.[76]

In the new tabloids, then, the reality was that, unlike sensational murders, everyday crime stories were rarely headline news but more often presented as gossip news, lacking in detail and substance, than as 'crime intelligence'. They were often buried among a diverse mass of other news including political news, social entertainment, bizarre stories or health issues, making them less distinctive within the landscape of the new tabloid journalism. Of the tabloids, the *Daily Mail* was

---

[74] 'Police: at Bow Street', *The Times*, 9 November 1903.

[75] 'News in Brief', *Daily Express*, 9 November 1903.

[76] 'The Unwritten Law', *Daily Express*, 14 November 1907; 'Unwritten Law Murder', *Daily Mirror*, 22 November 1907.

the one which strove most to maintain some of the older tabloid traditions. Designed to be 'lively but respectable', it used captions and textual brevity to make it reader-friendly, but it was arguably less melodramatic.[77] Yet, as Engels commented, it still managed to combine 'triumphalism … xenophobia … and of course crime, in equal proportions'.[78] In terms of crime and law coverage, though, the *Daily Express* was the more serious newcomer in bridging the gap between the traditional and the popular coverage of crime. It did have some access to lawyers as informants for its journalists, but this did not mean the title succeeded in preserving the accuracy of understanding that had characterised even the last decades of the previous century. For example, the text under the 1904 *Daily Express* caption IS THIS THE LAW? must have generated sighs amongst legal professionals about the legal sloppiness of the paper's staff when writing up reports from the summary courts. Two small boys were fined six shillings and sixpence each for stealing apples, and one father posed the question why they could not simply have been birched, as they had been a year previously for stealing currants. The Truro mayor, who was obviously the Chairman of the bench, was simply quoted as stating: 'we cannot birch them for stealing apples but we can for stealing currants'. Instead of exploring the legal dimensions to this statement (including comment on whether it was an example of 'justices' justice' or faulty law) as would have been usual in the previous period, the *Express* reporter merely claimed that he was unable 'to find any authority for this remarkable statement' and added that if it correctly represented the legal situation then 'the law is indeed an ass'.[79] The reader was left unenlightened by any follow-up to the case, again marking a difference from the previous period, when such comments were usually relentlessly pursued by newspapers with a consciousness of a legally informed readership to satisfy.

Press and police

Back in 1870, a detective had made the point that it was not uncommon for wanted individuals to be 'detected through the publicity given to the case in the press', adding that 'English newspapers were worth more than

---

[77] Conboy *Press and Popular Culture* p. 103.

[78] Ibid citing M. Engels (1996) *Tickle the Public: One hundred years of the popular press* (London: Victor Gollancz) p. 60.

[79] *Daily Express*, 23 October 1904.

all the police in Europe'.[80] Where there was no mystery over a culprit, print publicity could hinder the escape of such 'fugitives from justice', thereby 'facilitating their arrest'. Where a prosecution indicated the possibility of other like crimes committed by the defendant(s), the widespread broadcasting of such information, including 'the circumstances of its commission and detailed descriptions of the person suspected', aided the detection of culprits because of the way that newspapers 'by their enormous sweep' collated 'little links in the chain of circumstances until evidence of so complete a character is woven that...a prisoner is convicted' in a trial.[81]

The rise of the new breed of professional journalist wishing to focus on crime and the development of detective policing combined to create enhanced opportunities for collaboration between press and police, though the relationship was not always smooth initially. From the 1880s, journalists had complained of the reluctance of the police to keep them informed officially.[82] The police were, up to 1914, regularly on the receiving end of criticisms in the press, both for that reluctance to share information which journalists argued should be in the public domain and for their conduct of high profile cases. Police management of the 1888 Whitechapel murders, for instance, drew regular condemnation. Failure to identify 'Jack the Ripper' was generally agreed to encapsulate their incompetence.[83] Faced with this, the reaction of those journalists most determined to focus on crime and unable to challenge effectively the near monopoly on reportage from the courtrooms of the lawyer–reporter (certainly in London and on the Assize circuits) was to turn themselves into what Hall Richardson called himself: 'press-detectives'.[84] It was a strategy which brought them into close touch with individual police officers investigating crimes, and it is in that practical contiguity that the individual close relationship between journalists and policemen (and, later, women) has its roots.

The rise of new scientific techniques brought a fresh excitement to police-managed investigatory processes under the aegis of an expanding

[80] *Daily Telegraph*, 9 April 1870.

[81] J.A. Cairns (1922) *The Loom of the Law, The experiences and reflections of a Metropolitan Magistrate* (London: Hutchinson and Company) p. 270.

[82] C.T. Clarkson and J. Hall Richardson (1889) *Police!* (London: Field and Tuer), pp. 281–285.

[83] See L. Curtis (2001) *Jack the Ripper and the London Press* (New Haven, CT: Yale University Press).

[84] J. Hall Richardson (1927), *From City to Fleet Street. Some Journalistic Experiences of J Hall Richardson* (London: Stanley Paul), p.11.

detective police force from the end of the nineteenth century. As Wiener points out, it enabled detectives, police or private, real or fictional, to assume the 'imaginative center stage', taking over from the iconic criminal such as Dick Turpin and Jack Sheppard.[85] The new professional journalists targeting crime reportage unashamedly exploited this factor in expanding their coverage of the investigatory process, instead of the courtroom trial, even though the official attitude of the police authorities remained hostile to collaboration with the press beyond carefully crafted appeals for information.[86] The Metropolitan Police Commissioner went so far as to issue an order, in 1897, prohibiting the communication to journalists of any information known to the police.[87] In practice, this prohibition was unworkable as it operated against the interests of everyday detective work, so the order was rescinded in 1903 in the face of a reality that information had continued, unofficially, to be purveyed by officers. It is a measure of the close relationship being developed between professional journalists with an interest in crime and police officers that, as early as 1907, the National Union of Journalists was bringing pressure on the police by campaigning for formal press passes permitting access into police stations. Their objective was to regularise or 'professionalise' this relationship.

The Metropolitan Police refused to sanction the relationship officially by permitting such privilege until 1919, when it finally established a press office under pressure from politicians concerned about the relationship between the police and the press.[88] By then, informal arrangements for the passage of information from policemen to journalists were long entrenched and on a large scale, and the existence of a press office had little impact on the daily realities of managing crime intelligence by passing on information over drinks in public houses or similar informal venues. It established a habitual relationship enduring into the twenty-first century whereby, regardless of burgeoning official police channels for communicating crime intelligence, journalists

---

[85] M.J. Wiener (1994) *Reconstructing the Criminal: Culture Law and Policy in England 1830–1914* (Cambridge University Press) p. 220.

[86] Often these only appeared after the appearance of a defendant in the summary courts, making such appeals in effect part of the formal criminal justice process.

[87] H. Shpayer-Makov (2009) 'Journalists and Police Detectives in Victorian and Edwardian England; an Uneasy Reciprocal Relationship', *Journal of Social History* 42(4), 963–987.

[88] S. Chibnall (1981) 'The Production of Knowledge by Crime Reporters', in Cohen and Young, *The Manufacture of News*.

and police officers frequently preferred to use their traditional informal channels.

Conclusion

The popular representation of crime in the twentieth century had increasingly become conceptualised as posing 'intellectual puzzles' capable of a scientific resolution outside the courtroom by specialists, including trained policemen. The implication was that such resolutions, followed by arrests and charges, could not then be effectively challengeable by the defence within the trial process. This, not the particularised moral violations or judgments of the individual evident in the nineteenth century, was the new 'informed' crime intelligence of the day.[89] By the eve of the First World War, crime intelligence was no longer mainly presented through the revelation of evidence in the courtroom, filtered through qualitative judgments based on character assessments. Instead the focus was increasingly on the pre-trial excitements, where the trial simply confirmed and expanded an understanding of a particular criminal incident. This served to diminish the importance of summary cases to the journalist, and was the start of an enduring relationship between the investigative forces of the press and the police that has shaped modern media presentations of crime intelligence as a collusion between two forces which still contextualises the formal criminal justice process.[90]

---

[89] Ibid p. 224.
[90] 'Plebgate' seems to underline this. See Chapter Eight.

5
New Perspectives and New Informants: 1914–1939

Introduction

The interest of professional journalists in pre-trial investigations was fundamental to the construction of a new set of relationships within the broad area of providing crime intelligence. Increasingly crime reportage was to be characterised by conflicting standards of behaviour and ideas of responsibility towards the community in shaping and presenting its subject matter for consumption. The involvement of lawyers in crime reportage during the nineteenth century had been encouraged by the belief that this ensured that coverage of a case would not breach safe limits. A first generation of professional journalists reporting from the courts worked with legal professionals and largely observed those same conventions. But those restraints and practices did not survive the war and the final withdrawal of legal professionals from active involvement in crime reportage. As a result, the interwar years were characterised by tensions between journalists and their police informants, and their view of what constituted acceptable reportage, and the legal profession. Senior figures in the legal profession increasingly criticised the ways in which some members of the various police forces shared details of their investigations with journalists that would previously only have come into the public domain during the formal trial process.

Crime news in war and peace

The delay in official recognition of a relationship between press and police (via establishing the Metropolitan Police press office in 1919) is partly explained by the reality that, between the declaration of war on Germany in August 1914 and the Armistice at the end of 1918, the reportage of crime committed within mainland Britain diminished rapidly and significantly in terms of the content and space devoted to coverage, particularly in Britain's national titles. The Boer War had already shown how the power of the media could be utilised to exploit the supportive interest of the public.[1] There was a conscious will on the part of British government to ensure that what developed into the First World War should be 'well' reported; in other words, that titles took a positive and helpful perspective on reporting the war as a matter of patriotism. During the war years, censorship of sensitive news brought newspaper owners and editors into ever closer collusion with government and politicians to create newspapers and periodicals that would publish news which, without being dishonest, could boost morale while simultaneously informing readers of events in the war with news of losses balanced by stories of heroism and 'Britishness', as opposed to the awfulness of the Germans. The increasing scale of involvement of virtually the whole population in the war effort meant that newspapers had little impetus to focus on anything but war and war-related news.[2] It is in this context that the 1916 acquisition by Lord Beaverbrook of the *Daily Express* needs to be understood.

By the end of the war, for the population as a whole, the habit of consulting newspapers for important information, reliably reported, had been further hardened, with the tabloids enjoying an enhancement to their reputation, raising it to near the level of the more sober broadsheets. Above all, female readership of papers had increased across all classes, thanks to the thirst for information for menfolk on the front, at sea or in the air. Yet, for all the expansion of readerships and the fortunes to be made, newspaper publishing was an increasingly difficult enterprise in commercial terms, especially for the tabloids with a less automatically loyal readership than the broadsheets.[3] One consequence was that the competition for readers ensured that older restraints and wartime imperatives were dispensed with in the interwar period. From the start of peacetime reportage, the understanding of editors and journalists (and proprietors) was that, to be publishable, sensational news needed to be entertaining in some way (shocking or merely amusing) rather than instructive. The consequences for the new

---

[1] For a discussion of this, see K. Morgan (2002) 'The Boer War and the Media (1899–1902)', *Twentieth Century British History* 13(1), 1–16.

[2] See, for instance, D. Williams (2008) *Media, Memory and the First World War* (Montreal: McGill-Queens University Press).

[3] See R. McKibbin (1998) *Classes and Cultures. Britain 1918–1951* (Oxford University Press) pp. 505–507.

relationships forged between professional journalists and the legal profession before the war were not positive, further promoting a reliance on the police as the key source of crime intelligence for newspapers.

Interwar attitudes

By the early 1920s, the 'new' journalism that had characterised the tabloids was no longer new: it had become *the* established style of newspaper reportage across all newspapers. Additionally, the so-called 'era of the Press Barons' had produced a further impact on the older broadsheets, in terms of influencing the attitudes and motivations of their editors and proprietors and, consequently, the shape of their output. The Press Barons had, between them, acquired a monopoly on mass readership, leaving the broadsheets to fight for a more elite readership. Their extraordinary commercial success generated an unprecedented increase in newspaper readership between the two World Wars. It also precipitated the aggressive newspaper circulation wars of the 1930s, making that 'the defining decade for the direction of popular daily newspapers' and the expansion and commercialisation of popular newspaper markets.[4] There were some older mass papers, notably weeklies such as the *News of the World*, in an 'intermediate' position; with mass readerships which they maintained and so with less imperative to abandon all the characteristics that, in the dailies, had become largely restricted to the broadsheets, something which had implications for the continuance of an older style of populist crime reportage for much of the interwar period.

Rivalry for readers

During the First World War, public demand for information about news from the Front generated a momentous increase in the combined circulation of the national newspapers. By 1923, the escalating domination of the tabloid cartel ensured that tabloid sales finally surpassed those of the provincial press. As publishing costs increased and competition from the radio for news reportage began to have an impact, the market position of a smaller number of leading national titles became more unassailable, as numbers of titles were forced to close despite the fact that, nationally, newspaper circulation was still rising between the wars (from 3.1 million in 1918 to 10.6 million in 1939).[5] Amongst the

---

[4] Conboy, *The Press and Popular Culture*, p. 113.

[5] K. Williams (2010), *Read All About It! A History of the British Newspaper* (London: Taylor and Francis), pp. 152–155; see also Eldridge et al., *The Mass Media and Power in Modern Britain*.

weeklies, the *News of the World* maintained its pole position as the most widely read Sunday paper throughout the period, with a circulation of circa 1.5 million in 1910 and 3.4 million in 1930 and continuing to rise through that decade.[6] But the tabloid dailies, with a wider range of audiences in terms of readership classes, were hot on its heels. The *Daily Mail* had hit a million copies during the First World War and 1.96 million by 1930. The *Daily Express* achieved 500,000 in 1921, up to 1.5 million in 1930. By 1939, virtually everyone had access to a Sunday paper and two-thirds of all adults regularly read a national daily paper. The *Express*, *Mail* and *Herald* had ignited the 1930s press wars, but it was the *Daily Mirror* under Bartholomew that was to be the ultimate victor, producing the most widely read paper, from 1.3 million in 1937, to 3.7 million in 1947, to an all-time high of 5.2 million in 1967. But such commercial expansion came at a heavy cost, both financial and reputational.

Against a background where people began to look to the radio for immediate news, various additional non-news strategies to enhance the entertainment dimension of newspapers or to enhance their attractiveness to readers in other ways became important. On 1 December 1930 the *Daily Telegraph* halved its price to 1d, doubling its sales to 200,000, but this tactic was negligible compared with the antics of the tabloids, who offered a bewildering variety of free gifts and incentives to poach their rivals' readers and keep their own core.[7] Another favoured tactic was to offer the chance to win money through a variety of entertaining 'stunts' or competitions.[8] Crime intelligence did play a role here, but not as news. Instead, the appeal was to the growing genre of crime fiction, as crime mysteries offered the perfect forum for interactive entertainment. For example, the *Daily Mirror* offered prizes encouraging those who read their 'brilliant new series of detective mysteries' to become amateur sleuths, such as by solving the identity of 'Who is Guilty?' in the fictional series 'The Judge's Posy'.[9] Only those with considerable resources and power to attract advertising could compete, and by 1937 the five leading companies in the industry controlled 43 per cent of all titles.[10]

---

[6]   A. Bingham (2009) *Family Newspapers? Sex, Private Life and the British Popular Press 1918–1978* (Oxford University Press) p. 19.

[7]   See D. Griffiths (2006) *Fleet Street: Five Hundred Years of the Press* (London: The British Library) pp. 240–242.

[8]   M. Hampton (2004) *Visions of the Press in Britain, 1850–1950* (Chicago: University of Illinois Press) pp. 41–42.

[9]   E. Temple Thurston, *Daily Mirror*, 12 December, 28 December 1928 et seq.

[10]   Eldridge et al., *The Mass Media and Power in Modern Britain* p. 28.

Appearance and audience appeal

Physical presentation was also important in attracting readers. Just as the appeal of *The Times* had enhanced its success in the mid-Victorian era, the success of the *Daily Express* was partly a result of the decision of Arthur Christiansen (its new editor in August 1933) to offer a more visually appealing and accessible paper containing clearer layouts and cleaner print to enhance its entertainment value. Others, notably the *Daily Mail*, copied it. This was also the great era of the *Daily Mirror*, which moved on from its original 'unique selling point' as an illustrated picture-paper to relaunch in 1934, under Guy Bartholomew, as a more populist downmarket paper (ameliorating, though not abandoning, its socialist leanings). Bartholomew introduced a bold appearance and sensationalist style using 'short dramatic paragraphs, and blazing, exciting headlines' deliberately intended to attract a working-class readership and particularly suited to the often shocking nature of crime news.[11]

However, the need to give substantial space to advertising also involved a further squeeze on the amount of space available for news, including crime reportage.[12] During the interwar period, the habit was becoming established of listening to evening news bulletins for headlines, reading daily newspapers for the details behind those headlines, and Sunday papers for further detailed considerations. This further encouraged a habit of providing short, pithy and amusing news items to fill in the space around advertising and more substantial narrative reports. Again, crime often provided such items, as in the amused but pithy coverage of the 'extraordinary' bigamy case in the *Daily Mirror*, in which a woman remarried her husband after divorcing him for bigamy – and then found he had committed bigamy again.[13]

Crime correspondents and the police

All of this radically changed the nature of the potential for direct legal contributions to the production of news reportage generally, especially since journalists were already in the habit of turning to other 'professionals' (notably the police). This was unequivocally the age of the professional journalist. There were still a few with legal training, notably

---

[11] See E.A. Smith (1970) *A History of the Press* (London: Ginn and Company) p. 99.

[12] See J. Curran (2002) *Media and Power* (London: Routledge) p. 102.

[13] 'Divorced Pair Remarry. Alleged Bigamy of a Man Given a Second Chance', *Daily Mirror*, 23 September 1922.

Edmund Clerihew Bentley, who had read law at Oxford but never prac-
tised because he had determined to become a professional journalist and
writer. Bentley brought that training to his leader writing for the *Daily
Telegraph*, but, for all his personal interest in crime, he did not think
of himself as a lawyer and was not a specialist crime reporter. Leading
professional journalists usually had specialisms, and this included those
who became crime reporters, even though it increasingly failed to carry
the *cachet* that crime reportage had enjoyed in the days when it was
acknowledged as a leading attraction to readers. Politics and foreign
correspondence now carried more glamour. Men like Arthur Beverley
Baxter, who started as a leader writer on the *Daily Mail* and rose to
become editor of the *Daily Express*, might take a sustained interest in a
particular crime event (in his case, the fate of Edith Thompson in 1922),
but on the whole crime reportage was no longer the most desirable berth
in reportage.

For those who did become specialists in reporting crime, it was not
unusual for them to start their careers in provincial papers, where they
acquired their early skills in crime reporting and to some extent law (by
observation) through attending the police courts. An interested junior
reporter could also pick up leads and connections there to stand him (it
remained a predominantly male area) in good stead as his career developed. Peter Ritchie-Calder famously became a reporter at 15½ years,
specialising in police court crime coverage in Glasgow, where he became
a special crime reporter at 18 before moving to London to work as the
crime editor for the *Daily News*, then the *Daily Herald* and finally the
Daily Chronicle.[14] However, he had no particular contact with barristers or the judiciary, despite his specialism. His contacts were with the
police. The same held true for Percy Hoskins, who began his career in
1923, aged 19, by working for the *Evening Standard* before moving to the
Daily Express in 1932.[15]

Joseph Meaney of the *Daily Express* could probably lay claim to
being the epitome of a respected chief crime reporter of the interwar
era. His memoirs reveal that during his career he attended over 500
murder trials at the Old Bailey and Assizes, and on numerous occasions witnessed the judge don his black cap and utter the immortal
words 'and may the Lord have mercy on your soul'. His career started

[14] Royal Commission on the Press (1948) Minutes of Evidence cmd.7328
19 February p. 1.
[15] 'Percy Hoskins', *Oxford Dictionary of National Biography*. For more on Hoskins
see V. Davis (2004), 'Murder, We Wrote', *British Journalism Review* 15(1), 56–62.

before the First World War and so he witnessed the trial of Crippen. Post-war he investigated the crimes and attended the trials of Henry Jacoby and Ronald True, and was responsible for the *Daily Express* debate over the 'justice' of reprieving True (on the grounds of insanity) while failing to reprieve Jacoby (on the grounds of youth and previous good character).[16] Equally, with Beverley Baxter, his editor, he was active in the cause of Edith Thompson, having witnessed the revelations at her trial with Freddie Bywaters for the murder of her husband, as discussed later in this chapter.

As the previous chapters have revealed, there was already both a close relationship between professional journalists and policemen (especially the 'professionals' who worked in CID) and a concern about that relationship, as the press had come to draw more on information derived from the police rather than the courts. The attempt to regulate that by setting up formal channels of communication such as the Metropolitan Police's press office made minimal impact on the established informal links between the police and the press. It is difficult to find precise details of what were clearly extensive and substantive levels of communication between journalists specialising in crime reportage and the police. It was not, in the interwar period, something which the police authorities took seriously enough to purge by using the courts. As with the legal profession in the previous century, the reality was that when the police passed on information to the press (officially or unofficially) they were able to promote a positive picture of the police as a general force for good in society and also as individuals in terms of their ability to 'solve' crime and apprehend villains.[17] A supportive (though never completely uncritical) press was an asset in gaining the consent of people to be policed. Thus, within bounds, it was not in the interests of the police to regulate too closely the relationship between individual police officers and journalists; nor was it in the interests of journalists such as Hoskins, Arthur Tietjin or Calder-Ritchie to criticise the police (at least as an institution) too closely. For such reasons, when the case of Sergeant George Goddard came to court for accepting bribes from nightclub 'Queen' Kate Meyrick, it was reported as if he represented a single and singular example of police corruption. As the *Daily Express*

---

[16] See, for instance, 'Fighting Time to Save Jacoby', *Daily Express*, 6 June 1922. Jacoby was hanged on 7 June.

[17] For comments on this in the earlier period, see H. Shpayer-Makov (2011) *The Ascent of the Detective: Police Sleuths in Victorian and Edwardian England* (Oxford University Press).

leader put it, the way the police had dealt with the case ensured that 'its repetition was unlikely'.[18]

Crime correspondents and the legal profession

In his memoirs, Joseph Meaney was revealing of the very different interwar relationship between journalists and members of the legal profession: one lacking in any personal intimacy:

> No-one ever gets blasé looking at the curtain falling for the last time on unhappy wretches who killed for lust, jealousy, revenge, robbery. Not even judges like Darling and Avory ever passed the death sentence without showing some human feeling.[19]

Unlike previous memoirs, there are no stories revealing the characters behind the judgments; discussing Darling's (at times, inappropriate) wit or Justice Avory's encyclopaedic knowledge.[20]

Those lawyers who were on good terms with journalists attending the courts could make indirect contributions to crime reportage, but lawyers were less likely to mix in media circles and with newspaper proprietors than they had been in the days of Serjeant Ballantine or Montague Williams QC. Lawyers were no longer publicly familiar figures in the same way; seldom featuring in biographical articles or 'gossip' items in the periodical press. *Vanity Fair* did, in the early interwar years, publish a handful of cartoons by Bert Thomas of prominent lawyers (notably Justice Darling and Lord Birkenhead), but that was a rare survival. And, while cartoons were regularly published in the tabloids which made fun of the law and the criminal justice process, they contained no indication of the wide familiarity with their names or visual appearances that had characterised Victorian and even Edwardian cartoons.

Equally, the new journalists had less appreciation of the niceties of the law. Meaney's career started before the First World War and so he was

---

[18] 'The Goddard Case, Today', *Daily Express*, 30 January 1929. For more on the Goddard case see C. Emsley (2005) 'Sergeant Goddard: the story of a rotten apple or a diseased orchard?' in A. Srebnik and R. Levy (eds) *Crime and Culture: an historical perspective* (Aldershot: Ashgate) pp. 85–104.

[19] J. Meaney (1945) *Scribble Street* (London: Sands) p. 7.

[20] Darling was a well-known character; he had actually featured in a contempt of court proceeding in 1900 where he invoked the arcane form of 'scandalising the court' against the editor of the *Birmingham Argus* for an editorial describing Darling as an 'impudent little man in horsehair'.

more informed than later journalists (as well as the ordinary citizen) about the significance of legal practices, as in his retrospect on proceedings after the passage of a death sentence. Yet even he emphasised the human dimensions (as above) rather than the legal dimensions to the decisions reached:

> People who go to criminal courts, and attend murder trials, like I do, are better able to form an opinion of the guilt or innocence of a man or woman in the dock than the average newspaper reader can weave out of the condensed reports...scores of people owe their liberty to the human machinery of the Court of Criminal Appeal, and about half a dozen men sentenced to die have walked out of the green-curtained dock of the Lord Chief Justice of England's Court to – the freedom of the streets.[21]

Meaney did refer more explicitly to the legal dimensions in his depiction of how a Home Secretary reached decisions about reprieve. He referred to it as the 'final tribunal', taking place in the Home Secretary's private room in Whitehall. There he 'has a conference with his legal advisers' where they 'examine the whole case together with any notes the judge may have sent', looking for 'any reasonable cause why the Home Secretary should advise the King to exercise his prerogative'.[22] But, ultimately, the emphasis remained on the human dimension to justice:

> The Home Office despite its austere and cold atmosphere, doesn't send a man, and particularly a woman, to the gallows, unless the crime full deserves the punishment...the 'good old days' were the 'bad old days' compared with the way criminals are treated now![23]

All this meant that, from the perspective of legal professionals, their involvement in news publication was substantially different from that at the start of the century.

Barristers no longer thought of reporting crime, and few actively engaged in crime-related journalism (including writing leaders). For one thing, the purpose of editorials and opinion pieces had changed, particularly in the tabloids. Political comment remained a staple, but

---

[21] Ibid p. 37.
[22] Ibid.
[23] Ibid p. 38.

otherwise morally-shaped reflections on various topics of the day were the usual foundation for such comment. While that could and did involve comment on crime, there was no editorial inclination to inflect this with informed legal comment outside increasingly rare comment in the broadsheets, usually on Bills introduced into Parliament to amend aspects of the criminal justice process.[24] The majority of the interwar comment published, even in *The Times*, reflecting directly on legislative issues and the criminal justice process took the shape of published Letters to the Editor from a wide range of legal professionals.[25] Luminaries such as Henry Bodkin Poland and Lord Birkenhead shared the correspondence columns with lesser lights in a series of discussions throughout the interwar period about the operation of and potential for reforms to the criminal justice system; these substituting for what would earlier have formed the substance of a number of editorial comments.

For instance, proposed changes to the criminal justice system (including removal of grand juries and the legal presumption that married women acted under their husbands' direction) in the Criminal Administration Bill 1923 were touched on once in a very general *Times* editorial on 1 March, but thereafter its discussion was conducted through a series of letters published in that paper between figures such as Lord Birkenhead (the Bill's sponsor) and Judge Atherley-Jones.[26] There was no real discussion of the Bill in the tabloids, though it was touched on

---

[24] For the first *Times* editorial that provides such detailed expert comment on new criminal legislation that it is probable was written under close legal supervision, see 'Reforms in the Law', *The Times*, 28 February 1924. It is not claimed this is the first editorial commenting on crime (see, for instance, 'The Increase in Bigamy', *The Times*, 25 July 1919) and it is possible also that some legal perspective was asked for in 'The Plea of Insanity', *The Times*, 20 April 1920 and 'Whist and the Law', *The Times*, 2 March 1921; 'The Grand Jury System', *The Times*, 4 January 1922; 'The Law of Divorce', *The Times*, 14 February 1922; 'Crime and Insanity', *The Times*, 27 November 1923; but it is a measure of how reduced such legally orientated editorials dealing with crime had become. There were more dealing with civil matters, however.

[25] See, for instance, 'Criminal Law, Francis Y. Radcliffe and T.A. Lacey', Letters to the Editor, *The Times*, 12 March 1921; 'Hardened Offenders. W.D. Morrison', Letter to the Editor, *The Times*, 22 June 1929; 'Penal Reform. Edgar Sanders', Letter to the Editor, *The Times*, 23 November 1938; 'Criminal Justice Bill. Albert Lieck', Letter to the Editor, *The Times*, 29 December 1938.

[26] 'Evolution of Law', *The Times*, 1 March 1923; 'Trial by Jury. L.A. Atherley-Jones', Letter to the Editor, *The Times*, 31 May 1923; 'Trial by Jury, Birkenhead', Letter to the Editor, *The Times*, 4 June 1923; 'Trial by Jury, L.A. Atherley-Jones', Letter to the Editor, *The Times*, 7 June 1923. The Bill did not pass and Grand Juries survived until 1933.

in the *News of the World*.[27] As this underlines, a working relationship between the two professions to shape the nature and content of crime reportage was significantly less intimate than in the Victorian and even the Edwardian period. The new proprietors and editors in the tabloid press were unconcerned about this development. True, *The Times*, and to an extent the *Daily Telegraph* and *News of the World*, retained contacts with certain individual lawyers, who provided the specialist material for their law reports. The broadsheets remained willing to publish letters from legal professionals, which appeared regularly in relation to prominent criminal cases, providing comment on outcomes, such as the Home Secretary's decision to reprieve Ronald True, convicted of murder in May 1922. True's defence had been insanity; this had been rejected by the jury, but Edward Shortt had involved three further medical specialists to advise him and, as a result, commuted the death sentence to imprisonment in Broadmoor on the grounds of insanity. The case caused a substantial tabloid furore, but the sustained legally informed debate over the law and insanity and the impact on the justice process of allowing medical experts to override jury decisions was essentially restricted to the broadsheets.[28]

Legal strategies for controlling the press

However, though the practising professional as lawyer–reporter and even lawyer–journalist was no longer a feature of the media landscape even at *The Times*, lawyers were still involved in newspaper production, but in a part-time advisory capacity. In the interwar period they were mainly hired (often at a quite junior level in their careers, with all the implications that had for their expertise and the respect shown for the law by the press) to advise on aspects of the law, especially concerning the law on libel and contempt of court, in relation to stories written by their professional journalists or to provide occasional specialist legal advice columns for their readers (though these were not usually long-surviving features).[29] They

---

[27] 'Trial by Jury', Editorial, *News of the World*, 2 June 1923, for instance.

[28] See 'Insanity and Crime. Sir Bryan Donkin on the Report', Letter to the Editor, *The Times*, 29 November 1923; 'Insanity and Crime. Birkenhead', Letter to the Editor, *The Times*, 26 May 1924; 'Insanity and Crime. Herbert Stephen', Letter to the Editor, *The Times*, 3 December 1927. For a more detailed discussion of the case, see D. Carswell (2012) *The Trial of Ronald True* (Gale MOML archive first pub. W. Hodge 1950).

[29] Often this was more a feature of the popular periodical press aimed at female or family reading. See A. Bingham (2004) *Gender, Modernity and the Popular Press in Interwar Britain* (Oxford: Clarendon).

were there essentially as functionaries to advise journalists and editors on how to avoid overstepping the mark of legality in the stories they aimed to publish.

This again brings up the issue of contempt of court proceedings against newspapers for stories they published which were held to impede a proper delivery of justice within the courts. Under the amended laws of libel from 1888, newspapers could publish fair and accurate reports of public meetings. In 1889, Halsbury had pronounced that press reportage of court proceedings 'going beyond' an enlargement of the court was justified. For him there was a 'positive duty' to inform readers about criminal cases including comment on the actual justice process, because, by definition, criminal cases constituted matters of public interest.[30] But that judgment had been given when there was an expectation that the in-court reporters would be legally qualified. Subsequent legislation, including various Official Secrets Acts,[31] and the use of contempt of court proceedings had increasingly sought to curb the freedom of the press to explore pre-trial narratives as the professional journalist had replaced the lawyer–reporter.

Yet it was not reportage from the criminal courts that saw the first legislation specifically attempting to regulate news from the courtrooms, but the reaction to proceedings in the Divorce Court, which resulted in the Judicial Proceedings (Regulation of Reports) Act 1926. The purpose of this legislation was not to protect the process of justice delivery but, rather, to 'prevent injury to public morals'.[32] The main focus was to prevent the publication of 'indecent matter' when it was revealed, as part of the necessary justice process, in the Divorce Courts. Henry Fenn's memoirs of his Victorian and early Edwardian days as a reporter in the Divorce Courts revealed that the close relationship between the journalists and the legal professionals working there was based on a trust in the 'soundness and discretion' displayed by journalists, ensuring they would not overstep the mark when writing up the 'distasteful' details that explained why a divorce had, or had not, been granted. He quoted Lord Mersey as insisting on the need for judicious publicity, which 'helps to keep people straight', and Justice Bucknill agreeing that journalists 'knew when to stop' without 'suppressing anything that can reasonably be held to be essential or desirable that the public should know'.

---

[30] *Macdougall v Knight* [1889] AC 194 at 200.
[31] The first, the Official Secrets Act 1889, had restricted the passage of information between civil servants and the press.
[32] Introduction, Judicial Proceedings (Regulation of Reports) Act 1925.

Fenn added that 'unsavoury' detail was included only where its omission or even modification would 'entail, or imply, misrepresentation of the facts'.[33]

The publication of details relating to sensational coverage given to the divorce of Lord and Lady John Russell in 1922 and again in 1923 had played a key role in convincing politicians and leading legal professionals that curbs on the press needed to be introduced in the national interest. The core of the case involved the birth of a child when, according to Lord John, the marriage had not been consummated, requiring an examination of the physical relationship between the couple. The tabloids had reported the case in lavish and titillating detail as it involved members of the aristocracy (by now, gossip relating to the upper class was another news item with strong reader appeal).[34] The importance of this Act for reportage from the criminal courts was that it established a precedent that, in the public interest, legislation to control reportage could and should go beyond the law of libel and contempt of court proceedings. Looking back, Blumenfeld, who had originally been supportive of the *Daily Express* coverage, mused that this legislation was 'amply justified' and accepted by all 'reputable' newspapers.[35]

Perverting the course of justice?

The fundamental issue was the potential for repercussions stemming from unrestrained publicity. The consequences of a journalist's actions were not just confined to the issue of the personal reputation of the journalist, the editor or their newspaper. Irresponsible journalism could directly and negatively impact upon the actuality of a fair trial, arousing the spectre of miscarriages of justice. In the view of contemporary legal professionals, the revelations about the subjects of their 'investigations' in the columns of the press effectively and regularly undermined the rule of law in this period. It has to be acknowledged that not all journalists were viewed as being irresponsible in this sense, especially in the interwar period. Some, like Joseph Meaney, the leading crime reporter for the *Daily Express*, and his editor, R.D. Blumenfeld, were more influenced by and knowledgeable of an older tradition of respect for the legal profession and the rule of law. Generally, therefore, Meaney's reportage was within the bounds of

---

[33] H. Fenn (1910) *Thirty-Five Years in the Divorce Court* (London: T. Werner Laurie) ch. xxxiii, esp. pp. 289–291.

[34] For a thorough discussion, see Bingham, *Family Newspapers*, pp. 137–139.

[35] R.D. Blumenfeld (1933) *The Press in My Time* (London: Rich and Cowan) p. 134.

acceptability, if only narrowly so.[36] However, others who were ignorant of (and, it has to be suspected, uninterested in) the details of the law regularly, and at times recklessly, transgressed across the boundaries of responsible reportage in the interests of a good story.

What, from the perspective of a good journalist of this period, constituted responsible reportage? The dilemma was that the reportage which could make a journalist's reputation as a crime reporter was that which was also most likely to arouse the concern of legal professionals, because it was quite literally a matter of life or death. Murder trials, especially sensational ones, were a real temptation to overstep the mark of responsible reportage by including the human interest framework to a crime in ways that infringed the prospect of a fair trial. If Joseph Meaney at the *Daily Express* respected this, Norman Rae, who had joined the *News of the World* as an ambitious crime reporter in the early 1930s, was less scrupulous and unashamedly went beyond the role of reporter or journalist, as his first major story, the investigation of Buck Ruxton (discussed later in this chapter), and his post-1945 career were to underline.

There had, in earlier periods, been a number of occasions when editors or journalists (notoriously including Horace Bottomley) had been examined before the courts for a possible contempt of court in relation to their coverage of a criminal case, but these were relatively infrequent and were more likely to involve local than national titles.[37] Even the tabloids generally avoided official legal criticism for overstepping the mark. While the Crippen trial had been accompanied by some actions for contempt of court in relation to the trial, these were surprisingly few given the extensive pre-trial coverage, particularly in the tabloids, over the sensational detection and arrest of Crippen and Le Neve.[38] The

---

[36] Meaney, *Scribble Street*. See also 'Police Inspector and Journalist', *The Times*, 30 September 1927.

[37] See 'Kings Bench Division', *The Times*, 16 December 1908 (featuring Horace Bottomley); 'Mr Bottomley's Contempt of Court', *The Times*, 27 February 1912. Unusually, R.D. Blumenfeld of the *Daily Express* was also subject to a call for a rule *nisi* against him in relation to the South Wales Riots, but judgment was given for him: see 'Kings Bench Division: South Wales Miners', *The Times*, 2 March 1912. See also 'Newspaper Proprietor Arrested for Contempt of Court', *The Times*, 15 January 1900 (the paper being the *Tottenham and Wood Green Journal*); Leader, *The Times*, 11 November 1901 (involving the *Weekly Despatch*). The latter report made reference to 'the worst methods of … "American" journalism'; 'The South Wales Riots. An Editor's Application', *The Times*, 21 February 1912 (relating to the *Neath News*).

[38] See 'Kings Bench Division. Contempt of Court: Crippen Trial', *The Times*, 18 August, 20 August, 26 October 1910, relating to a charge against the *Daily Chronicle*, not one of the leading national titles.

line drawn by the court in the light of the increase in pre-trial coverage was to make a distinction between newspaper attempts to 'minister to the idle curiosity of people' and their efforts to 'assist in unravelling the case', where the latter was something (as discussed in the previous chapter) widely accepted as the proper role of a newspaper.[39]

The Times pointed out in response to the lamentations of the President of the Institute of Journalists on the difficulties this posed for them that it was important to make such distinctions because the issue involved was 'contempt, or at least an inadequate regard for the interests of persons' appearing in court accused of grave crimes; and thus the objective was to 'prevent undue interference with the "administration of justice"', preventing the possibility of a fair trial. It accepted that 'never was there greater temptation than now to forget, in the desire to meet the pressing demands of readers' that defendants had rights as well as readers. There needed to be, perhaps, a more careful distinction between an accidental and occasional overstepping by a newspaper which was normally 'scrupulous' in observing the rules pre-trial and the infringements of one which 'habitually hovers on the limits of fair comment and often exceeds them', but it was something which, in the interests of justice inside and outside the courtroom, needed to be properly dealt with.[40]

What had to be avoided was 'trial by newspaper', as Mr Justice Darling put it when considering a charge for contempt against Robert MacDonald of *Lloyds News*. That paper had sought out the wife of a man accused of murdering his young son, and published an affidavit from her on the grounds that it exculpated her from any suspicion of involvement, and was justified on those grounds. John Starchfield was subsequently acquitted of murder and so, it was further argued, no harm had been done. However, the point was again made that national titles had a substantial responsibility, given that 'very large numbers of people ... of the class from which the jury would be drawn' would have read their reporting in such cases, and thus, just because apparently no harm had been done, it could not be claimed that it was not a contempt of court, because it still amounted to an interference with the formal justice process.[41] During the First World War, no actions against newspapers had been brought for such excesses, with the sole exception of war-related

---

[39] 'Kings Bench Division. Contempt of Court: Crippen Trial', *The Times*, 26 October 1910.

[40] Leader: 'Contempt of Court', *The Times*, 9 November 1910.

[41] 'Kings Bench Division: An Editor Fined for Contempt', *The Times*, 22 April 1914.

incidents such as that concerning the trial of Sir Roger Casement[42] and pre-trial comment in the *Graphic*. The offending issue had not actually been published, and so, while the rule *nisi* was awarded, neither a fine nor an order for costs was issued.[43] Censorship – both official and self-imposed – in the interests of the war effort kept even pre-trial coverage of the 'Brides in the Bath' murders relatively restrained.

Once that had been lifted, cases against newspapers did begin to reappear with fair regularity, as in the example of the Sandhills Murder of 1919, when newspapers were again reminded that the courts would not 'permit the investigation of murder to be taken out of the hands of the proper authorities and carried on by newspapers'.[44] Post-war, the tabloids increasingly featured in such court cases brought by the Director of Public Prosecutions in relation to inappropriate publicity which potentially perverted the course of justice. This was a point taken up by Marshall Hall in his defence of William Gray, accused of murdering Irene Munro with his friend Jack Field on Crumbles Beach, near Eastbourne, in August 1920. The case against the men was heavily dependent on circumstantial evidence, in the shape of witness testimony confirming that the murdered girl had been seen with two men and many identifying those men as Gray and Field. Marshall Hall said it was 'deplorable' when newspapers 'arrogated to themselves the functions of detective officers instead of rendering their valuable aid in assisting the apprehension of people': in other words, newspapers were encouraged to respond to requests from the police to publicise a desire to find certain people (named, or described), but should not create an independent investigatory agenda.[45] Mr Justice Avory agreed that this constituted a 'pernicious practice' which was merely 'pandering to the prurient proclivities of the public', rather than advancing the cause of justice.[46]

This condemnation did not stop the tabloids from continuing to write up sensational crime during the pre-trial period – and even during sensational trials – in ways that regularly and consistently found editors in

---

[42] Hanged as a traitor for his role in the Dublin Easter Rising in 1916.

[43] 'Kings Bench Division. Contempt of Court by the *Graphic*: the Casement Trial', *The Times*, 20 October 1916.

[44] 'Kings Bench. Sandhills Murder Charge. Newspaper fined £1000', *The Times*, 20 January 1920. The newspaper in question was the Manchester-based *Empire News*, not a national title. The case involved the murder of Mrs Kathleen Breaks by her lover Frederick Holt in February 1920; Holt was convicted and hanged in April 1920.

[45] 'Beach Murder: Sir E. Marshall Hall's Speech', *The Times*, 18 December 1920.

[46] 'Beach Murder: Judge's Summing Up', Ibid.

the dock. Only two years later a second Crumbles murder, that of Emilie Kaye by her lover Patrick Mahon (a complex case requiring, during the trial, the best efforts of Spilsbury to unravel the forensic mysteries at its heart), resulted in a large number of newspaper editors being hauled up for contempt of court, unusually including the *Manchester Guardian* and *Evening Standard* as well as the *Daily Express*, *Daily Chronicle* and *Norwich Mercury*, representing a spread of national broadsheets and tabloids and provincial titles. In giving his judgment, the Lord Chief Justice commented that newspapers had arrogated to themselves the 'duty' of employing reporters as 'amateur detectives' who combined 'an ignorance of the law of evidence' with a 'complete disregard of interests whether of prosecution or defence'; publishing the results of their enquiries and consequent speculation simply to 'cater for the public appetite for sensational matter'.[47] During the interwar years, the fines for contempt rose steeply. Up to 1914, such fines had stood at around £50 to £100 plus costs per case for cases considered to be serious contempt. In the early 1920s, fines of £1,000 were regularly handed out, as to the *Evening Standard* in the Crumbles case (which had actually taken a witness under its 'protection', in a forerunner of what was later to become regular tabloid strategy).[48]

There was, in the 1920s, a certain sympathy with editors such as Blumenfeld, who was known personally to many of the senior judges who sat in judgment on such cases, because it was realised that it was pressure from proprietors which was largely responsible for such reportage. But that diminished by the mid-1930s. In the wake of the circulation wars of the early 1930s, Samuel Storey MP addressed the issue of the way that the 'struggle for sensation' entailed 'intrusions into private grief' and the 'utter lack of good taste' which were the 'principal characteristics of a large and widely read section of the Press'; a process

---

[47] 'High Court of Justice. Kings Bench Division. Motion to Commit Editors for Contempt: the "Crumbles" Case', *The Times*, 20 May 1924; 'High Court of Justice. Kings Bench Division. The "Crumbles" Case: Editors Fined for Contempt of Court', *The Times*, 24 May 1924.

[48] Ibid. See also 'High Court of Justice. Kings Bench Division. Heavy Fines for Contempt of Court', *The Times*, 21 April 1931. Cases involving campaigning journalism of some kind, interestingly, were far less likely to be successful in gaining rulings for contempt. See, for instance, 'High Court of Justice. Kings Bench Division. The Rodeo Summonses: Rule for Contempt Refused', *The Times*, 24 June 1924, on the grounds that the offending newspaper articles simply expressed public opinion that such spectacles were cruel, not unlawful, and so it was not an attempt to pervert the course of justice.

which was encouraged by the public willingness to continue reading such matter.[49] The issue was even dramatised in a 1935 play 'Murder Gang', which became the first British film, 'Sensation', to explore the news-making process and deliberately exaggerate the intrusive practices of crime journalists to highlight the issue. *The Times* reviewer described the play as a 'vivid, veracious and disgusting picture of crime reporting' but criticised the authors for 'allowing themselves so much propagandist licence that in the end it deranges the values'.[50]

Such fictional representation confirmed concerns that the sensational reportage of crime necessitated an internal investigation into its impact on police work. The 1938 Report of the Home Office Departmental Committee on Detective Work and Procedure was covered (rather smugly) by *The Times*. It highlighted the conclusions of the investigation that, while sometimes, as was long established, 'publication of the details of a criminal case is necessary and the assistance of the Press very valuable', generally such publication carried real risks. It reminded readers that the police were *not* obliged to share information with the press, and to publish unauthorised detail (improperly obtained) hindered the police in their work and so put in jeopardy the 'interests of justice' and also caused 'unnecessary pain or anxiety to innocent members of the public'.[51] Discussions continued up to the eve of the outbreak of war about whether new legislation was needed and, in that case, how to guarantee a free press (a key marker of British democracy) while curbing its excesses when it came to crime reportage.[52]

Shifting the framework for crime reportage

The general collapse in levels of crime reportage during the First World War had amounted to a mix of 'proper' feeling about what was considered appropriate to publish and competition for space. Practically speaking, where 'crime' continued to be used in newspaper headlines in these years, the coverage of domestic incidents was largely replaced by an emphasis on reporting what were (or were claimed to be) German war atrocities or 'crimes'. Against this background the old daily diet of coverage of petty criminality was seen to be uninteresting as well as unsuitable; after all, given that the nation was involved in a great 'moral

---

[49] 'The Freedom of the Press', *The Times*, 5 November 1936.
[50] 'Entertainments', *The Times*, 16 November 1935.
[51] 'Press and Crime Reporting', *The Times*, 24 September 1938.
[52] 'Government and the Press', *The Times*, 29 June 1939.

enterprise', it was not in the 'public interest' to publish news which was a distraction from the real issues of the new everyday reality. It also did not make commercial sense, as it was estimated that in this emergency what readers wanted was the latest, best and most detailed war or war-related news from the Home Front. There was, of course, crime which was specifically enabled by the developments of war, including the introduction of various forms of rationing. But it was also considered important to domestic morale to keep coverage of any war-related criminal activity, such as black-marketeering and other similar crimes, minimal, to avoid depressing or inflaming the wider populace.

The press coverage of the arrest, trial and execution of Edith Cavell for assisting Allied soldiers was in accordance with the 'crime news' of this period: the Germans as a nation or race were irrefutably the criminals; Edith Cavell the innocent victim who was also representative of the best British qualities: courage, decency, patriotism and duty.[53] Against this background, only the most sensational of domestic crimes was likely to attract anything approaching sustained coverage in the press, certainly in terms of tabloid reportage with its focus on pre-trial depictions of the progress of investigations.

One did fit this criterion, the so-called 'Brides in the Bath' or 'Drowned Brides' murders in 1915. George Smith had drowned one bigamously married wife, Bessie Mundy, in May 1912, a second, Alice Burnham, in December 1913, and, finally, Margaret Lofty, whom he drowned in December 1914. Reading the report of Lofty's tragic death, Burnham's father was struck by the similarities and alerted the police. Following their investigations, Smith was arrested in February 1915. From then until his execution in August, tabloids and even broadsheets covered regularly, and in considerable depth, the police investigation, including the exhumations of his previous wives, the inquests and the testimony of Bernard Spilsbury. Despite Marshall Hall's best efforts at defence, Smith was convicted. In the appeal, when arguing the trial had been unfair, Marshall Hall insisted that this was due to the press coverage: 'one of the great difficulties that the case presented was due to the wide publicity which was given to it before the trial' which meant that it was 'almost impossible for anybody to exclude from his mind entirely the prejudice created against the appellant' in that coverage.[54] However, there was no

---

[53] See 'British and German Methods', *The Times*, 25 October 1915.
[54] 'Drowned Brides Case', *The Times*, 30 July 1915; also J. Robbins (2010) *The Magnificent Spilsbury and the Case of the Brides in the Bath* (London: John Murray).

case brought for contempt of court in relation to that press coverage, and a survey of both tabloids and broadsheets reveals a distinctly more sober, if still extensive, coverage than had been the case for Crippen, for instance. It rather suggests that Marshall Hall's complaint was more defence tactics than genuine belief.

In reshaping newspapers for peacetime content, there was no longer an expectation from either editors or journalists that crime would, on a daily basis, provide the sensationally entertaining news that attracted and kept readers. After all, four years of the virtual disappearance of everyday crime news between 1914 and 1918 provided proof that the substitution of sport and non-criminal human stories worked. Only very sensational crime stories with a strong human interest focus could hope to take and hold the headlines, as in the example provided by the arrest and trial of Mrs Beatrice Pace for the murder of her husband in 1929.[55]

'First class' murders

Murder was now *the* staple of tabloid and also broadsheet crime coverage. Besides the case of Mrs Pace, the dramatic detail of the 'best-seller' criminal trials such as that of Edith Thompson and her lover Freddie Bywaters in 1923 for the killing of her husband, the trial of Frenchwoman Madame Fahmy in 1924 for the murder of her husband, an Egyptian prince, and Dr Buck Ruxton for murdering his wife and maid in 1935 filled many columns in both types of newspaper. Such demands tested the professionalism and moral purpose of professional journalists in both tabloids and broadsheets, given the importance of the pre-trial coverage of such cases. Even broadsheets such as *The Times* provided more detailed pre-trial coverage than had previously been the case. When the culprit in the murder of Irene Munro in 1920 was still being sought, their 'special correspondent' did not confine himself to the limits of the coroner's court. He recounted how one witness had told him that she had seen a 'powerful motor-car' parked for some time near where the body was found, and included comments from some of her girlfriends about a mysterious Frenchman whom Miss Monroe

---

[55] For a detailed analysis of how this event played out in the press, see J. Carter Wood (2012) *The Most Remarkable Woman in England. Poison, Celebrity and Trials of Beatrice Pace* (Manchester University Press). Because this text explores the reportage of this murder so extensively, it was agreed that it was redundant to do more than mention it here. Its coverage entitles it to be classed as one of the first class murders discussed below, and as such it partook of those characteristics.

was supposedly seeing. As a subsequent report underlined, he was very clearly seeking relevant evidence on his own account, not just about the perpetrators but also about the extent to which the murder victim had brought her fate on herself. He recounted how he had talked to a carter who had passed her, 'leaning on the street railings' outside her lodgings, and recalled that she had smiled at him and, when he 'responded', she had then 'waved her hand at him', thus giving 'an idea of the girl's attitude towards strangers'.[56]

It was not always pre-trial coverage that obsessed the tabloid press in such cases and commanded considerable column inches. The actual trial could still, as it progressed, reveal a human interest story that had not been picked up before proceedings opened, as with the Ilford Murder trial, better known as the trial of Edith Thompson and Freddie Bywaters. Most of the pre-trial coverage in tabloids as well as broadsheets, even in the particularly interested *Daily Express*, was subdued and related to revelations at the inquest and the initial committal. The *Daily Express*, though placing it on the front page, initially expected little from the case, providing only a sober headline 'Wife in Dock'.[57] The trial itself revealed sensational material in the shape of Thompson's letters, which disclosed a projected poisoning plot against her husband. This was covered in detail by all titles, but it was the death sentence on Thompson as well as Bywaters that stirred up the tabloids to extensive coverage, given the judge's comments on Thompson and the need to avoid sentimentality.[58]

The Times in its leader described the murder as a 'simple and sordid' case.[59] Subsequently it covered her failed appeal, dwelling on the legal points involved, thereafter confining itself to brief reports (such as the number of petitions for Thompson's reprieve) apart from a dignified leader protesting about 'sections of the Press' and its encouragement of an 'artificial and unhealthy excitement'. The ensuing 'campaign of publicity' was a 'grave discredit to British journalism'. As the murderers were under sentence of death, it argued, their plight was made worse

---

[56] 'Beach Murder. By Our Special Correspondent', *The Times*, 26 August 1920; 'The Beach Mystery, From Our Special Correspondent', *The Times*, 3 September 1920.

[57] 'Wife in the Dock', *Daily Express*, 7 October 1922.

[58] For a fuller discussion of the case and the execution of both Thompson and Bywaters, see A. Ballinger (2000) *Dead Woman Walking. Executed Women in England and Wales 1900–1955* (Aldershot: Ashgate).

[59] 'Ilford Murder', *The Times*, 12 December 1922; 'The Ilford Murder', Leader, *The Times*, 12 December 1922.

by the way in which the press 'paraded in print' details which fed the 'morbid appetite of part of the populace'. For *The Times*, there was no question of their guilt and no extenuating circumstances that warranted further scrutiny.[60] The rightness of the death sentence for both Bywaters and Thompson was, however, extensively debated in the tabloids. The *Daily Mirror* and *Daily Sketch* were more sympathetic to Bywaters (the only son of a widowed mother), led astray by an older woman.[61] The *Daily Express* and the *News of the World* were particularly urgent in their efforts to get a reprieve for Thompson, seeing her as the less guilty party and dwelling on her physical beauty and youth.

One murderer provided opportunities for both pre-trial investigations and post-trial sensationalism that reveal the extent to which some journalists were willing to go in order to get a 'scoop': Buck Ruxton. In October 1935 both broadsheets and tabloids, including the *News of the World*, headlined the discovery of body parts in a Scottish ravine.[62] The Ravine Murders, as newspapers initially headlined them, provided what the *News of the World* labelled as 'one of the journalistic sensations of the present century', partly due to the efforts of Norman Rae, who combined his journalism with investigation of a level which was unheard of until then. The body parts of what were identified by forensic scientists in Edinburgh as two individuals had been wrapped in sheets of newspaper.[63] These included sheets from the *Sunday Graphic*. Ruxton used his knowledge of the press to suggest to the police that, since the event had taken place in the North, they investigate whether those newspaper sheets were from 'slip' editions (those printed for a particular area). When they informed him that they were indeed from a slip edition for the Morecambe area in Lancashire, he evaded his fellow journalists and, using his particular knowledge (including further relevant information from the police), headed off for Lancaster, where (as a local *News of the World* correspondent had told him) there were reports of two missing women from the household of Dr Buck Ruxton, a respected Lancaster GP. Meanwhile, fellow journalists like Donald Mallett from

[60] 'Ilford Murder Petition', *The Times*, 27 December 1922; 'Murder and the Law', 6 January 1923.

[61] 'Is Edith Thompson To Live? Petition For Reprieve of Bywaters Being Prepared', *Daily Mirror*; 'Save Young Bywaters', *Daily Sketch*, 13 December 1922.

[62] See, for instance, 'Scottish Ravine Mystery. Double Murder Theory', *The Times*, 1 October 1935.

[63] Initially thought to be a man and a woman. See 'Man and Woman in Ravine May Have Been Drugged and Murdered', *Daily Express*, 1 October 1935.

the *Daily Express* initially remained in Scotland, observing proceedings there, including the arrest and bail of a potential suspect who was then interviewed by Mallett.[64] The *Mirror* was still concentrating on that area in the reportage of 10 October, though the *Daily Express* did announce that it was believed that the 'man and woman...were murdered in the north of England', and that they expected a 'dramatic outcome' in the next 48 hours, confirming this in their next edition, which specifically mentioned Lancashire and two missing women.[65]

By this time, Rae had already made contact with Ruxton, an Indian *parsi*, to investigate what had happened to his wife and servant, with Ruxton denying he was guilty of murder.[66] Rae was, in this, actually ahead of the police, whose investigations (including gaining and using fingerprint evidence from Ruxton's home) finally enabled them to arrest Ruxton on 13 October. Rae had already revealed the Lancaster connection to *News of the World* readers the same day, though with sufficient restraint to keep the police on side. Thus, it was tabloids such as the *Daily Express* which enjoyed imparting the 'sensational developments' in the 'Moffat Ravine Mystery' and Ruxton's arrest.[67] However, it was Rae and so the *News of the World* that enjoyed the most sensational subsequent coverage, as Rae had earned Ruxton's trust, leading to the promise of his story (including expenses for his defence). During his trial and subsequent appeal, Ruxton regularly wrote to the *News of the World*, protesting his innocence. Though by now, as he later recounted, Rae was personally convinced of his guilt, he ensured that these were regularly published.

According to Rae's own account, following Ruxton's execution in May 1936, Rae received a letter from an intermediary which (according to the newspaper report Rae went on to publish) was labelled 'not to be opened' until after Ruxton's death. It turned out to contain Ruxton's confession. According to the *News of the World*'s version, he recounted: 'I killed Mrs

[64] 'Police Suspected Me of the Ravine Crime – Brighton Hint. Released Man Tells Me of Spotlight Ordeal', *Daily Express*, 5 October 1935.

[65] 'Operating-Table Death of Ravine Victim?', *Daily Mirror*, 10 October 1935; 'Woman in the Ravine Crime Not More Than 25. Hunt for Murderer Narrows', *Daily Express*, 10 October 1935; 'Ravine Girl Clue. Police Officer Goes North', *Daily Express*, 11 October 1935.

[66] His original name was Buktyar Rustomji Ratanji Hakim. For more on the case see S. D'Cruze (2007), 'Intimacy, Professionalism and Domestic Homicide in Interwar Britain', *Women's History Review*, 16, 5, 701–722.

[67] See 'Ravine Riddle: Doctor Arrested', *Daily Express*, 14 October 1935; also 'Ravine Crime Victim. From Our Special Correspondent', *The Times*, 14 October 1935, giving more precise details of the arrest process.

Ruxton in a fit of temper because I thought she had been with a man. I was mad at the time. Mary Rogerson was present at the time. I had to kill her.'[68] It may appear odd that Ruxton requested his confession be sent to the *News of the World*, as Rae was, in many ways, primarily responsible for his conviction; and even stranger that he made a confession. Rae accounted for it by saying that, as a *parsi*, Ruxton needed to purge himself of his evil and refused to die with a lie on his lips; and, further, that he knew that his confession was guaranteed to be published, instead of suppressed, if sent to the paper.[69] Whatever the truth of the confession, Rae showed considerable skill in both using the police and keeping their approval, and probably thereby managing to evade complaints leading to contempt of court proceedings against his newspaper.

Sensational unsolved murders

There were also a number of unsolved murders in this period, giving opportunities to the tabloids in particular for substantial discussion and speculation about the human interest stories contextualising the killings. The Croydon arsenic murders, uncovered in 1929, provided one such example. Throughout 1929, pieces regularly appeared in all national newspapers. The case involved the suspicious deaths of three members of the Duff and Sydney families, and the inquest required the involvement of experts such as Sir Bernard Spilsbury, which always made for interesting copy. There were a good range of suspects, including the surviving daughter and son and the housekeeper. At the inquests on Mrs Sydney and her daughter Vera, Thomas Sydney responded to the Coroner that, being innocent, he 'would not mind' being charged with the deaths of his mother and sister. He would 'have the experience of going into a gaol', which would be useful to him in his lectures afterwards, and he expected he would 'get his expenses back in writing up for the Press'; a comment which provides an fascinating indication of public expectation of how crime reportage worked at the time and the new importance of personal interviews adding to the human interest.[70]

The two Brighton Trunk murders had also provided good copy in the last half of 1934, despite remaining unsolved, and despite the trial of

---

[68] J. Ritchie (1993) *150 Years of True Crime Stories from the News of the World* (London: Michael O'mara Books) p. 173.

[69] Ibid, also D. Webb (2009) 'Caught by the Slip: Part 7 of my life in a Newspaper Reference Library', *Life Traveller's Tale*, http://intheprint.blogspot.co.uk/, accessed 1 September 2012.

[70] 'The Exhumations at Croydon', *The Times*, 7 January 1929.

Tony Mancini (aka Cecil England) for the second crime. The failure to identify the woman found in the first trunk occupied many column inches in the last days of June and early July as the newspapers 'helped' the police in seeking to identify the headless and armless torso.[71] The publicity then led to the discovery of a second body, as breathlessly announced by all the tabloids, and more soberly by the broadsheets. The *Daily Express* claimed it was responsible for uncovering this crime. Its 'special correspondent' informed readers: 'I first placed the Scotland-yard team at Brighton in possession of the "Daily Express" clue'; which was that his enquiries had persuaded 'an attractive young married woman living here' to inform him of her concerns about the disappearance of her friend, Violette Kaye. As a result, her address was searched and a body found.[72] Though the reports of trials such as that of Tony Mancini for the murder of Violette Kaye were given in less detail in the tabloids, the fact that they stretched over many more days (largely thanks to the time required to go through the expert testimony of forensic specialists such as Spilsbury) kept them in the public eye for much longer, to the delight of newspaper proprietors. Mancini's trial, for instance, lasted from 10 to 14 December, ensuring column inches from 11 to 15 December.[73]

The daily diet of murder

Murder was the only crime which could rely on regular and at least reasonably extensive coverage, because of the ongoing public fascination with homicide and the titillation provided by the outcome. The representation of murder cases in terms of the headlines, by-lines and accompanying text visibly encouraged amateur sleuthing by readers, as the Brighton Trunk Murders has already shown. Nor was that exceptional, as this *Daily Mirror* example from 1930 illustrates:

STRUGGLE WITH
A MURDERER
Police Theory of Ferocious

---

[71] The discovery of a body in the Left Luggage office of Brighton station was announced in the press on 19 June 1934: 'Woman's Headless Body in Trunk. Torso in Brighton. Legs in London', *Daily Express*, 19 June 1934; 'Police Trace Trunk Makers. Was Victim of Brighton Crime a Convicted Woman?', *Daily Mirror*, 2 July 1934.

[72] 'Trunk: Another Woman's Body Found. Sensational Result of *Daily Express* Clue', *Daily Express*, 16 July 1934.

[73] 'Trunk Jury Decide in 2½ Hours', *Daily Express*, 15 December 1934. In 1976 Mancini admitted he had killed Violette.

Attack on Moneylender
LACE AROUND NECK
Aged Victim Battered to Death
In Lonely House[74]

These headlines allowed readers to envisage the crime according to the headlines, and they were then informed that 'Hull police have so far failed to find a clue to the murder of Samuel Henry Smith, a money-lender at his home in Parkfield-avenue, Hull.' This was followed by a systematic list of 'evidence' for the reader to use in investigating further on their own account:

'His assailant escaped without arising suspicion'

'In addition to his head being battered a bootlace was tied twice around his head'

'His cashbox, lying on the table, and his pockets had been emptied'

'Mr Wilfred Thompson [the deceased's granddaughter's fiancé] went to the house on Monday night and found the house in darkness'

'He found Mr Smith lying dead in his shirtsleeves a short distance from the foot of the staircase'

'Residents in the neighbourhood heard no sound of quarrelling on Saturday night'

'Police discovered a Sunday newspaper and a morning newspaper lying on the floor unopened'

'The police have not yet found any weapon,' and so on and so on.

Compared with modern crime reports, the level of detail shared with the public here is staggering. Public understandings of the real life authenticity of the law and the criminal justice process therefore became distorted, and the reportage played a significant role in that development.

The passing of a death sentence in the court ensured that a guilty verdict was always accompanied by subsequent newspaper discussion of whether or not there would be an appeal, whether the appeal would be allowed, and whether the Home Secretary would commute the sentence to life imprisonment. Particularly in more mundane murder cases, the amount of column inches (even in the broadsheets) reduced significantly, and not all trials involved the need for expert testimony

---

[74] *Daily Mirror*, 5 November 1930.

stretching proceedings out over several days. The painstaking reportage of a trial, witness-by-witness and speech-by-speech, was condensed by the crime journalists responsible for writing up the trials in favour of more 'interesting' human details. This enhanced the continual diminution of public comprehension about the finer details of the criminal justice process and the outcome of the consideration of a sentence by the Home Secretary. Encouraged by the implication in fictional crime from Agatha Christie to Dorothy Sayers that all murderers were convicted and then executed, there was an increasing public ignorance of and interest in the realities of legal procedure at this time, including the reality that most murderers did find themselves reprieved and that it was only in 'first class' sensational murders or ones involving other factors such as robbery that execution was likely.[75] Execution rates did go up post-1918, but still remained low in relation to the number of sentences passed.

Other crime reportage

Apart from murders, solved and unsolved, there was little consistency in the coverage of crime. Items covering stories which involved celebrities of some kind, or seemed amusing and occasionally educative in some way, would find their way into the tabloids, but outside murder it is not possible to say that any type of crime was more likely to be featured. On the whole, only provincial titles retained regular coverage of events in the magistrates' courts, even in London. In terms of the reports of court proceedings, it is evident from the legal detail and terminology used, or rather not used, that most were singularly written by journalists. Crime reporters regularly chose to report crime stories which offered them opportunities to use a first person narrative, offering a more personalised and intimate account, as if they were talking directly to the reader (usually without legal 'embellishments') of a crime event. In a typical example, under the headline 'Girl Hears Fiancé Cleared of "Trick" Charges', the *Daily Express* staff reporter emphasised the personal dimensions to the crime narrative in his interview with a man wrongly arrested for fraud and subsequently released by the police. Roger Searing was interviewed at his home in Shepherd's Bush, with his fiancée Joan,

---

[75] See 'News in Brief: Reprieve for Charles Tellett', *The Times*, 12 March 1921; 'News in Brief: Reprieve for Sentenced Newsvendor', *The Times*, 9 August 1921; 'News in Brief', *The Times*, 8 December 1921 (noting the reprieve of John Boss). Tabloids did not note any of these reprieves.

who 'was sitting beside him when I spoke to him' and 'he told me last night of his arrest and the 8 hours he spent in a cell'.[76]

Generally, unless particularly serious, domestic violence rarely made the newspapers as a crime story. Juvenile crime remained a concern, but substantial reportage tended to be a feature of the broadsheets more than the tabloids, especially when it came to covering government reports and statistics. That holds true for most government reports on crime and crime-related activities, unless it was possible to provide a titillatingly sensational aspect, as in the example of the report of the Horsbrugh Committee on the activities of adoption agencies in the wake of the Adoption Act 1926, which legalised adoption in the UK. Front page tabloid stories, such as that headlined in the *Daily Mirror*: '"Adopters" Buy Children. Sell Them into Vice', described the forthcoming report as 'sensational', revealing 'bogus adoption scandals' and 'grave abuses' which it argued revealed extensive child trafficking. Writing (again) in the first person, the journalist told readers what 'The secretary of the NSPCC revealed to me yesterday'.[77] The approach of the broadsheets was more sober, concentrating on the report's recommendation for enhanced regulation and a ban on 'foreign nationals' adopting and taking British children out of the country. There was no mention of vice and trafficking.[78] These new informants used expressive and emotive 'stories' as a device for publicising their opinions about the criminal justice system and contextualising their reports.

Conclusion

The new informants of the interwar tabloid press continually pushed against the boundaries of responsible journalism, seemingly oblivious in some cases to the impact and repercussions that their style of journalism might exert on those unfortunate enough to come under their lens. Close relationships with individual police officers regularly aided their ability to focus on pre-trial journalism. However, if the requisite information and 'crime intelligence' was not forthcoming from either official or unofficial sources (either way, primarily the police), then these reporters would turn 'police' investigators and, as detective journalists, become the interrogators themselves. Ill-advised payments and sponsorship of those accused of criminal offences put at risk any claim to

---

[76] *Daily Express*, 16 February 1938.
[77] ' "Adopters" Buy Children', *Daily Mirror*, 30 June 1937. This was not followed up.
[78] 'Adoption of Children', *The Times*, 7 July 1937.

professional objectivity, as did the invocation of sensational, speculative and exaggerated contextualisation. Thus, the tactics of some members of the press cohort represented a serious and dangerous disrespect for the rule of law, resulting in an enhanced potential for newspapers and their staff appearing in the courts charged with contempt of court carrying the danger of miscarriages of justice. This was in contrast to broadcast news, because a code of regulation on the reportage of news and related broadcast journalism had been in place from the start.

6
Enhancing Sensationalism: 1939–1960

Introduction

This was a period when the challenge of broadcast journalism increasingly required strategic rethinking by print journalists and editors in order to keep newsprint relevant as a way of delivering news. One significant result was an enhanced emphasis on crime intelligence. The importance of broadcast news throughout this period was, for differing reasons over time, considerable, but can be summed up in the greater immediacy of its headlines at points in the day when people were accustomed to looking for news from morning or evening papers. Lacking an ability to compete on immediacy, newspapers had to rely on the detail they provided to flesh out those headlines. Here, they had enhanced opportunities to do this in ways that, it was believed on the basis of past experience, would attract and keep the most readers: by presenting those details in the most sensational ways possible. It was also to their advantage that print journalists were not constrained by a code of conduct when generating their reportage, as broadcast journalists were. Renewed editorial emphasis on sensationalism in reportage to attract readers encouraged further excesses. Coming after a period when crime news had been increasingly restricted to murders in daily practice, a wide range of criminal events were once again included in newspapers. There are clear echoes of the Victorian emphasis on crime, but this time the sensationalism had no accompanying didactic purpose. This reportage was essentially only to entertain. The scope of the change between pre- and post-war reportage is illuminated by examining crime reportage during the Second World War.

Crime and war – again

Broadcast news made relatively little mention of crime during the war, with the exception of war-related atrocities performed by the enemy.[1] However, the freedom from 'news-breaking' enjoyed by print journalism gave it the space to interpret especially what it considered to be 'entertainment' news (which, as gossip rather than news strictly speaking, conventionally gave journalists greater room for comment and speculation). This continued, even if restricted to an extent by the exigencies of war. Censorship, allied to restrictions on newsprint pages to save paper, ensured that once again domestic crime took a low profile in the everyday affairs of most national and provincial newspapers. As with broadcast news and as in the previous war, most typically comments on 'crime' related to German, Italian and then Japanese atrocities: what became known as war crimes.[2] In purely domestic terms, outside *The Times*, coverage of 'crime' in the tabloids, Sunday titles and even the *Daily Telegraph* mainly related to comment in information and propaganda-related pieces about the conduct of the civilian population in connection with issues such as profiteering, waste or careless talk rather than 'crime' in a formal legal sense; describing conduct likely to lead to a prosecution.[3] Yet it was acknowledged, as a way of contrasting 'civilised' law-abiding Britain with its enemies, that 'Two of the things that still go on in war are crime and punishment' and consequently that 'Justice must not give way to an air raid.'[4] As one feature in the *Daily Express* on a front page otherwise dominated by war news put it, 'Marvellous is the quality of British justice, slow and painstaking are the processes of our law.'[5] Britain might be at war, but her justice process carried on regardless.

This consciousness that justice had to continue 'to be seen to be done', but that its daily processes had to be contextualised against the background of the more important events going on, regularly manifested

---

[1] For more comment on radio and early television broadcasting, see A. Briggs (1995) *History of Broadcasting: II, The Golden Age of Wireless* (Oxford University Press); S. Street (2002) *A Concise History of British Radio 1922–2002* (Oxford: Blackwell).

[2] This started quickly; see 'Opinion. Crime', *Daily Express*, 5 September 1939.

[3] For instance, 'We Will Always Expose This', *Daily Mirror*, 23 September 1939.

[4] 'Judge and Prisoner Go Down to the Cells. Each With His Gas-Mask Box', Hilde Marchant, *Daily Express*, 14 September 1939.

[5] 'This Is the Story of ANTONIO MANCINI A British Citizen', William Blakely, *Daily Express*, 3 October 1941.

itself in the details of crime reportage. Covering the trial of Mrs Florence Ransom for murder, the *Daily Express* coverage included a dramatic personal account of how their reporter, Hilde Marchant (one of the first and best women to work in Fleet Street),[6] 'went along to the Old Bailey to see the law take judgment of one woman's life' but instead witnessed the court in process during a siren alert. More remarkable, given that the case was 'one of the biggest murder trials in years', was that the courtroom itself was largely empty apart from those actively involved in the trial. The *Express* went so far as to reflect that 'perhaps there is so much death around us' that the usual curiosity about the details of a murder was 'exhausted'.[7]

The reportage of Antonio Mancini's[8] appeal in 1941 against his conviction for the murder of Harry 'Scarface' Distelman in a London club was similarly contextualised against the backdrop of war. The reporter here, William Barkley, reflected that Mancini's conviction had come 'ten days after Hitler's millions made their brutal assault on Russia'; the dismissal of his case by the Court of Criminal Appeal came 'when the Germans were threatening Smolensk', and the final act in the drama came 'with the Hun hammering at the defences of Moscow'. It was made plain that the case was open and shut, but still his appeal had been properly and thoroughly considered, even though, by comparison with greater moral questions, it was of trifling merit: 'Was there provocation? That was the question. Not whether Hitler was provoked into the slaughter of millions.'[9]

The courts continued to be busy during the war, and, generally in small, sparse paragraphs, a range of crimes were reported. These included manifestations of everyday crime, including teenage gang assaults, domestic violence and theft. Murder was always likely to assume a higher profile, though there was no sensational equivalent of the 'Brides in the Bath' murders to dominate headlines. The domestic impact of war and its management also produced particular wartime offending, including looting from bombed buildings and various forms of fraud and black-marketeering. Even though the latter was rhetorically identified

---

[6] See A. Sebba (1994) *Battling for News: the Rise of the Woman Reporter* (London: Hodder and Stoughton).

[7] 'Meanwhile, One Life Was Fought For ... ', Hilde Marchant, *Daily Express*, 13 November 1940.

[8] Antonio Mancini or Tony 'Babe' Mancini was not the same Tony Mancini acquitted of Violette Kaye's death, discussed in the previous chapter.

[9] 'This Is the Story of ANTONIO MANCINI A British Citizen', *Daily Express*, 3 October 1941.

by some as a form of 'treason', coverage was comparatively restrained in terms of both language and extent. For example, when six Sheffield looters were sentenced to penal servitude, the *Daily Mirror* headline was a restrained, purely informative 'Looters Get 36 Years in Gaol'; and the accompanying text was equally factually orientated.[10]

Given such restraint, it is not surprising that growing concern in the late 1930s about the style and content of tabloid newspaper reportage (including its emphasis on murder) was largely suspended during the war years. Critical commentators like George Orwell rejoiced in the reduction in the use of 'screaming headlines'. They predicted that this austerity in wartime reporting style heralded a permanent style change in the coverage of crime whereby 'the sensational nonsense' of the pre-war tabloids would disappear for good in the improved post-war world.[11] But those hopes were rapidly dashed with the post-war removal of restrictions on newsprint, because there was also a revival of commercial pressures and competition for audiences and advertisers. Sensation-enhancing headlines and accompanying stories, including murder and other crime reportage, resumed their regular appearances.[12] Post-war, headlines became bolder and the illustrations more lavish as an antidote to wartime asceticism. Within the tabloids, analysis across nine national titles in 1947 confirmed the return of interest in crime stories amongst the leading tabloids.

Post-war realities

It was over the next two decades that newsprint coverage of crime in both tabloids and Sunday papers reached levels of prominence that bear comparison with the days of Victorian crime reportage. But, if there are quantitative similarities, the qualitative comparisons of the crime intelligence were different. In the nineteenth century, political and national news dominated the headlines of most papers apart from in a handful of crime 'specialist' titles, notably the *Illustrated Police*

---

[10] 'Looters Get 36 Years in Gaol', *Daily Mirror*, 4 March 1941. See other typical tabloid wartime crime headlines, including: 'Blacketeer Gets 3 Years Jail and £2,000 Fine', *Daily Express*, 8 May 1942; ' "Suicide" May Have Been Murder', *Daily Express*, 16 July 1943; ' "I Killed Her" statement in sack murder', *Daily Mirror*, 24 March 1944, 'L.C.C. Sent A Child of 7 To Live With Evil Girls', *Daily Mirror*, 16 November 1944.

[11] G. Orwell, 'As I Please', Opinion Column, *Tribune*, 21 April 1944.

[12] G. Orwell, 'The Decline of the English Murder', *Tribune*, 15 February 1946.

News. Such news still dominated the front pages and leader columns of the broadsheets; but it did not, reliably, do so in the tabloids and Sunday papers. Famously, coverage of the death and funeral of Queen Mary was not given priority over the discovery of the bodies at 10 Rillington Place and the hunt for their murderer, John Christie.[13] The politician and legal journalist A.P. Herbert was one amongst many who were openly critical of this abandoning of a traditional emphasis on politics as a way of contextualising and locating crime reportage in the wider news context, including what was happening legislatively in this period.[14]

In the legislative background to this resurgence in crime reportage, there was a renewed law and order debate amongst the political and legal classes (broadly conceived). This did manifest itself in both the tabloid and broadsheet quality press, but rather differently in terms of content and quantity. In the immediate post-war period, there was a perception of a rise in crime that was, in the atmosphere of the new Welfare State, both surprising and concerning to those politicians and other interested commentators writing mainly in the broadsheets; those who had expected that the bright new world of that Welfare State would reduce working-class criminality. Instead, the post-war climate, bringing with it a steady rise in the public visibility of crime at least partly due to enhanced reportage of it, entertained real concerns about persistent criminality. There were fears that increasing crime, linked to other corruptions that had survived the war, would taint British peacetime society. This renewed debate resulted in considerations that produced, amongst other responses, the enactment of the Criminal Justice Bill in 1948, with its far-reaching suggestion for the abolition of both corporal punishment and hanging. Broadsheets such as *The Times* gave it substantial consideration via coverage of the Parliamentary debates and reader responses (especially from lawyers) in the shape of Letters to the Editor.[15] Despite its apparently controversial nature, the Bill received minimal attention from the tabloids. There was some comment when the proposals for the abolition of hanging were replaced by restrictions on its use, but little more than

---

[13] 'Race Against Time to Trap Horror Killer', Howard Johnson; 'All Day They Paid Tribute', *Daily Mirror*, 31 March 1953; 'Christie: Murder Charge', Arthur Coor; 'A Grieving Son Bows Low', *Daily Express*, 1 April 1953.

[14] 'Broadcasting's challenge to the Press' *The Times*, 25 June 1957.

[15] For insights into these debates, see M. Ginsburg (ed.) (1959) *Law and Opinion in England in the C20th* (London: Stevens and Sons).

that.[16] Parliamentary debate was apparently not sufficiently sensational to interest the tabloids.[17]

One major legislative development in this period, however, did attract more general attention from all sections of the press: the impetus to decriminalise homosexuality. In 1952, Hugh Cudlipp, editor of the *Sunday Pictorial*, denying any underlying sexual or commercial exploitation, ran an expose of the 'homosexual problem' entitled 'Evil men'. The series helped expedite public discourse about homosexuality,[18] precipitating an essentially newspaper-orientated debate that emerged around the trial, in 1954, of Lord Montagu of Beaulieu, Peter Wildblood and Michael Pitt-Rivers for homosexual behaviour. Intended by the police and the Home Secretary as a public demonstration of their determination to stamp out the 'plague' of unnatural vice amongst British men by targeting elite examples, the media reaction to the trial was unexpectedly sympathetic and reasonably muted. It was, essentially, a debate about the real criminality of such behaviour, featuring figures such as the Archbishop of Canterbury, who called on *The Times* for journalists, editors and owners of newspapers to establish a moral vanguard.[19] But such moves to restrict reporting of homosexual cases to 'spare the public from full reporting' were decried in the *Express* as counterproductive, given 'the whole purpose of sentences is to deter others by making an example.[20] How can an example be made without 'full publicity?'[21]

While the point made was the same as that made in divorce case reportage, it also signalled a shift in public morality which was not reflected in the law; leading to the establishment of the Wolfenden Committee. As well as homosexuality, heterosexual prostitution was

---

[16] 'Govt Wants to Keep Death Penalty. Crimes of Violence Increasing', *Daily Mirror*, 28 November 1947; 'Death Penalty Goes For 5 Years', *Daily Express*, 15 April 1948; 'Govt. Will Bring Back Hanging', *Daily Mirror*, 10 June 1948; 'Government to give experiment on 2 types of murder a 5-year trial', *Daily Mirror*, 5 July 1948.

[17] 'Broadcasting's Challenge to the Press', *The Times*, 25 June 1957, quoting A.P. Herbert on the issue.

[18] J. Bengry (2012) 'Queer Profits: Homosexual Scandals and the Origins of Legal Reform in Britain', in H. Bauer and M. Cook (eds) *Queer 1950s: Rethinking Sexuality in the Post-war years* (Basingstoke: Palgrave Macmillan).

[19] 'Exploitation of Sex', 25 November 1953.

[20] This idea of protecting the public from unpleasant details is something that is evident, and explains, a lack of lingering detail in many salacious cases that would be readily covered in later periods. For example, the murders by Mary Bell in the late 1960s attracted muted and principally factual coverage by both quality and tabloid newspapers.

[21] 'Why Bar Publicity?' 27 March 1954.

another concern for the Committee in the wake of the well-publicised trial of one of the notorious Messina brothers in 1951 for living off immoral earnings. Ultimately, the Wolfenden Report made front page news for the *Daily Mirror*, who unequivocally supported its recommendations on the management of prostitution, urging its readers 'Don't be shocked by this report, It's the truth, it's the answer, IT'S LIFE'.[22] *The Times* similarly published a substantial editorial broadly supporting its recommendations on prostitution.[23] The *Daily Express* was less enthusiastic about the recommendations, especially on the proposal for introducing 'lax laws for homosexuals'.[24] Yet generally, like the debate over the suspension of hanging, which resumed in the late 1950s and resulted in the enactment of the Homicide Act 1957, discussion of the moves towards homosexual toleration was generally not used to sensationalise related crime reportage.

Arguably, this was because there was no need: there was so much intrinsically sensational crime news to hand that crime reporters and editors did not need to engage with areas inflected with political debate that might not engage their readers' interest. The practical riposte to the unease of the political and legal elite about the apparent narrowing of news resulting from the sensationalising practices of the tabloids was the claim made by Sylvester Bolam, editor of the *Daily Mirror*, that the sensationalising of news (which, in his case, meant mainly crime news) was a 'necessary and valuable service'. For him, it was actually in the public interest, because he argued that sensationalism did not involve 'distorting the truth' but, rather, providing a 'vivid and dramatic presentation of events', simply to impress them forcefully on the mind of the reader. It was putting events in 'familiar, everyday language' and so (especially given the use of illustrations and cartoons to point up the message) making them accessible to the ordinary citizen.[25] In particular, editors like Bolam looked to crime to make the sensational news that was required to compete with radio and television broadcasts.

Bolam's comment reveals the realisation of tabloid and Sunday newspaper editors and proprietors that the more restrained public service ethos surrounding the BBC and its news delivery (which continued once commercial broadcasting opened up in 1955) had provided newspaper journalism with one area where they were without competition.

---

[22] 'VICE. OFFICIAL', *Daily Mirror*, 5 September 1957.
[23] 'Sex and Punishment', 5 September 1957.
[24] 'Vice Move Rejected', 30 June 1960.
[25] Editorial, *Daily Mirror*, 30 July 1949.

It illuminates also a contemporary recognition that the process of sensationalising the news was at its most effective when human interest
narratives were contextualised with editorial opinion pointing up the
shocking dimensions of the narrative. The advantage possessed by
broadcast news services was the rapidity and emphasis on information: but newspapers had the space and time to dwell on the detail and
the ability to provide sustained interpretation of news information. In
practice, the demand for sensationalism ensured that detail and interpretation were most easily focused on either crime in the formal sense
or crime-related enterprises associated with immorality and corruption
(which, while socially offensive, has never been automatically criminal
unless targeted by moral campaigners).

Yet newspapers needed to be identified as providing accurate as well
as sensational information, especially as broadcast news provided an
independent 'check' on their veracity. Sir William Haley had declared
in 1957 that broadcast news would 'show us up if we twist, or lie, or are
careless'.[26] Consequently, all titles were at pains to announce themselves
as accurate and reliable. In this period there was, on the whole, still a
will to believe that what was read in the press was a fair representation
of the 'truth' of an event.

Crime reportage: the Royal Commission view

The resumption of post-war newspaper publication habits, free of
wartime censorship and other restrictions, was scrutinised by the first
Royal Commission on the Press, set up to thoroughly examine the
power of the press in order to decide on the possible need for regulation
in the public interest. Ultimately, the British press was, in many ways,
invigorated by the Commission's conclusions. Its apparent endorsement of newspaper standards practically justified the decision to leave
the newspaper industry largely to regulate itself.[27] The main focus of the
Commission's considerations had been on the political dimensions of
newsprint, which, by virtue of the lack of party political tensions then
surrounding the criminal justice process, did not include crime news in
any significant way. It did, though, reflect broadly on sensational journalism in association with the content of various titles. In this context,
its Report reveals that as an everyday newsprint category, related to
entertainment, crime intelligence was not something that worried the

---

[26] *The Times*, 25 June 1957.
[27] Hampton, *Visions of the Press 1850–1950*, p. 42.

Commission.[28] Indeed, apart from the continuing concern about sala-cious matters, mainly in relation to reportage from the Divorce Courts, there was little consideration by policy-makers about crime reportage in general, and certainly not the publication of legal detail.

Against the background of the frenzied coverage of Neville Heath's crimes in 1946 and the even more immediate issues surrounding the tabloid reportage of John George Haigh's crimes in 1949, the Commission reflected that, while it was 'opposed to sensationalism as such', it acknowledged that 'of course there is no way of handling a murder which eliminates the sensational, particularly when it has affected a large body of public opinion and people are apprehensive about their children'.[29] It made no comment on the legal accuracy of such sensationalism or how it might affect the workings of the criminal justice system. Instead of commenting on the potential issues about 'trial by newspaper' in this style of reportage, the Commission Report pronounced that the extensive law reports from the various law courts which continued to appear in *The Times* were, in terms of their news value, 'relatively unimportant'.[30]

Implicitly, the legal profession seems to have concurred, suggesting the extent of the distance between the profession and the world of newsprint. The apparent perspective of that profession when it came to crime news is equally informative. The long-standing belief amongst legal professionals, that journalists reporting from the courts would be well-educated men who subjected themselves to a high degree of self-censorship in order to avoid damaging the justice process, proved hard to erode even in an age when much of crime intelligence in the newspaper columns was focused on pre and post-trial coverage. While comments may have been made in private, there was no public lobbying by lawyers for controls in this area: clearly libel law and contempt of court proceed-ings were considered sufficient to keep the excesses of the press in check, used as they were in both the Heath and the Haigh cases, if to little real effect in terms of their impact on the habits of journalists, as this chapter will discuss later.

One issue considered by the Press Commission concerned the quality and status of journalism as a 'profession'. This is an interesting

---

[28] Royal Commission on the Press 1947–1949 (1949) Report (London: HMSO) Cmnd 7700.

[29] Royal Commission on the Press. Minutes of Evidence Cmd. 7462 15 April 1948 pp. 1–2.

[30] Ibid p. 266.

indication of how journalism had failed to sustain that late Victorian and Edwardian expectation of professional status sought for by both newspaper proprietors and journalists themselves; a world in which crime reportage with its emphasis on news from the courtroom was seen as a pinnacle to be achieved only by an educated few. As touched on in the previous chapter, many mid-twentieth-century crime reporters were neither university educated nor formally trained in journalism.[31] The Royal Commission identified this as the reason why so many journalists linked with sensationalism and crime reportage were lacking in a spirit of public service. Tom Drieberg MP, formerly a journalist with the *Daily Express*, gave evidence that there were two types of journalists: the 'good and genuine' and

> the eager, go-getting, ambitious, slightly careerist type who is often attracted to journalism, perhaps with the hope of becoming a crime reporter, I do not think he is concerned very much with values or with absolute truth.[32]

His diagnosis was confirmed by Frank Singleton, editor of the *Bolton Evening News*, who highlighted the fact that such men regularly used their financial resources to pay for information and access to crime scenes.[33] Such comment, however, was not substantially and specifically reflected in the Commission's Report.

Criticisms and responses post-1949

By the mid-1950s, crime news had, outside sport, become the most significant news category. Critics like Richard Hoggart deplored the 'overuse' of personalisation in such coverage replacing the old 'healthy' appetite for a good murder story, producing something artificial and lacking in substance.[34] He specifically blamed a new breed of journalist for this development.[35] Even within the newspaper industry there was

---

[31] There was also the issue of training. See M. Conboy (2011) *Journalism in Britain: a historical introduction* (London: Sage) pp. 168–169.

[32] Royal Commission on the Press. Minutes of Evidence, 1 April, 1948 p. I.

[33] Royal Commission on the Press. Minutes of Evidence Cmd. 7462 15 April 1948 pp. 1–2.

[34] R. Hoggart (1957) *The Uses of Literacy. Aspects of Working Class Life* (London: Chatto and Windus) pp. 149–152.

[35] Ibid p. 187.

some disquiet about these practices. Sir William Haley, editor of *The Times*, voiced his concerns about the impact of such reportage on the 'ordinary man'.[36] Mass circulation titles were irresponsibly and 'cumulatively' building up 'an attitude of mind in the new generation which can be disastrous unless it is counteracted', he claimed.[37]

This indicates a new hostility, not just competition, between the popular and the quality press, as the latter began to label the former as being exploitative. The quality press advocated, in Haley's words, a return to responsible, properly informed journalism, using the old claim of the Victorian editors that 'popularity need not spell irresponsibility'.[38] This was the context in which, at the beginning of the 1960s, the Press Council recognised the place of the broadsheet (or, as it was becoming labelled, 'quality') press in restraining 'excesses in the midst of excess' and preserving 'minimum decencies in a free-mannered, free-thinking, loud and intrusive age' by requesting that the 'class' newspapers take a key role in the Council.[39] These vehicles could, it argued, better maintain standards than the establishment of a strict journalistic code of conduct, because they had not given in to the temptation to indulge in unnecessarily sensational journalism.[40]

The popular press ignored such high thinking in favour of continuing to appeal to those 'baser instincts' amongst its readers. Yet the tabloid press was also extremely sensitive to the criticisms of its broadsheet peers. The *Daily Mirror* ran a series of articles rebutting the suggestion that crime news should not feature so heavily in the press, or at least not in the way that it was presented in the popular press. It insisted: 'It is no good saying there is too much crime published in the Press or that the newspapers make too much of horrors like the Christie case. The world is as it is. The newspapers are bound to reflect it or give a false picture.'[41] Their argument was that 'the public is legitimately interested in these subjects' and a title could only survive if it supplied 'the information the public seeks'.[42]

---

[36] Cited in F. Williams (1957) *Dangerous Estate. The Anatomy of Newspapers* (London: Longmans, Green and Co.) p. 277.

[37] Ibid p. 278.

[38] 'Second Chance', *The Times*, 29 June 1955.

[39] 'Strengthening the Press Council', *The Times*, 10 November 1960.

[40] 29 June 1955. Haley had real insights into the nature of competition from broadcast journalism, having served as Director-General of the BBC, 1944–1952.

[41] *Daily Mirror*, 12 November 1953, *Sex, Crime and the Press*.

[42] Ibid.

There was, as a result, a further emphatic difference between the coverage of crime stories in the popular press and their presentation in the quality broadsheet titles. Amongst the broadsheets, the *Daily Telegraph* did continue its traditional interest in reporting crime including its human interest dimension, but the paper's 'sensationalism' was comparatively restrained, old-fashioned and increasingly conservative. *The Times* and the *Manchester Guardian* continued to stand largely aloof from crime stories divorced from the legal framing of the courtroom unless they could be considered *bona fide* news, judged on the basis of whether they constituted items such as would appear in radio and television broadcasts. When reporting from the courtroom, it was easier to contextualise salacious or unsavoury content as essential testimony which (as with the coverage of cases from the Divorce Courts) had to be included in order to make the workings of the justice process plain to readers. Not all the tabloids were as consistently and powerfully devoted to the extremes of sensationalism. The *Daily Express*, with its respectable and more middle-class readership, generally (but not always) comparatively avoided the excesses of the more 'downmarket' Sunday and tabloid titles for whom crime was the vehicle for conveying a wide range of information about the seamier side of British life.

Editors and proprietors

Maintaining standards was one of the key roles of a newspaper editor. One proprietor, Lord Thomson, claimed: 'I do not believe that a newspaper can be properly run unless its editorial columns are run freely and independently by a highly skilled and dedicated professional journalist.'[43] But the issue of how to maintain standards was not an easy one in the face of commercial pressures without interposing a heavy editorial hand on content, including (perhaps especially) crime reportage. Some post-war tabloid editors had been in position since well before the war and retained some of the values of that period, notably Christiansen of the *Daily Express* (1933–1957). Others, such as Hugh Cudlipp, editor of the *Sunday Pictorial* from 1937 and *Daily Mirror* from 1952, and his brother Reginald, editor of the *News of the World* 1953–1959, drew on no such traditions to shape their policies. Yet these titles could include informative items; packaged in ways that gave a sensational gloss to an essentially unsensational item in order to encourage readers to look

---

[43] J. Curran and J. Seaton (2003) *Power Without Responsibility: The Press and Broadcasting in Britain* (London: Routledge) p. 102.

at a story they might not otherwise pursue. At times, when it suited him, Hugh Cudlipp adopted this strategy (successfully pioneered by the Victorian *News of the World*). For example, a typically titillating headline, 'Why Public Fall Out With The Police', led readers to the comments of Sir Joseph Simpson, included to contextualise their summary of the annual report of the Metropolitan Police Commissioner.[44]

New initiatives relating to crime reportage aimed to refresh the market for Sunday papers. Under the influential guidance of Stuart Campbell (who was, practically speaking, in editorial control from 1947, though only formally becoming editor in 1957), *The People* expressly set out to crusade against criminal and moral wrongdoing, and revamped the idea of the individual exposé of (un)deserving individuals. Reflecting on this development on Campbell's retirement, *The Times* acknowledged that

> Where the old crusading newspapers had been content to set out the facts unearthed by inquisitive reporters, *The People*, under Campbell, produced the evidence itself. His exposures always disclosed how the investigation had been carried out; they read almost like police court depositions or detectives' reports.[45]

The power of these men not only extended to shaping the newspaper in their own vision but provided cohesion in a very real sense within the industry. When journalists were accused of having acted inappropriately in pursuance of a crime story (for example, hounding the relatives of a soon to be released murderer), it was not the individual journalists who were called to account by the Press Council but their editors. Invasion of the privacy of relatives of victims or perpetrators of offences was taken very seriously by the Press Council, and editors were regularly censured by the Council when their journalists engaged in harassment.[46] Interestingly, this resulted in a return to a degree of journalistic anonymity in the area of crime reportage. Because of the potential for criticism of individual journalists as well as editors, many 'scoops' involving intimate details of a crime narrative were published without a specific by-line. This tactic did not always work, though. In 1956, Duncan Webb (described as a 'crime reporter') as well as Harry Ainsworth, his editor, were named in a writ for contempt of court.[47]

---

[44] 'Why Public Fall Out With The Police', *Daily Mirror*, 23 July 1959.
[45] 'Mr Stuart Campbell', *The Times*, 3 February 1966.
[46] See, for example, *The Times*, 17 February 1961 p. 22 for a number of complaints addressed by the Press Council.
[47] ' "Probe This Case" – Lord Goddard', *Daily Express*, 27 July 1956.

Reflecting on all of this in 1957, Francis Williams, ex-editor of the *Daily Herald* and the Controller of Newspapers and Censorship during the Second World War, noted that journalists were certainly freer but they were also 'more vulnerable than the barrister, the solicitor, the doctor' to pressures from within their own field. The failure to professionalise journalism properly meant that, while 'the preservation of the strictest ethical and professional standards in the press' was 'no less important to society' than it was with the established professions, the reality was that the journalist, being dependent upon 'the goodwill of a single employer', might find it more difficult to 'resist pressures' to reduce those professional standards.[48]

Williams made an important point. The emphasis of editors on the public thirst for salacious detail was difficult for any ambitious journalist to resist, particularly as the column inches in the tabloids and Sunday papers increased significantly in the two decades after the Commission's Report. Such titles set up what were effectively crime offices, with each title having several reporters focusing on crime stories rather than the handfuls of specialist crime reporters who had been active interwar. When Campbell became editor of *The People* (later the *Sunday People*) in 1958, he initiated a phase of investigative crime journalism which was to set the template for modern media exposés. Even the respectable papers, such as the *Daily Telegraph*, found it necessary to expand their coverage of crime stories, if in a more restrained fashion than that employed by the tabloids. Their argument was generally that such exposés served to uncover the real extent of sin, immorality and corruption surrounding and enabling actual crime and that they were consequently in the public interest. The pressure to provide sensational and personally intimate detail to flesh out crime stories was so intense it drove at least one prominent journalist to leave: Harry Procter of the *Sunday Pictorial*. Procter acquired distaste for the crime stories that he was so good at writing, and, when his editor, Colin Valdar, and the overall *Mirror* proprietor Hugh Cudlipp refused to let him step down from his role as crime reporter, he resigned.[49]

The investigative journalist

By this time, what is now labelled investigative journalism as a general field was firmly established in Britain. Reflecting back on his understanding

---

[48] Williams, *Dangerous Estate*, p. 268.
[49] H. Procter (1958) *The Street of Disillusion. The Author's Life as a Journalist* (London: Allan Wingate).

of journalism in 1929, J. Hall Richardson had made a distinction between what he considered journalism and 'publicity'. By the end of the interwar period, crime reportage now very firmly perceived itself, and was externally perceived as, entertainment, marking a real break with previous standards in popular as well as elite crime reportage.[50] The modern investigative journalist readily eschewed legal detail for the excitement and spectacle of 'true' crime narratives. As post-war criminal enterprises blossomed, they offered opportunities for actual infiltration to suitably motivated journalists. Those willing to go to such lengths to involve themselves in the 'story' won headline-grabbing scoops while producing also the poignant narrative detail only close proximity to those involved in a criminal event could bring. *Time Magazine* wrote of Duncan Webb's investigations in 1955 that:

> In almost 20 years of covering crime he has been slugged, kicked, lunged at with knives, shot at, knuckle-dusted and was once the target of a speeding automobile that raced onto the sidewalk of a narrow Soho street and tried to smash him against a building.[51]

Crime reportage has always been well suited to the talents of the investigative journalist, given that it is by definition an attempt to expose to public scrutiny what someone wishes to hide from that gaze. By this time, there were too many important crime reporters to be individually named and listed in this chapter; however, amongst the most significant were Norman Rae (discussed in the previous chapter), along with Harry Proctor, Percy Hoskins, Rodney Hallworth, Stanley Firmin, Duncan Webb and Murray Sayle. None were from educated upper-middle or upper-class backgrounds; many came from relatively humble backgrounds, and went into journalism on an apprentice basis. As a result, their training in law was minimal, and, while some (notably Percy Hoskins) had a better grasp of the nuances of the justice process, others (such as Rae and Hallworth) were not even interested in the niceties of the law.

The contrasting coverage by Hallworth and Hoskins of the John Bodkin Adams case is illuminating in this respect, taking into account not just their reports at the time but also their retrospective reminiscences. In his text, Hallworth accepted, largely uncritically, the police version of events: he recalled being briefed in a pub by Detective Superintendent Hannam on the investigation. He went on to interview the ordinary

---

[50] Hall Richardson, *From the City to Fleet Street*.
[51] 'The Press: Twenty Years of Crime', *Time Magazine* 10 January 1955.

citizens who worked for and encountered Adams in his daily medical business in Eastbourne, and built up a deeply unflattering picture of him which was later reproduced in the columns of the *Daily Mail* both before and during Adams' murder trial. The book shows little grasp of the criminal justice process and no appreciation of the reasons why Justice (later Lord) Devlin made the points he did in directing the jury in what has become known as the 'double effect doctrine'.[52]

By contrast, Hoskins recounted in his *Two Men Were Acquitted* how he had been originally convinced of Adams' innocence and ensured, therefore, that the *Daily Express* reportage of the case was balanced by placing the emphasis on coverage of the trial rather than the wider narrative. In refusing to join the frenzy against Adams, Hoskins depicted his own career as being at stake. He recounted that, because he had let other papers seize the initiative in reporting the juicy details of the case, Beaverbrook had it in mind to sack him but had relented when Adams was acquitted (hence his book's title).[53] It helped, of course, that Hoskins had invested in Adams' innocence to the extent that he had befriended him during the trial and was consequently able to secrete him away and pay him £10,000 to give exclusive interviews to the *Daily Express*, making up for their pre-trial lack of sensationalism.

Investigative journalist Duncan Webb established himself as a superlative crime reporter through his sustained focus on the nation's criminal underworld, particularly in London. By contrast, Stanley Firmin, the *Daily Telegraph*'s leading crime correspondent, was its more respectable face. Retiring, both Webb and Firmin recounted their experiences and crime coverage in books for the mass market in a further acknowledgment of the sustained market for true crime stories.[54] In practice, for investigative crime reportage to be successful, individual journalists generally needed the collaboration of the police in their activities. It was the early consciousness of the importance of close relationships with the police that had led to the establishing of the Crime Reporters'

---

[52] R. Hallworth and M. Williams (1983) *Where There's A Will ... The Sensational Life of Dr John Bodkin Adams* (Jersey: Capstan Press). The double effect doctrine establishes that if the primary effect of medication is to ease pain and make a patient more comfortable, then the secondary effect that that medication will shorten life, possibly dramatically, is not the basis for a murder conviction. See M. Warnock and E. MacDonald (2008) *Easeful Death. Is There a Case for Assisted Dying?* (Oxford University Press).

[53] P. Hoskins (1984) *Two Men Were Acquitted. The Trial and Acquittal of Doctor John Bodkin Adams* (London: Secker and Warburgh).

[54] S. Firmin (1955) *Murders in our Midst* (London: Hutchinson) p.15.

Association in 1945, with the aim of giving both an identity and an air of quasi-professional legitimacy to specialist crime reporters. Its advertised purpose was to formalise and so to improve relations between its members and the police. It lobbied for, and achieved, a situation where the police would give favoured briefings to journalists admitted to this body as a mark of mutual trust and confidence.

The press and the police

This was, in other words, an era when relations between journalism (especially individual journalists) and the police flourished on a number of levels. Formal police briefings were conducted by a new breed of media-conscious press relations staff in police forces and given to selected journalists, while the Crime Reporters' Association boasted of the access its members had to Scotland Yard. But, in practice, contacts were more widespread and less regulated than ever before, and spread beyond the relatively small elite that constituted the Association. Stanley Firmin actually styled himself the mouthpiece of the Yard to underline the closeness of the relationship he wished readers to understand he had with senior police sources. However, even such members of the Association did not confine themselves to information gleaned from Scotland Yard. Norman Rae, the leading crime reporter for the *News of the World* even before the outbreak of war, was reputed to visit police stations in order to leave small sums of money with individual constables as a way of persuading them to earn more by passing him news. Many seem to have done so (as Clive Emsley has pointed out, low police pay had, from the nineteenth century on, made individual officers vulnerable to temptation).[55]

More senior policemen (including CID detectives) also seem to have been willing to go beyond the official line, providing trusted journalists such as Rae or Harry Proctor with 'unofficial' information which would help identify culprits and build a sound case against them, even if the publicity that consequently surrounded that case amounted to trial by newspaper. The journalist with the closest ties to the police was Tom Tullett, chief reporter of the *Daily Mirror*'s Crime Bureau during the 1950s, who had previously served as a member of the Criminal Investigation Department at Scotland Yard.

Leading crime investigative reporters were undoubtedly useful to the police because they were not hampered by police codes of conduct

---

[55] ·C. Emsley (2009) *The Great British Bobby: a history of British policing from the eighteenth century to the present* (London: Quercus).

in searching out evidence and building good stories. The *Press Gazette* commented in 2005 that Norman Rae was 'probably more successful at solving crimes of the time than Scotland Yard's finest'.[56] For this reason, very probably, police trust in journalists continued largely unabated during this period; even though that trust could (spectacularly on occasion) come unstuck, embarrassing the police and damaging their reputation for competence as well as for honesty and efficiency. But, on the whole, crime journalists were reluctant to embarrass the police as a body, preferring to maintain the established line that police corruption was not institutional but confined to a number of cases of 'rotten eggs'. Thus, a series of trials in the mid-1950s featuring corrupt police officers was not reported as being indicative of something endemically wrong in the nation's police forces. The scandal was not uncovered by tabloid or Sunday title investigative reporters, but by a petition to the Home Secretary from a convicted petty criminal Joseph Grech which revealed a web of police corruption in London. Although the *Daily Mail* in particular was prepared to leak the details of an internal Scotland Yard investigation by Superintendent Herbert Hannam, this was not capitalised on by leading investigative journalists from either the Sunday titles or the other tabloids to reveal the potentially shocking extent of police corruption.[57] What is striking about the coverage of the resulting trials during 1955 and 1956 is the relative restraint with which this police wrongdoing was depicted. For example, the *Daily Mirror* glossed over how the offending of Detective-Sergeant Tommy Mills (who had abused his position in the Criminal Records Department to pass information to criminal contacts) had been uncovered and the extent to which Scotland Yard's investigations had been undermined by Mills. Its focus, instead, was on how other Scotland Yard detectives had finally been able to 'smash' Mills' network.[58]

In explaining the willingness of the police to work with journalists, it should be remembered that police officers, particularly ordinary constables, received relatively little formal legal training. For ordinary constables, it was not part of their job (certainly in this period) to be sensitive to the nuances of how publicity might affect the course of any subsequent criminal justice proceedings. They needed to be informed

---

[56] 'Reg Cudlipp – Former Editor, News of the World', *Press Gazette*, 9 February 2005.
[57] *Daily Mail*, 17 November 1955. For further details, see D. Thomas (2006), *Villain's Paradise. A History of Britain's Underworld* (Harmondsworth: Penguin).
[58] 'Rogue Worked in Rogues' Gallery', *Daily Mirror*, 17 March 1956.

only of 'all aspects of the criminal law, together with those procedures which govern the processes of law enforcement, which are of particular concern to the police'.[59] In practice, it was a matter of learning definitions and then applying them; there was a rather obscure line in daily practice between officially sanctioned use of the media and a more unofficial enabling of the media to help them detect criminals and 'solve' crimes. Criminal activities were understood by the police as public events requiring the oxygen of publicity in the interests of justice for the whole community. This helped further to undermine official instructions not to talk to journalists. Nor were the public unhappy at the clear evidence that the police were using and being used by individual journalists to solve criminal cases. A long tradition of detective fiction had accustomed readers to thinking that the police worked better with the input of amateur detectives, whether private investigators of some kind or investigative journalists.

The press and the legal profession

There was, during this period, something of a resurgence in legal journalism in newspapers and periodicals; though not at the levels of the nineteenth century. Legal journalism had never entirely disappeared; figures like Sir Patrick Hastings had always made occasional journalistic contributions.[60] But this contribution expanded as a number of noted legal figures, including Fenton Bresler, A.P. Herbert and Henry Cecil, took advantage of both print and the broadcast media to make contributions as freelancers. In print, they wrote for a range of titles rather than being linked to any particular paper; their pieces amounted more to reflective comment on legal issues and their popular impacts than to a clear focus on crime-related news. What their writings do not include is any indication that they mixed with, or enjoyed good relationships with, the crime reporters already discussed here. Apart from anything else, as the reports from the actual trials underlined, it was rare for the 'star' investigative reporters to sit in the courtroom listening to the details of

---

[59] A point made in the Preface to the successor to *Moriarty's Police Law*, the key text in the post-war period, J. English and R. Card (2005) *Police Law* 9th edn (Oxford University Press) p. v.

[60] In his autobiography Patrick Hastings commented that, though he had a respect for journalism, he had never enjoyed it; his hero was Northcliffe and, in comparison, post-war editors and journalists fell short. P. Hastings (1954) *The Autobiography of Sir Patrick Hastings* (London: Roy Publishers) p. 60.

a case. Most reports, even from high profile trials such as that of Bodkin Adams, were authored by an unnamed staff reporter.[61]

True, there were times when the legal profession still found it useful to invoke the power of the press. In the mid-Victorian period, they had used their roles as lawyer–reporters and journalists to ensure the debate was sustained over habitual criminality, the ending of transportation and the development of penal servitude at home.[62] A century later, their unhappiness with the reforms to sentencing and the penal system generally under the Criminal Justice Act 1948 also appeared in the quality press. It is likely that individual judges, knowing that any extreme language used by them in the courts was likely to be reported, ensured that their rhetoric was quotably hostile. Judge Tudor Rees, for instance, was reported in *The Times* as insisting that the courts had been partially emasculated in their powers of punishment and endorsed the ideal of deterrence and 'vigorous action'.[63] A subsequent editorial confirmed that the matter had entered the popular arena substantially due to the press attention given to the negative statements made by members of the judiciary.[64]

Contempt of court

Overall, the majority attitude of legal professionals towards investigative crime reporters, certainly on the basis of comments made in contempt of court or libel proceedings, was not complimentary. What caused most regular offence until well into the 1960s was the enhanced degree of salacious or personally intimate detail that regularly accompanied stories in the tabloids and Sunday papers. The potential for such detail became an important factor in journalistic calculations to identify a crime story that would hit the headlines. It was no longer enough for a case to feature a gruesome murder: there needed to be, somewhere, some accompanying sexual or other intimate titillation for a story to dominate the headlines. The old belief amongst politicians and legal professionals that there was a consensus shared with the press that 'unsavoury' detail that was

---

[61] See 'Dr Adams Will Not Be Called', Percy Hoskins and Arnold Latcham, as front page news; 'On Evidence of Nurse's Notes Mrs Morrell Did Not Die A Morphine Death – Defence Doctor', *Daily Express*, 4 April 1957 p. 9. This is typical of the reportage of the trial: Hoskins commented but was clearly not consistently present to report the daily proceedings.

[62] See Chapter 2.

[63] 'Serious Crime in Surrey', *The Times*, 15 March 1950.

[64] 'Punishment for Violence in Crime', *The Times*, 20 March 1950.

extraneous to any crime narrative would be excluded finally disappeared during the 1950s. The tabloids and Sunday titles, notably the *News of the World*, now showed themselves ready to print what would previously have been considered unpublishable. This enthusiasm for sleaze and other inappropriate material convinced the Press Council that it needed to decry the use of what it termed the 'unwholesome exploitation of sex by certain newspapers and periodicals'.[65]

However, irrespective of the affront to public decency, in and of itself, publication of sexually titillating matter in association with a criminal (rather than divorce) case did not necessarily amount to something which could form the basis for legal proceedings against a newspaper. In May 1945, Mr Justice Humphries had said that 'it was desirable that editors of newspapers should reserve their comments on a criminal case until it was over' (which instruction included proceedings in the Court of Criminal Appeal).[66] But tabloid and Sunday paper editors, proprietors and journalists soon showed their willingness to ignore this advice; evidence given to the Royal Commission confirms the lack of interest they felt in providing coverage of criminal cases in a way that satisfied the legal profession. The *News of the World*, once proud to claim credit for the legal soundness of its crime reportage, had been one paper grilled on this issue during the Royal Commission inquiry. Its then editor, Sir Arthur George Waters, had been asked whether he could 'recollect the last occasion on which the courts commended the *News of the World* for publishing reports of court proceedings?' Water's response was that it had been 'Mr Justice Cassels' who had done so, but, tellingly, he could not recall what had been said.[67]

Given such attitudes, it was only a matter of time before serious contempt of court proceedings were again launched against a tabloid editor. Various charges were brought, and thoughtfully dealt with by the courts (not always to the disadvantage of the newspapers). Between 1945 and March 1949 George Haigh made an application alleging contempt of court against the editor of the *Daily Mirror*, for publishing, in three separate

[65] 'Press Council view on "Sex Exploitation"', *The Times*, 28 October 1953.
[66] 'Law Report 15 May. High Court of Justice. King's Bench Division. Alleged Contempt of Court: Applications Fail', *The Times*, 16 May 1945.
[67] Royal Commission on the Press 1947–9. Minutes of Evidence Thursday 19 February 1948 cols. 7464–66. Sir James Cassels had been appointed judge in 1939. Ironically, Cassels also started his career as a journalist working on the *Morning Post* for 14 years as a parliamentary correspondent and as a sub-editor before being called to the Bar; hence he was well known in political and press circles.

editions on 4 March 1945, material that described him as a 'vampire' as well as asserting, not merely implying, that Haigh had committed other murders than the one he was charged with. Silvester Bolam appeared in court on 22 March 1949, when it was decided that the matter was so serious that the proprietors of the company should also be 'peremptorily' summonsed. Humphries LJ justified this by describing the content as constituting 'some of the most horrifying things it would be possible to read'.[68] The summoning of the proprietors was not new in such cases, but it signalled how seriously the court was taking this incident.

Sir Valentine Holmes, appearing for Bolam and the company, made no real defence to the charge that the reportage could only be described as 'a disgrace to English journalism as violating every principle of justice and fair play which it had been the pride of this country to extend to the worst criminals'.[69] For the first time, the court not only issued the heaviest fine ever levied against a newspaper (£10,000) plus costs but also sentenced Silvester Bolam himself to three months' imprisonment.[70] This outcome was justified by Goddard and Humphries, saying that it was the court's opinion that there had never, previously, been a case of 'such gravity' as this, nor a contempt of court of 'such a scandalous and wicked nature'. It did not constitute an error of judgment; rather, it had been a matter of policy: 'pandering to sensationalism' in order to increase circulation. The company directors were warned to control their editor, because, if they offended again in this way, they would find that 'the arm of that Court was long enough to reach them and to deal with them individually'.[71] As *The Times* leader of the same day reflected, to publish material which could prejudice 'the fair conduct of a case' was a 'plain abuse of the right to report news freely'.[72] Interestingly, the *Daily Mirror* itself simply published (small front page headline and column, continued on page 7) a sparse version of the Press Association account of the proceedings.[73]

---

[68] 'Law Report 21 March. High Court of Justice. King's Bench Division. Application Against Editor of the "Daily Mirror". R v Bolam *ex parte* Haigh', *The Times*, 22 March 1949.

[69] 'Home News. Contempt of Court. Editor Committed to Prison. Company Fined £10,000', *The Times*, 26 March 1949.

[70] Ibid.

[71] Ibid.

[72] 'Contempt of Court', Leader, *The Times*, 26 March 1949.

[73] 'Judgment Against the "Mirror"', *Daily Mirror*, 25 March 1949. Virtually no mention of the case and its outcome was made by other tabloids and Sunday titles.

Other contempt of court proceedings demonstrate the ongoing concern of the courts at the willingness of newspapers to pander to reader tastes for sensationalism by breaching the law in covering criminal and civil cases.[74] However, the enthusiasm for what was becoming known as 'cheque-book journalism' continued to entice tabloid and Sunday titles into running the risk of such proceedings, as in the reportage of the case against Dr Bodkin Adams.[75]

Comments made at a meeting of the Institute of Journalists in 1959 further underline the problems surrounding effective crime reportage when undertaken by legally uninformed reporters. Herbert Gunn, editor of the *Daily Sketch* and president of the Institute, argued that 'The difficulty most journalists had was that they were compelled to guess when comment was contempt.' This was exacerbated by the difficulties of consulting court lists to identify whether an individual they were interested in was already involved in the criminal justice process.[76] Regular mistakes in this area undermined the insistence of some of the better-informed journalists that contempt proceedings in criminal cases had a real potential for miscarriage of justice, as the defence could not, while a trial was in progress, proceed against publication of material that was considered prejudicial without consent of the Attorney General.[77] Even the quality papers had become alarmed at the consequences of political hostility to newspaper reportage of legal proceedings (civil as well as criminal).[78]

However, a real issue revealed in a number of contempt of court cases underlines the practical dimensions to the lack of comprehension that crime reporters had of the criminal justice process, something not effectively dealt with by the profession in the 1950s. For instance, Percy Elland of the *Evening Standard* and his crime reporter George Forrest appeared

---

[74] See 'Law Report 2 March. High Court of Justice. Queen's Bench Division. Judge on "Spiteful Article" in Newspaper', 3 March 1956.

[75] 'Drugs Killed Wealthy Widow', *Daily Express*, 22 August 1956; ' "I Will See You in Heaven" said Dr Adams', *Daily Mirror*, 21 December 1956. Interestingly, the Attorney General launched no contempt proceedings during this case, and Bodkin Adams only launched a successful case against *Newsweek*, the US news magazine, which resulted in restrictions on the circulation of foreign titles. See *R v Griffith* [1957] 2 All E.R. 379.

[76] ' "Restrictions" on Press Freedom', *The Times*, 4 June 1959.

[77] This had been a factor in the Bodkin Adams trial; Bodkin Adams was only free to proceed after his acquittal, which may explain the apparent support that Lord Goddard has been accused of showing towards him.

[78] See 'When Press Should Intrude. By Our Own Special Correspondent', *The Times*, 20 June 1958.

before Lord Goddard (again) to answer for slipshod reportage in the case of Albert Kemp, acquitted at Chelmsford Assizes of the murder of his wife. The case provides an informative survey of how court reportage was produced. According to the *Evening Standard*, one witness (Mrs Darmody) had announced that the defendant had asked her to marry him. In fact, she had made no such claim; a previous witness (Miss Briggs) had made such a claim, but her evidence had been disallowed. It was revealed that 'the reporter's habit was to take some notes in Court and then go and telephone his account to London, and then come back to court and resume reporting and go out again'. As the reporter was not interested in the legal niceties that had prompted the judge to disallow Miss Brigg's evidence, he had left the court to telephone his account, returning as Miss Briggs left. Mrs Darmody then delivered her evidence, which was later muddled by the reporter and the editor in London with the inadmissible evidence provided by Miss Briggs.[79]

In this case, Kemp had been acquitted, but it was agreed that the implications of such careless reportage methods were significant. This was proved in the postponement of the trial against Anthony Micallef for brothel-keeping as the result of an exposé of his activities written by Duncan Webb in *The People* while Micallef was awaiting trial. Ainsworth, the editor, and Webb himself insisted that they had no knowledge that Micallef was about to be tried. It turned out that, because Micallef was familiar with Webb, a freelance crime reporter had been sent to interview him and, according to his affidavit, no mention had been made by Micallef of his awaiting trial in that interview. It was put to the Court that 'Webb had made a careful search of the files in the library and the editor had made arrangements with the court reporters to let him know of any proceedings.' However, the instruction 'had not filtered down' and so the information was not passed on.[80] In the final judgment, after considerable examination, the Court decided that '*mens rea* did not need to be present to constitute contempt of which the Court would take cognizance and punish'. The Court was scathing in its condemnation of the attitude of the papers and their reporters, and, in particular, of their

---

[79] The Court agreed the reporter had made an honest mistake and the editor had no moral intention to pervert the course of justice, and so was 'lenient', imposing only a £1,000 fine and costs on the company, not the editor or reporter. 'Law Report 29 March. High Court of Justice. Queen's Bench Division. Kemp Murder Trial Report: £1,000 for Contempt', *The Times*, 30 March 1954.

[80] 'High Court of Justice. Queen's Bench Division. Contempt Proceedings Against "The People" Adjourned', *The Times*, 27 July 1956.

legal ignorance. The defence, according to Lord Goddard, amounted to an argument that it

> had come somehow for some reason to be the duty of newspapers to employ an independent staff of amateur detectives who would bring to a complete ignorance of the law of evidence a complete disregard of the interests whether of prosecution or defence.[81]

The Court was also highly critical of the editor for the attitude he had shown during the proceedings; Ainsworth was reminded that it was a matter of law that editors were responsible for what appeared in their papers. As for Webb, his attitude 'fell far short of that standard of care which persons indulging in that kind of reporting were bound to take'. While it was accepted both were ignorant of the court proceedings against Micallef and so would not be imprisoned, they should have been aware and so were heavily fined.[82] By the end of 1957, attacks on press intrusion were being made in Parliament and considerable pressure was brought to bear on the press to reduce its exposé tactics in both criminal and civil cases: to such an extent that even some legal voices were raised in concern. However, a 'Legal Correspondent' for *The Times* provided an article in the aftermath of the Bodkin Adams case in which he repeated Lord Denning's assertion that the newspaper reporter was 'the watchdog of justice'; and arguing that the Press could be trusted.[83] Not all were convinced, especially when it came to high profile cases.

Murder and other crime

In terms of column inches and profile, murder remained the most favoured crime story. The Thames Towpath murders, the multiple murders by John Christie, the killing of her lover by Ruth Ellis and the trial of teenagers Derek Bentley and Christopher Craig for the murder of PC Sidney Miles were amongst the cases which attracted substantial coverage. Much has been written elsewhere on the ways in which these sensational and other less sensational trials were covered by the press. In addition, apart from those cases already discussed (notably

---

[81] 'Law Report 11 October. High Court of Justice. Queen's Bench Division. Contempt in "The People". Owners Fined £1,000: Editor and Reporter £500 Each', *The Times*, 12 October 1956.
[82] Ibid.
[83] 'Heard In Camera. By a Legal Correspondent', *The Times*, 15 May 1957.

Bodkin Adams), none represented a significant change in the style of reportage. It would therefore be redundant to discuss them further here, given the availability of significant detail available in a range of other texts,[84] and that no single reporting incident stands out independently; thus, the reader is directed to other works specifically on this topic.[85] Unsurprisingly, however, whether murderous or not, cases which contained a sexual motivation or dimension remained a regular factor in sensational crime reportage.

Importantly, though there was a greater appetite for crime stories, interpersonal assault (especially domestic violence), unless linked to another crime issue such as juvenile delinquency or robbery, was rarely discussed. Items focusing on the levels of violent crime were still favoured by crime reporters, but these were lacking in human interest detail; it was the statistics which were the sensationalism. Domestic violence was one area of persistent criminality which, outside divorce court reportage, still failed to be a feature of post-1914 crime reportage. Essentially, it was too mundane a form of criminality to interest key crime reporters such as Hoskins, Rae or Webb.

While undoubtedly an everyday affair, juvenile delinquency and youth criminality did provide a constant theme for crime reportage throughout the period, and not just in the late-1950s era made famous by Cohen's moral panic model. The shock that those who were, because of their age, stereotypically associated with innocence could in fact be guilty of heinous crimes remained intrinsically sensational, arguably because the Welfare State was meant to eradicate the root causes of juvenile crimi-nality across all classes. But, in March 1950, tabloids including the *Daily Mirror* headlined the 'rising tide of youth crime, including cowardly attacks on women', as had the broadsheets in the light of a particularly vicious robbery with violence in which two teenage apprentices (and so in no real need of the money) had attacked an elderly woman on a bus who only narrowly escaped with her life.[86] *The Times* reported Lord Goddard casting

---

[84] See S. Chibnall (1977) *Law-and-Order News: an Analysis of Crime Reporting in the British Press* (London: Routledge); N. Root (2011) *Frenzy. Heath, Haigh and Christie. The First Great Tabloid Murderers* (London: Preface Publishing).

[85] For instance, Bingham, *Family Newspapers? Sex, Private Life and the British Press 1918–1978*; K. Soothill and S. Walby (1991) *Sex Crime in the News* (London: Routledge); C. Browne (1998) *The Prying Game. Sex, Scams and Scandals of Fleet Street and the Media Mafia* (London: Robson Books); P. Chippindale and C. Horrie (1999) *Stick It Up Your Punter! The Uncut Story of the Sun Newspaper* (London: Simon and Schuster).

[86] 'Youth Crime Shocks Nation', *Daily Mirror*, 3 March 1950.

doubt upon 'modern methods of dealing with young criminals' while the *Daily Mirror* effectively raised the same point: 'What is being done to tackle this problem? Who is investigating the causes? What progress is being made? The answer seems to be NOTHING, NO ONE and NONE.'[87]

The same apparent helplessness in the face of consistently high levels of juvenile crime that concerned the mid-Victorians was evident in the mid-twentieth century, with similar causes, from inappropriate reading matter to bad parenting and poor environments, being suggested. Equally, the print debate over management of juveniles post-conviction aired the same dilemmas. What in many ways characterised this period, in terms of its crime reportage, was its interest in the sensationally criminal dimensions to corruption and immorality (including that associated with celebrities and their lifestyles). This provided a regular focus for sensationalism besides murder. It also enabled justificatory claims that investigative crime reporters were exposing crime that needed to be prosecuted or wrongdoers who should be publicly shamed. Stories about the criminal activities of the Messina brothers with their string of London brothels regularly captured the front page headlines of the Sunday press thanks to the efforts of Duncan Webb. His inflammatory rhetoric deliberately sought to pressure the police into prosecuting the brothers, as when he exhorted them to 'ARREST THESE FOUR MEN', on the grounds that they ran a 'VICE EMPIRE' in the 'HEART OF LONDON'.[88]

One clear consequence of such stories was to familiarise readers of the tabloids and popular Sunday titles with the exploits and personalities of a series of criminals; especially those of a 'home-grown' variety rather than foreigners like the Messina brothers or the Maltese Michaleff. The coverage of the trial of Jack Corner, described as a 'gangster-boss' and familiarly known in the press as Jack Spot, who was cleared of a vicious assault on Tommy Falco, a bookmaker, emphasised his popularity with the crowds who gathered outside the Old Bailey and, implicitly, with the crime reporters for these papers.[89]

Conclusion

In one sense, what is interesting about the development of crime reportage after 1945 is how little was new in terms of substance. The

---

[87] 'Punishment Fit for Brutality', *The Times*, 2 March 1950; 'Youth Crime Shocks Nation', *Daily Mirror*, 3 March 1950.

[88] 'Arrest These Four Men', *People*, 3 September 1950.

[89] 'True or False? The Framing of Jack Spot', *Daily Express*, 19 July 1956.

emphasis on organised crime and the associated salacious sexual detail in newspaper coverage of such cases, all in the interests of cleaning up British society, represented an editorial shift, and the pioneers of modern murder coverage had established the basics of sensational reportage by the end of the interwar period. It is, rather, the emphasis on the dimensions of the crime narrative external to the formal criminal justice process that is so striking about the immediate post-war era. The fact that so few leading crime reporters spent significant amounts of time listening to the details of trials in the Assizes, preferring to attend the briefer initial charge or committal hearing in the magistrates' courts or even limiting themselves to the Coroner's Court, provides a telling indication of just how far crime reportage had departed from the standards established for it in the Victorian era. Yet, one survival of that era was still visible: law and order news was not yet heavily politicised. That was to become a feature of crime reportage in the last 40 years of the twentieth century.

7
Positively Criminal? Press, Police and Politicians: 1960–2010

Introduction

This chapter addresses a lengthier chronological period than any of the others; substantially because this is a period which, in terms of the details of crime coverage in the media, has been extensively addressed elsewhere by authors from Steve Chibnall to Maggie Wykes.[1] It would be redundant to rehearse again that which has been so thoroughly investigated and analysed by other scholars. Instead, the chapter highlights aspects of the presentation of crime reportage which stress the continuities and changes with the earlier periods discussed. It thus locates the crime reportage of the last half century in its historical–legal context in order to aid comprehension of how the crisis of public confidence in print journalism arose, leading to the setting up of the Leveson Inquiry, in the aftermath of the sensationalism surrounding the trial of Levi Bellfield in 2011.

Of the periods addressed, this has perhaps been the most difficult for the print press, as multiple forms of news delivery have opened up the crime news arena. As a result, reportage of crime in the media, in terms of breaking news, is rarely within the province of the print media.[2]

---

[1] See, for instance, Chibnall, *Law-and-Order News: An Analysis of Crime Reporting in the British Press*; M. Wykes (2001) *News, Crime and Culture* (London: Pluto Press); M. Wykes and K. Welsh (2008) *Violence, Gender and Justice* (London: Sage); C. Carter, G Branston and S. Allen (eds) (1998) *News, Gender and Power* (London: Routledge); also Soothill and Walby, *Sex Crime in the News*.

[2] An exception can be made in terms of online versions of papers such as the *Daily Mail* (with its current claim to be the world's largest online newspaper), which have, in the last five years in particular, regularly broken news on a rolling, 24-hour basis.

What the print media have had to concentrate on is essentially detailed reportage given further impact by journalistic commentary and reflection. In an era of plurality of types of news media, the economic pressures on the viability of actual physical print newspapers have steadily increased. Many titles (especially provincial ones) have closed, and surviving national titles compete for a diminishing readership.

As journalism came to be understood and studied by academics as an organisational process, the 1970s also saw burgeoning criminological interest in the activities of those who present crime news in various formats. With a range of new criminological insights came a greater journalistic self-awareness as the quality of their product came under scrutiny. By the late 1980s the *British Journalism Review* had identified and condemned a slide towards what it labelled as a 'contagious outbreak of squalid, banal, lazy and cowardly journalism whose only qualification is that it helps to make newspaper publishers rich'.[3] This underlines an 'in-house' perception of a gap between professional print journalists working for the tabloid and Sunday titles and those working for the 'quality' press. Crime stories were a particular target for such condemnation, but, if tabloids were the main target for this charge, surveys of crime reportage in the broadsheets suggest that they cannot be exempted. Part of the issue is that what is considered 'newsworthy', and capable of being sensationalised, has always depended on its reader appeal, but what constituted reader appeal on that basis was changing in terms of toleration for what in previous periods would have been condemned as prurient. The line between what was publicly interesting and what was in the public interest has always been difficult to draw, but in terms of competition for readers, and so survival, this became even more difficult to negotiate.

In broadsheet crime intelligence, there has been since the 1990s a manifestation to a degree of the Victorian ideal that informed reportage should be readable but also capable of being defined by audiences such as politicians and legal professionals as being in the public interest. Such legally intelligent coverage of crime, intended to challenge public understanding of the 'realities' of the criminal justice process, has, however, largely been confined to editorial commentary, opinion pieces and the more specialist law pages rather than the everyday diet of crime reportage that such titles also contain.[4] Even the broadsheets have succumbed to the will to keep high profile stories in the public view, as part of

---

[3] *British Journalism Review* (January 1989), 1(1), 2–6.

[4] B. Franklin (1997) *Newszak and News Media* (London: Edward Arnold) p. 5.

the process of keeping readers, though this has largely been a tabloid and Sunday title phenomenon. This has required a further blurring of the distinction between reportage and journalism, whereby reportage conveyed the factual content of a crime story and journalism provided opinion-led commentary on that story.

Sustaining high profile crime stories encourages journalists to reappraise the key elements of a particular narrative on a regular basis by re-presenting it from different angles, notably invoking critiques of government policy on crime management. Using sensationalised and ideologically framed rhetoric such as would have been familiar to Stead in his 'Maiden Tribute' campaign, and claiming the imperative of public interest, this has led to a series of panics linked to stories such as the murder of Sarah Payne.[5] From the 1970s on, crime intelligence in the tabloid press has increasingly relied upon commentators reflecting upon crime events rather than items written by specialist crime reporters – still further distancing such journalism from legal expertise. Figures like Littlejohn for the *Sun* and *Daily Mail* and Tony Parsons for the *Mirror* effectively transformed crime news into political opinion columns on crime policy, merely illustrated by particular cases. Littlejohn's piece concerning legislation on religious hatred effectively suggested that 'harmless white eccentrics' would be subjected to criminal prosecutions.[6]

Politically inflammatory opinion pieces may be nothing new, but historically they had rarely used crime news to argue party political points with such vehemence until this period. The *Mail*, a newspaper associated today with highly emotive crime coverage, was, until the 1970s, very much a *newspaper* in that sense, as was the *Daily Mirror*, with opinion pieces clearly separately located in the 'What the Mirror Says' section. The march towards brevity that characterised the last two decades of twentieth-century newsprint worked to emphasise only the sensational aspects of crime news, further redacting any legal commentary unless a political point was to be made. The result was that complex legal principles were susceptible to being subsumed beneath political thunder, as in coverage of issues such as insisting on a need for legislation to control dangerous dogs, say.[7]

---

[5] B. Franklin (2008) *Pulling Newspapers Apart; Analysing Print Journalism* (London: Routledge) p. 14; J. Davidson (2008) *Child Sexual Abuse: Media Representations and Government Reactions* (Abingdon: Routledge), pp. 87–89 in particular.

[6] 30 August 2005.

[7] Jewkes, *Media and Crime*, p. 89.

One thing, therefore, which does characterise this era of reportage was the emergence of a new political dimension to comment about crime. This resulted from the party politicisation of law-and-order issues from the late 1960s on. Inflecting that, a gulf has appeared between the quality and the popular press in attitudes towards crime intelligence. The former has benefitted from a renewed willingness to communicate with the press on the part of the legal profession, and so can better reflect the values and priorities of that profession, out of a mutual commitment to the principles of promoting open justice through public information. Popular print journalism, convinced that what keeps the tabloids in business is provision of the juicy details of sensational scandal (as provided by individual crime stories rather than thematic considerations of policy) accompanied by often alarmist rhetoric commenting on crime policy or aspects of individual cases, has had less interest in reflecting such principles in its columns.

Commercial pressures, editors and proprietors

At the end of the 1960s, newspapers came steadily under the steward-ship of commercially minded media conglomerates headed by figures like Rupert Murdoch. His vast media empire, News International, included print titles such as the *News of the World* and the *Sun*, acquired in 1969.[8] Despite competition from media and (increasingly) internet news sources, there was a belief in the importance of newspapers as a source of comment-inflected news. However, the symbolism and signifi-cance of a print press which was not only uncensored by government but independent of political control and the influence of outside inter-ests became diminished as newspapers were compelled to remain profit-able elements in the context of these large media enterprises with their responsibilities to shareholders. This has led to a landscape in which the diversity of newsprint offerings has been much reduced.

Recent entries into the market, such as *Metro* and *I* (a condensed version of the *Independent*), are characterised by ever more 'bite-sized' items. An associated shift towards a greater minimalism in terms of the complexity of newsprint offerings has also featured, most obviously in the continuing rise of attention-grabbing headlines. These increasingly moved away from factual, if summary, headlines towards impact-driven headlines. Emotive phrases were used to attract readers even though

---

[8] *The Times* and the *Sunday Times* were subsequently acquired by News International in 1981.

those headlines frequently bore little resemblance to the subsequent narrative, being representative only of a journalistic opinion rather than the facts of a story. Assessments of the impact this has had on standards of accuracy in reporting crime and the criminal justice process may be most critical when referring to the tabloid press, but the quality press of the last half century has also been guilty of inaccuracy, for instance, in relation to headlines. An enhanced audience impact could be the only justification for a misleading *Daily Telegraph* headline relating to a proposed overhaul of the law on murder which suggested that it would be possible for parents who killed paedophiles to 'plead not guilty to murder'.[9] Equally, the *Sunday Times* was one of five titles accused of contempt for its inaccuracy in reporting the charge against Michael Fagan, who broke into Buckingham Palace in 1982.[10]

Despite a rise in 'Infotainment' or soft news, crime reportage has continued to be a staple for both regional and national newspapers, scattered amongst and intersecting with human interest, celebrity, sporting and political stories. In many ways, crime news became indistinguishable from such contextual human interest narratives. It is not just that, as has long been the case, a minor crime committed by a famous figure regularly receives more coverage than a serious crime without interesting personalities involved. It is often the case that the crime dimension to a news story often gets hidden under reportage focusing on the celebrity aspects of the personalities involved. Thus, a rape committed by a footballer has been liable to being treated as a celebrity/sport story as much as a crime one; equally, criminal fraud by politicians has been subsumed in political news. The loss of crime specialists such as those operating in the mid-twentieth century is clearly substantially responsible for this. When a sexual assault is committed by a pop star, and that piece is covered by an entertainment commentator, the narrative very necessarily becomes primarily a celebrity rather than a crime story.

As in previous periods, the influence of proprietors upon newspaper content continued to be significant. But in this period, a new dimension was added in that the political attitudes taken by titles in reflection of

---

[9] 'Parents Who Kill Paedophiles Can Plead Not Guilty to Murder', *Daily Telegraph*, 28 July 2008.

[10] 'Fagan Report Inaccurate', *The Times*, 27 January 1983. The papers 'wrongly' reported he faced a stabbing charge, which could have had a 'quite incalculable effect on a jury'. The title was fined £1,000 plus costs, while the *Daily Star* received no fine but only costs awarded against it, suggesting a higher expectation of the quality press from the courts. Frances Gibb, 'Sunday Times fined for Fagan Reports', *The Times*, 12 February 1983.

the parties they supported began to shape their commentary on law-and-order (and so crime) issues. Political considerations consequently made a contribution to the choices of incidents and themes to cover, and to the specific emphasis and 'spin' of titles. Increasingly, the commentary on individual crimes and their management was used to provide illustrations of good or bad practice under the official policy of the day. Crime news has always been political, of course, but this was the first time that it was, on a sustained basis, relayed for public consumption through the lens of political allegiances. Previously, the political dimension had been that a government was always expected to demonstrate its interest in promoting appropriate legal reforms. But, as an examination of the actual debates in Parliament and the reportage of legislative initiatives in the press reveals, such debate was more governed by individual experience and belief than by party politics *per se*. Silverman's 1956 bill for the abolition of capital punishment, for instance, passed the Commons substantially on a free vote; while the opposition of the Lords was equally cross-party.[11]

From the late 1960s, however, the party allegiances of a title expanded to shade comment on a government's criminal policies and the reactions of the opposition. The tabloids became increasingly and didactically party sensitive in their crime presentations. In 1977, the *Daily Express* announced that the Conservatives were 'set to fight the next General Election campaign on law and order', including 'new stern laws to fight violence and vandalism'.[12] In the 1990s, the *Mail* trumpeted the Major government's 'Crusade of Decency' in fighting crime.[13]

Crime news as political rhetoric is not new, but crime news became something extensively drawn upon by political or general journalists to illustrate party political points and so influence an electorate. Choices became driven by individual crimes and issues believed capable of supporting or challenging party competence in managing crime. Labour, for instance, successfully positioned itself as the 'law-and-order' party, wresting that title from the Conservatives, by promising to be 'tough on crime and tough on the causes of crime'.[14] Then, with New Labour in power, the *Sun* commented on the 'Shock new crime figures which show

---

[11] The passage of the Offences Against the Person Act 1861 was equally non-party-political. It is worth noting that the classic media moral panic examined by Cohen demonstrates that there was no serious party political dimension to the 1950s debates. See Cohen, *Folk Devils and Moral Panics*.

[12] 'Law and Order!', *Daily Express*, 22 September 1977.

[13] 19 November 1993.

[14] Tony Blair (1993), 'Why Crime is a Socialist Issue', *New Statesman*, 10 January 1993.

that muggings are rocketing',[15] with an increase of 19 per cent in violent crime, as part of an attempt to toughen government policy.[16] In 2006, with the end of the first decade of Labour government in sight and Labour claims for considerable success in their criminal justice policies being made, Trevor Kavanagh wrote a scathing opinion piece: 'vicious assaults have quadrupled, rapes are up ELEVEN-FOLD, convictions are down – and dangerous criminals are being dumped in open prisons (which they promptly quit) because of overcrowding in real jails'. This was part of a campaign to persuade the Government to rethink the investment it was planning for the subsequent 2007–2008 period.[17] Despite concern about how newspapers wield political influence, it continues to be recognised by political campaign organisers as important that they should be allowed to do so. The fears that the Labour government had post-1945 about the potential effect that owner prejudices and political allegiances could have for a 'balanced' or fair presentation of news resurfaced in this period, with a new vigour; and there is some evidence that this did affect the access of some journalists to politically sensitive news-gathering.[18]

The shape of British newspaper reportage during the 1970s was also profoundly influenced by the American press, thanks to Watergate. It encouraged among journalists a self-perception of themselves as figures who could deliver justice where the criminal justice system had failed. Few things demonstrate this better in the British context than the exposure, in 2009, of the 'expenses scandal' uncovered by the *Daily Telegraph*. Occurring at the height of the recession, the assertion that those elected to govern had been bilking the public purse was guaranteed to elicit public outcry. The scene had been set in the early 1990s when the press had first highlighted numerous cases of political 'sleaze', albeit more in the moral than the criminal realm. But it fits into one of the central themes of modern news stories: that of emphasising crime victims and identifiable victimisation.[19] The expenses scandal was positioned as a

---

[15] 19 January 2000.

[16] *The Sun*, 26 June 2000.

[17] T. Kavanagh, *The Sun*, 29 May 2006; also 'A Nation Stalked by Fear', *The Sun*, 1 August 2007, demonstrating his ongoing campaign on this topic.

[18] R. Negrine (1994) *Politics and the mass media in Britain* (London: Routledge) pp. 42–54; Chris Walker recalled being refused a briefing on the grounds that he was one of 'Murdoch's men'; C. Walker (2005) 'Small Times, Bad Times', *British Journalism Review*, 16(2), 26–30.

[19] R. Reiner, S. Livingstone and J. Allen (2000) 'No more happy endings? The media and popular concern about crime since the second world war,' in T. Hope and R. Sparks (eds) *Crime, risk and insecurity: law and order in everyday life and political discourse* (London: Routledge) pp. 107–126.

crime against society as a whole and thus recruited a cohesive body of true 'public' outrage. Effective communication of the legal issues bound up with fraudulent activities of politicians was hidden to some extent by the use of colloquial language by the press. The terminology of 'fiddling expenses' was widely used across both broadsheets and tabloids as an expression which replaced the true legal terminology of false accounting; the terms 'fraud' and 'theft' were also used in numerous reports, offences that are legally distinct yet rarely elaborated upon in the press.[20] Consequently, 'fiddling expenses' now appears to have passed into common usage as a pseudo-legal term.

Contextualising the choice of the 1970s for the start of the chapter, the decade was also crucial because, once again, the Government decided to establish a Royal Commission on the Press in 1974. The remit was to 'inquire into the factors affecting the maintenance of the independence, diversity and editorial standards of newspapers and periodicals and the public freedom of choice of newspapers and peri- odicals, nationally, regionally and locally'.[21] Again, little of practical policy significance emerged. The key proposal emerging from the 1977 Report was rejected: that a written Code of Practice be drawn up. In the end, political will to tackle the issues raised by the Commission's Report was lacking, and the proposals for a tougher regime to regu- late both the potential for monopolies within the press and the publi- cation practices of individual newspapers failed to materialise, again. As a result, newspapers continued to be substantially successful up to 2011 in establishing a popular perspective that newspapers worked in the public interest, including when it came to reporting crime and the criminal justice process.

The issue of press responsibility for the content of news items was raised again just over a decade later; via a Departmental Committee set up under Sir David Calcutt QC in 1990 to investigate invasions of privacy by journalism. Its final Report once again insisted on the need for a better level of self-regulation at least, with the recommendation that the Press Council be replaced by a Press Complaints Commission.[22] Established at the start of 1991, the Commission had a Code of Practice drawn up by national and regional editors. Calcutt reported on it in

---

[20] Used in 1985 as a term for tax evasion; *The Times*, 28 October 1985, p. 10.

[21] Royal Commission on the Press, 1974–77 (1977) Report (London: HMSO) Cmnd 6810.

[22] See T. O'Malley and C. Soley (2000) *Regulating the Press* (London: Pluto Press).

1993 and complained then of its ineffectiveness, but political will to change things was wanting.[23]

Tellingly, throughout the debate, the issue of the impact of current press practices in reporting crime was not an issue: the discussions of breaches of individual privacy focused primarily on prominent individuals (including politicians) rather than on the issue of the damage done to the justice process by intrusive reportage of human interest aspects of criminal cases.[24] Calcutt had referred, in his original Report, only to the importance of investigative journalism in exposing crime, which was (he argued) very clearly in the public interest.[25] While there was an attempt to tackle the issue of damaging reportage of juveniles in legislation such as the Youth Justice and Criminal Evidence Act 1999 (which imposed further restrictions on reporting cases involving juveniles), there was still a faith that investigative journalism was crucial to the way in which the press contributed to the public interest. This belief is revealed in the Code of Practice, in its 1992 version, insisting that intrusions into individual privacy were justified in order to detect or expose 'crime or serious misdemeanour' and 'seriously anti-social conduct' (which, at least implicitly, led to or bordered on criminality).[26] In the revisions of the PCC's Code of Practice between 1991 and 2011, this perspective was not challenged. There was no substantial political will to engage with the fundamentals underpinning newspaper presentations of crime news because this was not something which alarmed the reading public, despite regular complaints by the individuals exposed to public scrutiny in the press in the course of crime reportage.

Crime in its media context

The continuing public thirst for personal detail presented as human interest information to contextualise an event ensured that crime reportage continued to be highly significant, as it was considered fundamental to a story's 'newsworthiness'.[27] In 1992, the *Reuters Handbook for Journalists* insisted on the importance of a journalist reporting a crime

---

[23] Ibid.

[24] For a fuller discussion of this aspect, see Rozenberg, *Privacy and the Press*.

[25] D. Calcutt (1990) *Report of the Committee on Privacy and Related Matters* (London: HMSO) Cmnd 1102.

[26] O'Malley and Soley, *Regulating the Press*, p.167.

[27] J. Galtung and M. Ruge (1965) 'The Structure of Foreign News', *Journal of Peace Studies*, 2(1), 64–91 at 70–71; but see also A. Bell (1991) *The Language of News Media* (London: John Wiley and Sons).

story interviewing eyewitnesses, but also seeking out 'authoritative' or official sources to give a story credence and depth in terms of its journalistic value.[28] Studies have shown more than double the percentage of crime stories in samples of tabloid and quality newspapers than had been featured in the mid-century.[29] This was largely because of the claim of crime reportage to be 'serious' news (especially with the politicisation of crime management strategies) while incorporating an approach to the human interest dimension which was most strongly associated with gossip columns and celebrity news in terms of the minutiae of human relationships.

From the commission of a crime to its formal resolution, there were myriad opportunities for revealing the stories of those even peripherally involved. Thus, criminal episodes have continued to act as a valuable source of copy for newspapers as well as other media formats. It is not so much that more crime, in terms of prosecutions brought, was being covered as that there was ever more extensive and dramatic coverage of each high profile crime, solved or unsolved, and often that reportage referred to the criminal justice process only through the actions of the police as part of that system. Reportage of the proceedings in the courts (especially of more minor offences) has not depended on the legal dimensions of a case but on a newsworthy human interest drama that is rarely legally framed. Minor theft such as shoplifting, unless involving a nationally (or, in provincial papers, locally) known figure, was essentially absent from the national press unless it reflected on issues such as economic policy or social deprivation issues. Individual convictions or acquittals and the grounds for that outcome where ordinary citizens were concerned were used only as illustrations of the wider issue.

Of course, as the previous chapters have revealed, treating a criminal incident as an unfolding drama was nothing new.[30] The framework provided by informed reportage of the criminal justice process was not missed, because of the diminished popular understanding of the legal

---

[28] I. Mcdowall and Reuters Ltd (1992) *Reuters Handbook for Journalists* (London: Butterworth-Heineman) p. 137.

[29] R. Reiner (2001) 'The Rise of Virtual Vigilantism: Crime Reporting Since World War II', *Criminal Justice Matters*, 43, 4–5; Reiner, Livingstone and Allen, 'No More Happy Endings?'; R. Reiner, S. Livingstone and J. Allen (2003) 'From Law and Order to Lynch Mobs: Crime News Since the Second World War', in P. Mason (ed.) *Criminal Visions* (Cullompton: Willan), pp. 13–32.

[30] Episodic delivery of crime stories had been a staple of earlier reportage but also, of course, of the developing genre of detective fiction as serialised in Victorian periodicals and subsequently.

dimension. Rather than the trial and the airing of evidence in the context of the legal process, it was the investigation of crime and identification of a suspect that were now seen as core to the everyday drama of crime. The trial was simply a forgone conclusion in many ways, given how much of the evidence had been pre-aired in the newspapers. The new information age developing from the 1990s brought with it an expectation of increasingly frequent instalments. The result was to promote strategies by which a frequent repackaging of core information was refreshed (and its inclusion justified) by associating it with new narrative detail on the human interest aspects of a case, in order to satisfy a public appetite for regular updates on high profile stories which catch the popular imagination.

This has ensured that the investigative dimension to crime reportage has remained crucial, but has further diminished the importance of the actual trial, as the types of case that it made sense to cover in detail via newsprint have decreased. With a much more limited resource in terms of investigative journalists available to research a crime, the emphasis in the print press (in line with televisual drama) was increasingly turned towards serious crime. This had the effect of even further reducing the press coverage of more mundane everyday crimes. The result has been the establishment of a skewed picture of the reality of the profile of crime and criminal activities, so that popular perceptions of both levels and types of crime committed on an everyday basis challenge the statistics of, for instance, the British Crime Survey.

In many ways, media presentations of the 'reality' of crime stories have made it easier for audiences to understand what they see as the criminal justice process, and to critique its workings. Both the issues involved and the actors in a crime drama are now packaged into a series of stereotypes which lack both complexity and a sense of how these relate to the effective delivery of justice. The necessary ambivalence of a criminal case before and during a trial, including any substantial discussions of legal interpretations of character and motivations, is no longer believed to sell even broadsheet newspapers.

Journalists and crime intelligence

In this period, journalism became once again more aspiringly professional, with the development of university courses in journalism and media studies. With the improvement in its status, a number of individuals who qualified in law chose, as in the nineteenth century, to practise journalism instead, including Joshua Rozenberg. Rozenberg read law at

Oxford, qualified as a solicitor and then turned to journalism (print and media), working for the BBC and eventually becoming Legal Affairs editor for the *Daily Telegraph*.[31] The fact that Rozenberg and similar figures can be found as legal editors for broadsheet titles certainly raised the quality of informed legal reportage in those newspapers. For example, enhancing his ability to present court proceedings accurately, Roger Verchaik both qualified as a barrister and worked as a court reporter before joining the *Independent*.[32] At first sight, it could be said, therefore, that the legal knowledge of a significant number of leading journalists has returned to almost nineteenth-century levels. Such figures have certainly made a genuine contribution to legal journalism: but that does not automatically conflate or have any impact on the everyday reportage of crime stories, even in the quality press. Figures such as Joshua Rozenberg, Roger Verchaik and Frances Gibb provide more specialist reportage with a focus on broad legal issues (true, regularly including criminal justice issues) rather than crime reportage as such.[33]

Thus, this evidence of quality at the higher levels of legal reporting did not really change the status of the everyday reporter providing crime stories, especially amongst the mass circulation tabloid titles. High-flying university-educated incomers to journalism were more likely to be interested in areas identified as glamorous in the context of the last half of the twentieth century. If not legally qualified, then (outside politics) the appealing posts included being a foreign correspondent or (increasingly) the related field of war correspondent. While crime remained an important area for editors and proprietors, the new intake of journalists did not look to crime investigative reportage as containing substantial potential for making an individual reputation. Indeed, apart from foreign and war correspondents, and to some extent political correspondents, a move away from specialist reporters and journalists has been taking place since the 1970s. The shift is most vividly illustrated by the actions of Larry Lamb, Murdoch's first editorial appointment to his newly acquired *Sun*. Lamb cut specialist staff as part of an explicit drive towards creating a more superficial (if controversial in its opinions) newspaper. Lamb insisted that 'The basic interests of the human race are not in politics, philosophy or economics, but in things like food and money, sex and

---

[31] He left the paper in 2008; and has recently returned to the BBC's *Law in Action* series.

[32] Verkaik is currently Security editor of the *Mail on Sunday*, an interesting move to a tabloid title.

[33] Gibb is currently Legal editor of *The Times*.

crime, football and television.'[34] Culls of specialist staff and reductions in staffing levels at many newspapers have made a reduction in detailed consideration and accuracy inevitable. One noted veteran journalist and section editor at a national daily newspaper reflected:

> the volume of stories we produce in a day has increased a lot. When I started out, in the days before the electronic revolution, I was producing one or two stories a day. Today it's not uncommon to be knocking out 5 or 6 in a day – and when you're doing that you rely more on the wires and on PR than you did before.[35]

It is no surprise that the idea of a dedicated crime journalist reporting and/or investigating crime news has steadily morphed into a journalist presenting their own opinion based on readily accessible information, however that access is obtained.

The investigative journalist, working for a campaigning newspaper, has not disappeared, however, even if they are rarely exclusively concerned with reporting crime in a strictly legal sense (morally offensive conduct, especially by prominent individuals, is regularly dubbed 'criminal'). Serious broadsheets such as *The Times*, *The Guardian* and the *Daily Telegraph* and the tabloids including the *Mail*, *Mirror* and the *Sun* (and, up to its demise, the *News of the World*) provided a context in which investigative print journalists could still see themselves as having a particular role in shaping public opinion about major issues. Crime was, overall, less regularly a focus for such investigation-based campaigns than in the two decades after the war. But the quality of that crime reportage, especially in tabloid titles, has been at best mixed in terms of its legal accuracy and ability to help the reading public understand the criminal justice system and its workings.

As the earlier twentieth-century experience underlined, without legal training reporters and journalists have regularly failed to represent the complexities of the legal issues in crime stories, or even to indicate that such complexities exist. Adam Wagnar, barrister and *Guardian* columnist, has deplored inaccurate press reporting of the Human Rights Act 1998 and commented on the lack of journalistic understanding of human

---

[34] Cited in J. Nicholas and J. Price (1998) *Advanced Studies in Media* (Cheltenham: Nelson Thornes) p. 92.
[35] J. Lewis, A.Williams, B. Franklin, J. Thomas and N. Mosdell (2008) *Quality and Independence of British Journalism; Tracking the change over twenty years* (Cardiff School of Journalism: Cardiff University) p. 4.

rights law and immigration. When coupled with editorial agendas, in some tabloids at least, desiring to see the abolition of the Act, the result has been what he has described as ill-informed and 'shrill' reporting which 'jars with the nuance of judge's decisions'. He argues that, where decisions reached in court are badly reported, they cannot be 'exposed to accurate scrutiny' by the reading public because they lack the information and so the understanding to do so properly.[36] The example of the *Daily Express* (a title regularly singled out for criticism on this front) is informative. The editor, Peter Hill, was determinedly opposed to the Human Rights Act and its impact after it came into force in 2000. In 2010 (the last full year of his editorship) stories included the claim that 'The human rights scandal is rooted in our subservience to Europe'[37] and that 'Human rights law is still protecting the terrorists.'[38] It went so far as to make the alarmist claim that human rights laws were 'helping Britain's enemies'.[39] There was no discernible effort by the title's journalists to understand the legislation so that they could use it to provide useful or measured criticism of its impact.

The treatment of Learco Chindamo after his release from his sentence for murdering Philip Lawrence in 1995 provides a useful example of how crime news can be very differently contextualised and evaluated. The *Express* presented his leave to remain under the terms of the Human Rights Act as yet another failure to protect the community from foreign criminals threatening individuals, while the *Guardian*'s Polly Toynbee lamented that the case was being used by the press for party political purposes in ways that sensationally misrepresented not just the individual facts of the case but also the wider crime landscape.[40] Consequently, it is unsurprising that readers have consistently failed to appreciate or approve of the use of human rights considerations in relation to criminal cases such as that of 39-year-old recidivist Congolese child rapist William Danga in 2011: 'Child rapist used "human rights" to fight deportation – then struck again,' screamed the *Mail*.[41] Danga used Article 8 of the European Convention on Human Rights and other

---

[36] 'Inaccurate human rights reporting will not help either side of the debate', 17 January 2011, *The Guardian* Legal Network (online) http://www.guardian. co.uk/law/2011/jan/17/human-rights-act-gurkhas?showallcomments=true&#co mment-9186717, accessed 19 March 2013.

[37] 18 December 2010.

[38] 19 June 2010.

[39] 19 May 2010.

[40] *Guardian*, 28 August 2007.

[41] 18 September 2011.

delaying tactics to prevent his deportation, to the expressed disgust of the judge, who failed to comprehend a previous decision not to deport him. The same rhetoric was used against Akindoyin Akinshipe, 'Nigerian rapist allowed to stay in UK',[42] despite the clear differences in the basis of their claims. Akinshipe had committed rape when aged 15 and, after serving his sentence, gained a university education, became a regular churchgoer and secured a job, thereby convincing the European Court of Human Rights that he had a legitimate right to remain.[43] Such reportage underlines the extent to which ignorance of the law compounds a long-standing determination to sensationalise the content of crime reportage and the more recent will to politicise crime management strategies. The extent to which politicians used crime management issues as a party political football ensured that editors had a real will to support different party agendas by investigating and reporting crimes which seemed to provide useful political ammunition as well as sensationalist narratives.

There have been exceptions where the popular press has sought to educate its readers on legal issues. From its relaunch as a tabloid in 1971, the *Daily Mail* positioned itself as the bulwark of British liberties. Its law and order perspective was valued by its long-serving editor David English, enabling the title to present itself as the mouthpiece of the 'reasonable person' against the excesses, absurdities or actual failures of the criminal justice process. Notable campaigns included the Tony Martin case in 2007[44] and, from 1997, a 15-year 'search for justice' for Stephen Lawrence, murdered in 1993. The *Daily Mail*'s crusade undoubtedly led to the 1999 Macpherson Report into police conduct in relation to the Lawrence murder and conclusion of 'institutional racism' within the Metropolitan Police (with implications for the UK police forces more widely).[45] But it was (in many ways) a sustained reportage that sought to inform readers of at least some of the legal nuances that underpinned the collapse of the 1996 trial. This relatively rare excursion into legal niceties was essential to this campaign, because the newspaper's objective was to secure legal reform in the abolition of the double jeopardy legal principle, which would permit the retrial of the key suspects in the Lawrence murder. Thus, the principle (effectively scrapped in 2005) had to be explained to readers. This development permitted

---

[42] *Daily Express*, 21 September 2011.
[43] *AA v UK* [2011] ECHR 1345. None of this reasoning appeared in the *Daily Mail* coverage; see J. Slack, 'Social Ties Keep Rapist in Britain', *Daily Mail*, 21 September 2011.
[44] *Daily Mail*, 15 March 2007.
[45] Home Office (1999) *The Stephen Lawrence Inquiry: Report of an Inquiry by Sir William Macpherson of Cluny*, Cmnd 4262-I, para. 46.1.

(eventually, on the discovery of new evidence) a retrial of Gary Dobson and David Norris, resulting in their conviction in January 2012.[46]

Journalists and the police

The most common source for the crime intelligence that could support sensationalist reportage continued to be the police; even though the print media were more regularly critical of their abilities to fight crime than in previous periods, as the wide publicity given to the Macpherson Report underlines. Certainly coverage of the police became more complex in this period, reflecting growing levels of public dissatisfaction with and even downright distrust of the police as an institution; something which was discernible from the late 1960s.[47] Tellingly, it was a quality broadsheet and not a tabloid that led the way in revealing that police corruption had become both systemic and involved more than using their position for financial gain. In 1969, *The Times* provided an exposé of police corruption, providing a front page headline supported by column inches detailing the extent of the corruption already uncovered in the Metropolitan Police, hinting at more and demanding a full inquiry.[48]

The importance of this story lay not only in the authority of the title publishing it, but also in its inference that, this time, it was not an incident involving a few corrupt officers but, with the involvement of senior officers, a systemic problem with the police. When the case came to trial, *The Times* happily reported the praise of its journalists voiced by Lord Justice Edmund-Davies, that 'it was, it would appear, mainly their intrepidity and skill which laid bare a hideous cancer which, if unchecked, could have done even greater and incalculable damage to law enforcement'.[49] This suggests that the close relationships between investigative journalists from the tabloids and their police sources had ensured that they had preferred to turn a blind eye to police corruption to maintain their sources on other crime news. But tabloids did begin to follow the example set by the broadsheets, though they still preferred to provide stories which encouraged their readership to view examples of corruption as atypical rather than typical of the institution as a whole.[50]

---

[46] See S. Wright, 'The Mail's Victory', *Daily Mail*, 3 January 2012.

[47] See Chibnall, *Law-and-Order News*, which discusses the issue at length.

[48] 'Tapes Reveal Planted Evidence. London Policemen in Bribe Allegations', *The Times*, 29 November 1969; also 'A Little Firm in a Firm', Editorial, *The Times*, 29 November 1969.

[49] *The Times*, 27 June 1973.

[50] 'TWO WICKED DETECTIVES. Jail for Yard Gangbusters who tried Blackmail', *Daily Mirror*, 6 March 1972.

There were several enquiries, reports and even trials dealing with police corruption during the 1970s and 1980s, including an exposé of corruption (principally bribery) in the Metropolitan Police's Vice Squad.[51] Coverage of Operation Countryman (1978–1984) and the subsequent trials indicating that corruption was endemic in the Metropolitan and City of London Police was actually more lavish in the broadsheets than in the tabloids. But both regularly discussed reasons why 'the good name and reputation of the Police have become a matter of grave public anxiety'.[52]

This greater willingness to give column inches to incidents or allegations of police criminality and/or incompetence is perhaps surprising, given the continuing pro-police agenda adopted by most tabloid newspapers. Neil Wallis (former deputy editor of the *News of the World* 1986–2009) reflected that, during his tenure with News International, its titles were 'always pro-police, pro-army and pro-law and order'; something fostered by the fact that its tradition of investigative journalism (increasingly undercover in the post-1945 era) and interest in exposing serious criminality and corruption meant that the 'close links' between the Metropolitan Police (and other forces) and titles like the *News of the World* continued to flourish.[53] The reality was that a close relationship was more than simply mutually beneficial to both the individuals concerned and the institutions. Use of the media (including newspapers) continued to allow the police to call upon the public for information to assist them in their investigations as they had done in the nineteenth century. Equally, there was a continuing police consciousness that positive presentation of their activities could be justified as a legitimate information-gathering exercise that cast them (individually and institutionally) in a favourable light at a time when they needed such.[54] There was even official endorsement of the relationship. The Home Office reiterated in 1982 that 'the public are entitled to accurate information in relation to serious crime through the media and the Police Service has a duty to report and comment on it responsibly'.[55] The official position

---

[51] 12,13 November 1976, 24 August 1977.

[52] 'The Police, The Law and the Public', 4 March 1972.

[53] Second Witness Statement of Neil Wallis to the Leveson Inquiry, Monday 2 April 2012.

[54] See Chibnall, *Law-and-Order News*; M. Fishman (1981) 'Police News: Constructing an Image of Crime', *Urban Life*, 9, 371–394; R. Ericson (1989) 'Patrolling the Facts: Secrecy and Publicity in Police Work', *British Journal of Sociology*, 40, 205–226.

[55] Home Office (1982) *The investigation of a series of major crimes* (Home Office Circular 114/82).

was that through regular briefings the police released limited details of individuals arrested and had discretion, where appropriate, to name suspects and confirm details uncovered by the press.[56]

A complication in all this was that the press did not have a monopoly over reportage; it was, generally, television or radio which 'broke' the news and also, increasingly, undertook investigative journalism. However, television and radio journalists did not have the tradition of closeness with police sources, and, as their news coverage of police corruption had underlined, they had no interests which were best served by ignoring suggestions of police incompetence or corruption. The familiarity between newspaper journalists and the police came under the media spotlight during the Yorkshire Ripper investigation. Details of a tape, allegedly from the Ripper, were leaked to the press. In the ensuing inquiry, one journalist suggested that close relations with the police could cause journalists to 'ignore' crime stories that should be made public. Consequently, there was the potential for that relationship to develop into a 'corrupt liaison'.[57] From the police perspective, in the internal inquiry that followed the publicity around the Ripper tapes, informal police disclosures were (again) condemned and it was (again) recommended that the flow of information to the press be controlled through a spokesperson.[58] The reality was that, while there was a change in terms of journalist relations with police sources, with press officers becoming more prominent as mouthpieces, relationships between individual investigative journalists and police officers continued, albeit (again) with a lower profile.[59]

Journalists and the legal profession

Compared with relationships with the police, a distance between most journalists and criminal justice professionals, in terms of personal relationships, continued. There was some contact of a genuinely personal nature within the broadsheet or quality press, thanks to the presence of legally qualified journalists in their specialist pages. Such men and

---

[56] Details are contained in the Communication Advisory Group Guidance (most recent 2010), Association of Chief Police Officers of England, Wales and Northern Ireland.

[57] P. Burden (1982) 'The Business of Crime Reporting: Problems and Dilemmas', in Sumner, *Crime Justice and the Mass Media*, pp. 1–7.

[58] Ibid.

[59] The Association of Police Communicators was established in 1998 to legitimise the role of press officers and other staff in police communication roles.

women are respected by the legal profession, facilitating informed contact between the two professions at this specialist level. Rozenberg's informed contributions to the broadsheet press won the Bar Council's Legal Reporting Award on four occasions. Equally, Frances Gibb, the Legal editor of *The Times* (now 'the only national paper to have dedicated law pages' according to its website), has provided well-informed legal coverage that has won the admiration of legal professionals. Such figures provide an interesting contrast with another legal professional who contributed enthusiastically to tabloid coverage of crime news. The infamous Judge James Pickles became a tabloid columnist on retiring from the Bench; though his ability to tap into current thinking in his profession was (at best) idiosyncratic, he was not popular with his fellow lawyers.

But even Pickles had little to do with everyday crime reportage from the courts or the criminal justice system in general. The party politicisation of crime management meant that reporting of the daily workings of the criminal justice system (particularly in the right-leaning tabloid press) was often critical of the legal profession as a whole, with particular individuals (especially judges) regularly being singled out for criticism. Individuals who were held to be 'soft' on sentencing and so labelled as 'failing' the victims of crime (especially violent and/or sexual crime) could expect excoriating comment as part of a drive to toughen up aspects of the criminal justice process. The blame heaped on legal practitioners underlines the fundamental lack of journalistic comprehension of the legalities involved in a criminal trial. The *News of the World* provided a typical example of 1980s tabloid outrage with the headline 'Lock him up for Good!' and the subhead 'Fury over soft sentence for monster who has attacked 38 little girls'; there was no discussion of the legal dimensions of the court proceedings or the reasons behind the sentencing decision.[60] Equally, while the legal dimensions to the political debates generated by such reportage were generally covered by broadsheet journalists, notably *The Guardian* and *The Times*, these were (continuing the twentieth-century habit) largely ignored by tabloid journalists.

The levels of criticism echoed that aimed at early Victorian practitioners, and had a broadly similar result. Alarmed by the effects on the public, in terms of levels of support for the legal profession, leading figures began to reassess their relationship with the media. The object was, once again, to promote a better public understanding of the workings of the

---

[60] 'Lock Him Up', *News of the World*, 9 March 1980.

criminal justice process (particularly the role of the judiciary) through better use of the media. But there was no question of using junior lawyers as reporters or even as advisors to reporters. Lord Woolf insisted that a free and independent judiciary with free and independent media was the surest safeguard of democracy, where 'the media exposes and the judiciary determines illegality'.[61] He accepted that, in addition to the official processes (including appeals) to prevent 'inappropriate' conduct by individual judges, a further 'protection' was provided by knowledge that 'inappropriate behaviour on the part of a judge can be exposure in the media'. Yet the judiciary (individually and institutionally) could not, he believed, be on too close terms with the media. There was a danger in conveying an impression that judges sought media approval. In that light, he approved of Lord MacKay's decision in 1987 to remove the Kilmuir rules, enabling judges to contribute to 'public discussion' without seeking official approval (though, with the exception of those sitting in the Lords, they should avoid appearing political).[62]

At the time of the suspension of the Kilmuir rules, Sir John Donaldson MR suggested something that amounted to a return to nineteenth-century habits; the core reportage would convey the charge, outcome and sentence, leaving it to clearly separated editorials or opinion columns to add commentary on the handling of individual cases, including sentencing decisions. In respect of such comment, Donaldson pleaded: 'Let criticism be well-informed, well-researched, and temperately expressed.'[63] Over the subsequent quarter century there have been genuine attempts by the judiciary to become more accessible and 'media-friendly', but the more measured approach favoured by the legal profession has not found a ready echo within the print media, especially the tabloid section. Measured and balanced assessments failed to make headlines, for a start. The tabloids preferred the attention-grabbing pronouncements of an iconoclast such as Pickles, who had already notoriously thumbed his nose at the official stance of judicial silence.

Pickles was a key source for what were dubbed 'no nonsense' law and order dictates. His comments (carrying the weight of authority of

---

[61] Lord Woolf (2003) 'Should the media and the judiciary be on speaking terms?' Speech (University College Dublin: Law Faculty, 22 October). http://www.judiciary.gov.uk/media/speeches/2003/should-media-judiciary-be-on-speaking-terms, accessed 19 March 2013.

[62] Ibid.

[63] Speech delivered to the Law Society 15 April 1987, reported in *The Times*, 16 April 1987.

someone who was on the 'inside' but who challenged that establishment) were loved by the tabloids. Their popularity with the public ensured that even the broadsheets began to echo his critiques of the legal establishment; as when *The Times* used a headline for a story on sentencing 'Something is wrong with our judgment.'[64] Sentences such as those imposed by Mr Justice Leonard in 1987 on the men convicted of the Ealing Vicarage rape case aroused popular outrage.[65] Yet, despite the impression given in the tabloids, cases such as this were atypical in terms of both the crime and the sentencing, something which further underlines the problematic nature of populist crime reportage from the perspective of the legal profession. The sensationalist focus on serious crimes ensured that the reality that they represented under 10 per cent of crime prosecuted, as well as failing to reflect sentencing practices for those found guilty, was not apparent to the majority of the reading public. Looking back over a decade of criticism, Lord Bingham reflected on the 'extraordinary paradox' that the judiciary and magistracy had consistently been 'roundly criticised for over-lenient sentencing during a period when they have been sending more defendants to prison for longer periods than at any time in the past 40 years'.[66]

Certainly, one side effect of the party politicisation of crime reportage was a scrutiny of the law, which regularly shifted the sensational emphasis from 'shocking' crimes towards 'shocking' laws. There was a determination to highlight what were being identified as legislative 'mistakes' as well as judicial missteps and a failure on the part of the criminal justice process to respond appropriately (according to the judgment of 'right thinking' people) to both types of crime and individual examples of crime. The result was that the press first established, and then regularly compounded, a popular perception that the criminal justice system as a whole (from police to prisons) was 'failing'. As well as issues surrounding sentencing practices, the inadequacies of legislation and police failures were regularly tropes underpinning the thrust of crime news, inflecting the ways in which individual cases were covered in various titles. Such themes were particularly explicit in the Conservative press when Labour

---

[64] 'Outside the Law: Something is wrong with our judgment', *The Sunday Times*, 19 April 1987. The controversy Pickles started lasted for over a year; see 'Judge speaks out against "soft" courts', *The Times*, 28 May 1988; 'Judges should never comment publicly on criminal trials', *The Times*, 19 October 1989.

[65] For instance, 'Outrage'; 'Criminal sentence', *Daily Mirror*, 3 February 1987.

[66] F. Gibb, 'Bingham attacks media fallacy of "lenient" sentences', *The Times*, 11 July 1997.

was in power: and in the Labour press when the Conservatives were in power. But, even when a Conservative government was in power, the right-leaning press was regularly critical of the established legal system in the context of arguing for legislation to force change on the system. It may seem (given the dominance of the Conservative leanings amongst the tabloid press, at least until 1995 and the rise of New Labour) that the newspaper press was generally hostile to the contemporary criminal justice process, as Lord Bingham's observation indicates.

The legal profession did begin, very earnestly, to try to forge a new relationship with the media during the 1990s, fearing the impact on their reputation of ongoing criticisms. The dropping of the Kilmuir rules had encouraged members of the judiciary to be willing to talk, on the record, to journalists. In 1990, the Bar Council created its Legal Reporting Award to recognise journalists whose work contributes to a 'greater public understanding of legal issues'. Tellingly, though, no tabloid journalist has ever won that award.[67] And even in the broadsheets, and certainly in the tabloids, criticism of individual legal professionals has continued in stories that constitute crime reportage as well as in legal opinion or commentary pieces.

The impact of sustained and politically inflected criticism of the criminal justice system through the medium of print journalism has been considerable, especially as it has also been allied to critical comment in other media formats. But it has been print journalism, using the authority and permanence of the written word, which has campaigned most vigorously for changes to 'bad' laws or for new laws to fill 'gaps' in existing legislation. Such pressure has played a major part in making governments feel compelled to preside over the enactment of apparently electorate-friendly legislation which has been rushed through the parliamentary process. Examples of such rushed, and so poorly drafted, 'kneejerk' legislation have included the Dangerous Dogs Act 1991, but also legislation to control the football hooliganism which flourished during the late 1970s and 1980s.[68] The media furore surrounding that put pressure on the Government to impose new legal sanctions, including the Sporting Events (Control of Alcohol) Act 1985, the Football Spectators Act 1989 and an order of exclusion from a football ground included in the Public Order Act 1986.

---

[67] Though one winner, Roger Verkaik, now acts as Security editor for the *Mail on Sunday*.

[68] See K. Reid (2003) 'Law and Disorder: Victorian Restraint and Modern Panic', in J. Rowbotham and K. Stevenson (eds) *Behaving Badly: Social Panic and Moral Outrage – Victorian and Modern Parallels* (Aldershot: Ashgate) pp. 82–84.

It must be added that such pressure emanated largely from the less legally aware tabloid press, and that the broadsheet press did regularly raise concerns about public order law being too readily expanded as a result of populist and sensational tabloid assaults on the status quo of the criminal justice process. Such commentary pointed to the potential for infringement upon the individual rights of those affected (but not necessarily directly targeted) by such legislation in ways which demonstrated that such titles still possessed access to legally informed columnists.[69] But, with their smaller circulations, such broadsheet concerns had far less success in imposing restraint than did the tabloids when pressing for action.

The wariness of legal professionals about being misunderstood (or having their comments misquoted) was still obvious even towards the end of this period. Judge Anthony Scott-Gall, for instance, was reported as 'stunning' Lewes Crown Court with his reflections on the defence put forward by 'an ASBO thug' seeking to avoid a jail sentence for criminal damage, an unrelated assault, breach of a suspended sentence and a two-year ASBO. The defendant, Dexter Vidal, had claimed he was kicked, in a drink-related tussle, by the sons of a woman police officer whose private car he had vandalised. Deferring sentence to see whether Vidal would remain out of trouble, as promised, Scott-Gall had contextualised the tussle by commenting that he was 'not surprised he was given a good kicking. It's what he deserved'; taking care then to address the press box and add 'Lest the press think the judge conducts a vigilante campaign against people that terrorise his neighbourhood and his car – he doesn't and they haven't.'[70] It is telling that this was not an example of the kind of criminal case that was usually reported nationally. What made it 'newsworthy' was the particularly quotable (from a journalistic perspective) judicial comment – which he then felt impelled to explain because he was resigned to being reported, but also plainly unsure that the context in which his comments were made would be fully and accurately reproduced in the press. It is that wariness and resignation which explain, on the one hand, the continuing use of contempt of court proceedings and, on the other, the relatively low penalties being imposed by the twenty-first century.

---

[69] *The Guardian*, 27 December 1984.

[70] 'Judge stuns courtroom by telling ASBO yob he "deserved a good kicking from victim's sons" ', *Daily Mail*, 16 October 2009.

Journalism, contempt of court and other illegalities

As in previous periods, an examination of contempt of court cases brought against journalists, editors and proprietors of newspapers is informative of the standards expected of crime reportage. Examination of cases brought suggests a diminished willingness, political and legal, to launch prosecutions against newspapers. Certainly 'unwholesome' revelations were no longer an issue: the public interest was no longer regarded as being challenged by publication of what, in a previous era, might have been dubbed 'sleazy' detail. In many ways, the most significant development lay in the events resulting in the passage of the Magistrates' Courts Act 1980 and the Contempt of Court Act 1981; enacted because both domestic circumstances and European law compelled government to try to clarify the law on contempt (especially the issue of public interest in freedom of speech in high profile criminal and civil cases) and to bring English legislation in line with European expectations.[71] English and Welsh contempt of court legislation had remained largely unamended (though not undiscussed) since the nineteenth century.

Contempt proceedings against newspapers (and later other media formats) during the twentieth century had been on the grounds that publications of certain reports or information had interfered with the administration of justice, with the increasingly frequent defence being that it was in the public interest that information be provided to a reading public. It was accepted by the courts that investigative journalism did not constitute, *per se*, contempt because there was, at times, a genuine public interest in exposures of criminal conduct which would otherwise remain hidden (i.e. the Profumo Affair). In 1974 the Philimore Committee had recommended the provision of a public interest defence of publication to a charge of contempt made against a newspaper provided any prejudicial impact on the justice process was unintentional.

The issue was how far investigative journalism should be able to publish information expressly contextualising an event actually within the criminal justice process. Perspectives on the tensions between freedom of expression in the public interest and the right to a fair trial, with the key evidence being tested in that arena, differed sharply between the legal profession and journalism. The priority for the former was to avoid trial by media, or, as Lord Diplock asserted in 1974, the key players in a case should be able to 'rely upon there being no usurpation

---

[71] *Attorney-General Appellant v Times Newspapers Ltd. Respondents* [1974] AC 273 at 307.

by any other person of the function of that court to decide it according to law'.[72]

The diminishing media interest in the actual trial process was disquieting, especially in the context of an increasing interest by the European courts in UK court outcomes. What made new legislation seem urgent was the 1979 publication, by the *Sunday Times*, of criticism of the proposed court settlement in the long-drawn-out thalidomide case, substantially because of the danger that it would lead to public disrespect for the law.[73] The Contempt of Court Act 1981 consequently made interference (including through media publication) with active court proceedings an offence in an attempt to clarify the ambiguities of the existing common law; enabling a judgment to be made about potential danger to pending or ongoing court proceedings. Account could be taken of the public interest; however, what constituted that public interest remained undefined in practical terms, and so very much open to debate, as did the issue of how to judge intentional harm. Lord Hailsham insisted that the intention was to make the law on contempt not only clearer but also more 'liberal' in terms of freedom for the media to report issues of public interest.[74] If the press was, as Lord Denning had adjudged in 1955, a 'watchdog', was it a watchdog that needed some chains on its freedom of action?[75]

Lord Justices Watkins and Mann certainly believed so, in the light of what Watkins described as 'trial by newspaper, a form of activity which struck directly at a jury's impartiality' on the part of the *Sun* (especially as it published allegations inadmissible as trial evidence). The paper had taken up a rape case involving an 8-year-old girl in which the decision had been reached that there was insufficient evidence to proceed with a prosecution. It had financially aided a private prosecution resulting in the acquittal of the accused. In fining the paper £75,000, Watkins commented that 'the need for a free Press was axiomatic but the Press could not be allowed to charge about like a wild unbridled horse'.[76]

Another interesting test of the legislation, and of the relationship between press, police and the legal profession, came in a 1997 case

---

[72] Ibid, p. 72.

[73] *Sunday Times v United Kingdom* (1979) 2 EHRR 245.

[74] 'Parliament, December 9 1980; Lord Hailsham says new contempt measure will make law much clearer and more liberal', *The Times*, 10 December 1980.

[75] Lord Denning (1955) *Road to Justice* (London: Stevens and Son) p. 78.

[76] 'Law Report. Trial by newspaper was contempt', *The Times*, 20 February 1988.

relating to a *News of the World* investigation into counterfeiting. After setting up the criminals to gain the necessary evidence, the paper informed the police that they intended to publish the story. The police promptly pre-empted them by arresting the alleged culprits the day before the *News of the World* trumpeted its success in a detailed story outlining its investigations. [77] This meant that the paper was liable for contempt proceedings as it was an active case; the title and the key journalist were fined £50,000, to the fury of other editors and journalists who labelled the judgment a 'blow to investigative journalism' which let two criminals walk free and made the job of the police harder.[78] Since 1981, newspapers have 'escaped', or fallen foul of, contempt proceedings according to whether or not the judge considered the case active and the process of justice seriously damaged, or likely to be.[79] There was no attempt to prosecute the *Daily Mail* for contempt after it named the suspects in the Stephen Lawrence murder case, for instance.[80] Interestingly, in contrast with previous periods, the fines for newspapers and journalists convicted of contempt have been lower overall, and no newspaper editor or journalist has been sent to jail for publishing information as a signal of the grossness of their contempt.[81]

Yet prosecutions of the press for contempt of court continued to be undertaken; the long-standing concern of the legal profession about the impacts of trial by media seemed justified by a recent study revealing

---

[77] 'We Smash £100 Million Fake Cash ring', *News of the World*, 11 September 1994.

[78] The charge was that the story made it necessary to abandon the trial; the point made by the paper itself was that, had it behaved more improperly and published before the arrest, it 'would have been in the clear'.See F. Gibb, 'Editors rally to paper fined for contempt', *The Times*, 21 July 1997.

[79] Thus the Attorney General ruled out prosecutions of the press for contempt in the Peter Sutcliffe (Yorkshire Ripper) case: 'Sutcliffe Contempt Ruled Out', *The Times*, 11 June 1981.

[80] 'Contempt Threat to "Daily Mail" ', *The Independent*, 17 February 1997.

[81] For instance, the rejection of the demand to jail Paul Foot, editor of the *Socialist Worker*, and fine him (plus the publishers) £250 plus costs (amounting to around £8,000) for naming principal witnesses in the Janie Jones blackmail case; 'Mr Paul Foot fined £250 for contempt of court', *The Times*, 19 October 1974. Some journalists have, of course, been sent to jail for refusing to identify a source, which also counts as contempt. See 'Judge Will Not Jail Reporter', *The Times*, 4 June 1981, where the judge, refusing to jail the reporter Lundin, said he would 'normally commit such a witness to prison for 7 to 14 days' but would not in this case because of his 'journalistic ethics'. Lundin was later tried for contempt by the High Court but, after much debate, acquitted there also. F. Gibb, 'Journalist Cleared of Contempt', *The Times*, 20 February 1982.

that juries are both exposed to and influenced by media coverage of a case, and more than 60 per cent of this coverage comes from newspapers.[82] This suggests both that legislation is needed and that the press needs to ensure that crime reportage is genuinely responsible. However, for the period covered in this chapter, the Press Complaints Commission's Editors' Code of Practice expressly identified detecting or exposing crime as a public interest issue, and this 'in-house' validation encouraged continuing challenges to contempt legislation. Bob Woffinden has even suggested that, practically speaking, 'the media now are, by and large, free to publish as prejudicially as they wish, not merely without effective contempt of court restraints but without any restraints at all'.[83]

Crime stories

While murder remained a popular staple in crime reportage during this period, the greater tolerance of sexually explicit material meant that detailed coverage of rape cases, especially those involving children, was possible in ways previously not really tolerated in newsprint. In terms of the key murder stories of this era, those with enduring resonance have generally demonstrated the growing gap between populist and legal ideas of what constitutes justice. The 2000 trial of Tony Martin, the Norfolk farmer who killed one and wounded another would-be burglar, and was convicted of murder (not manslaughter), provides a crucial example of this. The tabloid media were outraged at the jury's decision on behalf of what they claimed (almost certainly rightly) was majority public opinion, and in so doing reignited public debate concerning the limits of the law.[84]

---

[82] C. Thomas (2010) *Are juries fair?* (London: Ministry of Justice Research Series 1/10).

[83] B. Woffinden (2007) 'Treating contempt with contempt', *British Journalism Review*, 18(2), 5–12.

[84] There was an interesting parallel case in 1865, when an eccentric East End physician, Dr Debenham, shot and killed a figure who turned out to be a drunken sailor and was charged with murder. The judge in that case, as in Tony Martin's trial, pointed out that the law 'would only excuse the taking of human life under very extreme circumstances'; and that in all cases, 'the law required that proper discretion should be exercised'. Debenham was actually acquitted by his jury, despite the startled remonstrances of the judge; indicating that popular support for extreme reactions by householders has a long-standing tradition. But the jury in 1865 indicated very clearly that it comprehended but rejected the strict legal position. 'Occasional Notes', *Pall Mall Gazette*, 13 July 1865.

The long-standing legal question at the heart of the case concerned the amount of force that could be lawfully used in defence of property. However, this dimension to the trial could not have been gleaned from reading the popular newsprint coverage of the case. Instead, the emphasis was on the 'justice' of his conviction in the light of the old adage that 'an Englishman's home is his castle'.[85] To a degree, the issue then became starkly politicised in party terms, as the Labour-supporting *Daily Mirror* accused the Conservative party of 'Pandering to the Lynch Mob'.[86] But it had a wider resonance, as the popular Murdoch press vigorously defended the position of the average working man seeking to defend his home.

The recruitment of the press to the 'positive Martin story' illustrates another modern development in relations between journalists and sources, namely the use of public relations intermediaries by those involved in high profile crime news. Malcolm Starr, press manager for Martin, channelled 'pro-Martin stories' to those who wanted to 'reflect the disgust of "all right-thinking people" '.[87] The *Sun* was ardently vocal, demanding 'Does anyone seriously believe this is justice?'[88] In the face of a continuing media barrage over subsequent years (through Martin's appeal, the reduction of his conviction to manslaughter, and his eventual release in 2003), successive legal arguments were made to justify the legal rationale underpinning Martin's trial and conviction, but without changing the attitude of the popular press. In 2005 the then Director of Public Prosecutions, Ken Macdonald QC, issued a clarification of the law in the Crown Prosecution Service's (CPS) statement on Self Defence.[89] But the popular mileage in such cases has been regularly reignited in the subsequent decade, most recently when Omari Roberts killed an intruder in a struggle at his mother's home in 2009 and the tabloids and broadsheets all leapt enthusiastically on the issues for popular justice that his actions raised.[90] In the face of continuing critical tabloid coverage of

---

[85] 'Fury at Martin verdict "raises risk of violence" ', *The Times*, 25 April 2000.

[86] 27 April 2000.

[87] T. Martin (2004) *Right to Kill? Tony Martin's Story* (London: Artnik) p. 165.

[88] *The Sun* also published numbers of letters from readers supporting Martin.

[89] http://www.cps.gov.uk/publications/prosecution/householders.html, accessed 19 March 2013.

[90] Daniel Boffey and Ross Slater, 'In my self-defence. How I fought off knife-wielding intruder and was forced to clear my name', *Daily Mail*, 25 April 2010; Helen Carter, 'Burglar murder charge dropped at last minute', *The Independent*, 19 April 2010. It has remained an issue. See Lucy Bogustawski, 'Man seized after shooting intruders at his East Midlands home', *The Independent*, 2 September 2012.

what was felt to be, popularly, an ongoing 'miscarriage of justice' when householders were prosecuted for taking action against intruders, the Conservatives decided to include a populist pledge in their 2010 election manifesto to revisit the law of self defence in this context.[91]

Age and gender have also provided substantial copy for tabloid titles. Several high profile crimes have given both investigative journalists and opinion writers substantial material to discuss the 'failings' of the criminal justice process in terms of what has been portrayed as an unwillingness or inability to deliver the 'justice' that has been held, popularly, to be required by the dimension of a case. One example with enduring mileage has been provided by the murder of Jamie Bulger, and the conviction of two young boys for that killing. Presentation in the press ever since their trial and conviction in 1993 has polarised around two approaches – one favoured by the broadsheet press (the issue of the age of criminal responsibility) and the other by the tabloids (concentrating on the 'evil' nature of the killers and so promoting a moral panic over child-on-child killings).[92] Key cases revealing a profoundly gendered approach to crime reportage have included the case of Kiranjit Ahluwalia in 1990. The criminal justice narrative included not just her original trial but also her appeal against conviction for murdering her husband. Broadsheet coverage provided careful legal considerations of the issues involved.[93] Ahluwalia's trial was, however, largely ignored by the tabloid press until it became politically sensitive during her appeal, when it began to be discussed in terms of whether or not it permitted or encouraged women to kill and get away with it.[94]

Generally, the tabloids have shied away from 'big' legal questions and instead favoured cases that have more readily fed into the simplistic tropes of 'bad' or 'mad' individuals.[95] Against this background, it is easy

---

[91] The result was the Crime and Courts Bill, introduced in May 2012, containing a clause which would penalise only 'disproportionate' action. See S. Lipscombe, 'Householders and the criminal law of self-defence', www.parliament.uk/briefing-papers/SN02959.pdf, accessed 19 March 2013.

[92] See J. Rowbotham, K. Stevenson and S. Pegg (2003) 'Children of Misfortune. Media Parallels in the Cases of Child Murders Thompson and Venables, Barratt and Bradley', *Howard Journal of Criminal Justice* 42(2), 107–142; B. Franklin (1999) *Social Policy, the Media and Misrepresentation* (London: Routledge), especially pp. 177–178.

[93] *The Independent*, 2 July 1990.

[94] M. McDonough, 'The Women Getting Away With Murder', *Daily Mail*, 24 September 1998.

[95] See, for instance, the case of Amelia Edwards, *The Mirror*, 28 May 2002.

to see how governmental rhetoric concerning the deterrence effect of legislative change commonly suffers from journalistic miscommunication bemoaning 'how we are beaten by the system'.[96] However, the killing of Sarah Payne in 1991 was the watershed case for the press in their coverage of child sexual abuse and another politically charged topic for reportage. The press has had a complicated relationship with sex crime since it was embraced as a reportable topic in the early 1970s. Sex crimes have been readily used as titillation by a print press driven by economics because 'Sex news teases and titillates with stories of the rich, famous, devious and dangerous but ultimately promotes both a conventional moral code and the law', such as was espoused particularly by the popular press.[97] After Sarah Payne's murder, press coverage was unrelenting and a campaign, spearheaded by the *News of the World*, demanded a policy shift towards public access over privacy in the case of convicted sex offenders. Various publications took a similar tack, deriding the Government for a lack of action.[98] The *Mirror* insisted, in alarmist tones, that the 'Police must warn parents of monsters'.[99] It was also readily susceptible to party politicisation, as Shadow Home Secretary William Hague showed when he lambasted 'the apparent powerlessness of our society to protect an eight-year-old girl playing only a few yards from her grandparents' home'.[100] As with the Tony Martin example, careful and considered legal analysis fell victim to the overriding newspaper quest for public attention. The *News of the World*, for instance, campaigned on the grounds that it was an unregulated, rather than an under-regulated, area of law.[101]

Conclusion

In this period press coverage rarely dwelled upon the legal nuances of crime news. The quality press still provided in-depth legal coverage in

---

[96] *The Mirror*, 26 July 1995.

[97] Soothill and Walby, *Sex Crime in the News*, p. 22; Wykes, *News, Crime and Culture*, pp. 144–145.

[98] There were press dissenters in this call for greater public access, most notably *The Guardian* and the *Observer*.

[99] *The Mirror*, 25 July 2000.

[100] 13 August 2000.

[101] Principally that the notification requirements introduced by the Sex Offender Act 1997 were not rigorous enough as regards the disclosure of information to interested parties (albeit on a confidential basis), e.g. head teachers, youth and community leaders, doctors and sports club managers, and the release of information to the wider community in exceptional circumstances.

its specialist law pages, but less so on its main news pages.[102] Despite this, the role of the press as mouthpiece, both informative and opinion-shaping, has not faded. Crime news, commentary and entertainment crime stories, such as sporting 'assaults' and celebrity drug-taking, continue to form the bulk of commentary in the press. Historically the press had tackled these issues as legal ones, but the modern press has increasingly adopted a soft sell approach; the modern public apparently prefers, or is at least proffered, the law as a subsidiary element. This kind of covert engagement is a distinctive feature of modern legal reporting. By subsuming legal issues within social commentary, crime news is still delivered, albeit surreptitiously and not always accurately. Sensational and emotive reportage has become more important as newspapers fight to retain their readership.

An increasing expectation of up to the minute reportage has also changed the landscape for newspapers. All have websites that are updated throughout the day. This fast-paced delivery brings with it the danger of inaccuracy, particularly given the loss of specialist legal commentators. What is particularly interesting in many of these modern reports is the lack of resolution, as criminal issues seem rarely to be resolved and confidence in the criminal justice system and its personnel declines. The print press of the past 40 years has conveyed the impression that the criminal justice system is inept, either through individual cases (James Bulger; Sarah Payne) or its institutions (the legislature, judiciary, police and the CPS), as revealed through investigations mounted by the press and later taken up by the authorities. Newspapers are swift to trumpet their successes, from the *News of the World* sex offender campaign to the *Telegraph's* exposé of MPs' expenses. Regrettably, it is increasingly rare to find positive messages about the criminal justice system.

---

[102] D. Rooney (2000) 'Thirty Years of Competition in the British Tabloid Press', in C. Sparks and J. Tulloch (eds) *Tabloid Tales: Global debates over media standards* (Maryland: Rowman and Littlefield Publishers) p. 102.

8
Online and Offline: Postscript 2011–2012

Introduction

As this text finally goes to print, there are on the table two different drafts for Royal Charters to regulate the press in the post-Leveson era. One, agreed by all political parties on 16 March 2013, was evolved without input from the newspaper industry itself; the other (published on 25 April 2013) was evolved by that industry. Both versions accept the need for a Royal Charter under which investigative journalism should be regulated. One thing is plain from both versions, however: the original point of the Leveson Inquiry (an exploration of the negative impact on the criminal justice process of unbridled investigative journalism, including the generation of information via inappropriate 'leaks' or improper – even illegal – means, including payments to informants) has been relegated to the background of the debate. This is despite the fact that Operations Weeting and Tuleta (investigating hacking and computer hacking) and Operation Elvedon (investigating payments to the police) remain ongoing, and could be used to generate substantial evidence to consider whether or not modern methods of investigative journalism have created a type of crime news which has distorted the criminal justice process. For instance, in January 2013 former Detective Chief Inspector April Casburn was convicted of misconduct in a public office for offering to sell information to the *News of the World* in September 2010, and sentenced to 15 months' imprisonment. Her defence, supported by many, has been that she asked for no money but simply went to the press as a 'whistle-blower'. What that action certainly indicates is the extent to which titles like the *News of the World* were an automatic resource for police officers wishing for something to be publicised.[1]

As the end of the twentieth century segued into the twenty-first century, newspaper reporting generally, and crime reporting in particular, was both privileged and challenged by two momentous developments, one legal and one technical. The Human Rights Act 1998 established press freedom from state-sponsored censorship (in terms of both access to, and the right to publish, that information) as a key element in that freedom of expression which marked democracies. Of course there were, within the Act, broad limits to manifestations of that freedom of expression. However, the failure of successive initiatives to establish a comprehensive code of conduct for investigative journalism which would have the practical force of law in terms of its ability to regulate the content and quality of that journalism ensured that, in practice, the Act enhanced rather than restricted the ability to publish ever more salacious detail in the advertised interests of the public's right to knowledge about certain individuals and issues.

The existing impetus to provide such sensational detail in the 'public interest' was enhanced, in ways that undermined traditional restraints, by the impact on the newspaper industry of the increasing range of technological advances during this period. New web-based platforms for dissemination of information helped to redefine what constituted 'news' and, in so doing, destabilised the commercial relationship between the industry and its customers. The 'new journalism' of the early twenty-first century was that provided by the 'citizen journalist'. This new breed of non-professional news reporters became increasingly active amongst the young, and thereby diminished the readership demographic, because it was younger readers who were turning away from the traditional print press to consume their news in a variety of online alternatives. In a spirit of 'if you can't beat them, join them', professional journalists increasingly contributed to these alternative news forums to amplify and inflect their contributions to print journalism. Consequently, the sophistication (in terms of depth, range and quality) of these alternative news forums varied widely. However, their themes remained broadly the same (if often at a more local or individual level) as in the commercial media.

---

[1] 'Met detective charged with misconduct in public office for "leaking information to News of the World" ', *Daily Mail*, 12 September 2012; 'Corrupt or just a scapegoat: is top detective locked up over role in phone-hacking scandal just a pawn in a political game?' *Daily Mail*, 9 February 2013.

This meant that political comment and gossip, sport and celebrity stories, and also crime news (if the conceptualisation of crime was usually less legally coherent than in newspapers) featured largely. It did have an impact on crime reportage, resulting in a renewed focus on trial events. Initially, the criminal justice process was happy to endorse the use of live text-based electronic communication by journalists or other accredited commentators. It seemed simply an extension of the twentieth-century habit of journalists leaving the courtroom to telephone in their stories, and had the advantage that they would neither disturb the court with comings and goings nor miss, thereby, any important details. It was assumed that a representative of the media or a legal commentator using such live communication technology from within the court would not pose a danger of interference to the proper administration of justice in an individual case. This was because the most obvious purpose of permitting such communications was conceived of as being to enable the media to produce fair and accurate reports of the proceedings.[2] Was this a way of supporting rather than replacing traditional formats for disseminating crime news?

The experience of the murder trial of Vincent Tabak indicates that, in practice, the result was less positive. During those proceedings, many journalists from a range of titles sent thousands of tweets from the press benches that described the evidence and speeches in real time. Rather than ending up with a tidy and legally informed summary of proceedings, Twitter followers had access to a raw, running report of what was going on in Bristol Crown Court in ways that both oversimplified the nuances of prosecution and defence, and failed to give a sense of justice being delivered.[3] As this trial underlined, real time news delivery without time for analytical reflection is limited to providing 'raw' commentary of proceedings, which contributes little to public security in the criminal justice process. The apparent intimacy of Twitter as opposed to the more formal process involved in traditional media reportage has also encouraged a range of ill-considered and, at times, illegal comments from 'citizen journalists', as the Twitter dissemination of a false identification of Lord McAlpine as a figure involved in a child abuse scandal showcases. As *The Guardian* put it, such careless dissemination of information

---

[2] Lord Judge (2011) *Practice Guidance: The Use of Live Text-Based Forms of Communication (including Twitter) from Court for the Purposes of Fair and Accurate Reporting* (Lord Chief Justice's office, 20 December 2011).

[3] 'How I tweeted the Tabak Trial', *Guardian Unlimited*, 2 November 2011.

[4] 'Lord McAlpine and the high cost of tweeting gossip', *The Guardian*, 27 November 2012.

ensured that 'tweets' would be at the forefront of libel litigation in the coming years.[4]

While libel is essentially criminal, it is not the key focus of this text. However, what such incidents reveal is the seismic shift in news consumption habits which has resulted from the development of electronic communications. This has also had implications for the shape and content of crime news. The newspaper industry has needed to become ever more competitive and publishers necessarily more innovative. News has increasingly been distributed by mainstream national and local newspapers in digital format via dedicated websites and downloadable apps as well as in print.[5] Proposed changes in legislation since 2011, such as the Justice and Security Bill, due to come into force in 2013, have been discussed in the popular press as well as in more measured terms in the broadsheet specialist law pages. This represents what many legal professionals see as an overload of criminal legislation and policy initiatives, and more intense political management of the criminal justice system; and this has been faithfully reported in those specialist pages. But elsewhere the superficiality of reportage from the courts has continued because non-specialist reporters covering crime stories have simply not been able to cope with the metaphorical quicksands of the criminal justice process. Stories have 'developed' on websites (including those of the tabloid and other press) with new information being added as a kind of 'topping' to an original story, as there is not the time to rewrite the contribution from scratch and so properly to update the available text.

Post-2011, there has been an even stronger emphasis put forward for public consumption on an essentially emotional sense of what constitutes justice rather than on one informed by a sense of the law. This has tended to mean that useful criticism of the criminal justice system has not formed part of that popular knowledge gained through the mass circulation press, especially that acquired electronically. This failure to grasp the legal dimensions to any incident defined as 'criminal' has been intensified by the endemic recording and reporting of crime stories by citizen reporters at the scene of incidents. Utilisation of mobile phone technology, with images and accompanying comment then openly disseminated through the internet, social networks, video platforms and so on, has provided competitive 'real-time' information streams

---

[5] A variety of charging systems have been introduced since 2011, first by *The Times* and the *Financial Times* but followed by other titles, including the *Daily Telegraph*.

which popular titles have enthusiastically incorporated without considering the broader issues raised in terms of safeguarding, for example, presumptions of innocence.

What citizen journalism also means is that the press (like television and radio) no longer enjoys absolute control over the actuality and transmission of crime news. Ultimately, and viewed with hindsight, the key event in these years was the trial of Levi Bellfield in the summer of 2011, and the associated revelations of phone-hacking which caused such popular outrage that they led to the demise of the *News of the World* and to the Leveson Inquiry. The public realised that direct or implicit endorsement by senior news editors of questionable journalistic practices and invasive strategies meant that such tactics were either already embedded in, or fast becoming regular features of, the investigative journalist's everyday tactics when it came to crime stories and not just celebrity gossip. What was seen as acceptable in relation to one group was not regarded as acceptable when it came to the victims of crime. The long-cherished moral high ground that the media in general, and newspapers in particular, had assumed since uncovering the Profumo Affair in the 1960s was washed away in a tide of public indignation. This precipitated the inescapable showdown, when the press would have to defend, justify and account for itself as a so-called professional crime news-gathering institution.

Neither 'crime intelligence' nor an intelligible approach to crime reporting?

The present Coalition government came to power in 2010 possessed of the legacy of an explosion in policy-led initiatives and legislation aimed at delivering Tony Blair's mantra that New Labour would be 'tough on crime, and tough on the causes of crime'.[6] The consequent excess of criminal law and procedure had, since the start of the twenty-first century, made it difficult for practitioners, let alone an interested lay person, to cope with and understand the details and nuances of the criminal justice process. In contrast to the informed reportage and 'crime intelligence' of the Victorian era, intelligible reporting of actual criminal incidents in ways that could reveal how changes to the criminal law were affecting outcomes had, genuinely, become virtually impossible. And, as has been pointed out in the previous chapter, popular crime

---

    [6] See C. Harris and K. Stevenson (2008) 'Inaccessible and Unknowable: Accretion and Uncertainty in Modern Criminal Law', *Liverpool Law Review*, 29, 247–267.

reportage had become increasingly superficial and devoid of sound legal content.

Take the media coverage of the consequences for criminal justice outcomes of the Crime and Disorder Act 1998 combined with the Police Reform Act 2002 and the Anti-Social Behaviour Act 2003. This had produced an increasingly complex, extensive (and in some respects misguided) crime management agenda. As agencies outside the formal criminal justice system acquired wide powers to deal with anti-social behaviour (an increasingly maligned and much derided term), huge numbers of Anti-Social Behaviour Orders were issued (16,999) between 1999 and 2008.[7] Predictably, the press were quick to highlight the more extreme and bizarre examples, such as 'Boy, 14, breached curfew order 193 times'[8] and 'The Farmer with antisocial pigs'; thereby turning what was intended to be a serious crime management strategy into a comedy in terms of its media presentation.[9] Well-intentioned but ill-advised police initiatives added to the ridicule; as with the *Mirror*'s hilarity in reporting that Lancashire Police had made a spoof video showing pensioners spraying graffiti and vandalising cars on a drink-fuelled spree to 'educate' youngsters that anti-social behaviour is not 'funny at any age'.[10]

The reality was that, by 2010, the original aims of crime reportage (informing accurately and so educating as well as entertaining the ordinary citizen – the usual Victorian formula) were long gone from people's memories. Realistically, a popular need for legal detail no longer exists. For good or ill, the individual citizen is no longer a key player in decisions about whether or not it is in the public interest to prosecute. Choices are driven by the Treasury, via the Crown Prosecution Service, and are informed as much by the public interest of economising on the criminal justice process as by the public interest of revealing the justice process at work. But, even so, the level of inaccuracy about criminal law in modern law reporting should concern the political community, as it already concerns legal professionals, because of the consequential rise of popular misunderstanding about the nature of justice and the point and purpose of the criminal justice process. That, in itself, was problematic because it

---

[7] Ministry of Justice (2010) *Statistical Notice: Anti-Social Behaviour Order Statistics*, http://www.statewatch.org/asbo/asbo_statistics_july_2010.pdf, accessed 19 March 2013.

[8] *The Telegraph*, 16 September 2008.

[9] *The Guardian*, 12 June 2005.

[10] 'Pensioners filmed "on the rampage" in anti-social behaviour campaign video', *Daily Mirror*, 25 October 2011.

has undermined popular respect for and confidence in the criminal law and its practitioners. Instead, people have tended to rely on the media (including newspapers) and their practitioners to act as the guardians of 'real' justice, trusting that journalists would investigate and uncover what the police and the legal system could (or would) not reveal.

Given that the definition of a crime is an action which damages the welfare of the whole community, and not just the target(s) of that action, the successes of investigative journalism, at least since the middle of the twentieth century, seemed to qualify journalists to act as 'crime-busters' and also revealers of 'crimes' that related to the will of the political classes to 'cover up' wrongdoing that was politically motivated or represented the overweening power of the legal system. A good example of a recent presentation here has been the publication by tabloid titles such as the *Daily Mail* of 'secret' arrests, prosecutions and sentences. The fight to reveal in print that a celebrity like Rolf Harris was arrested in late 2012 as part of investigations into sex abuse allegations sparked off by the revelations of Jimmy Saville's criminal activities under the umbrella of Operation Yewtree has gone hand in hand with revelations that two individuals were tried in their absence and imprisoned by the Court of Protection.[11]

This reflects a growing popular dissatisfaction with the criminal justice process, expressed through Twitter and social media, but also voiced in the commercial media (especially newspaper comment columns and interviews or letters). The feeling seems to be that 'real criminals' are not brought to trial, not convicted or, if convicted, given inappropriate sentences, encouraging a sense that the formal legal functions of the state are not working properly. Instead, 'trial by media' has been popularly established as the best way of dealing with such 'criminal' figures. That, in itself, should concern the legal and political classes, but what is even more concerning is the high potential for miscarriage of justice in such unbalanced and one-sided 'trials'. Mass circulation newspaper coverage of crime and criminality has, in the last 75 years, increasingly enhanced misunderstandings of the workings of the criminal justice process through the inaccuracy of much of its crime reportage. Challenged by contempt of court or other legal proceedings, newspapers can and do publish corrections and apologies. Unless forced, however, newspaper apologies rarely assume the prominence of original crime stories; something which can amount to a real miscarriage of justice for

---

[11] 'Rolf Harris arrest lifts lid on Fleet Street open secret', *The Guardian*, 19 April 2013; 'Agony of woman locked up for six weeks by secret court', *Daily Mail*, 24 April 2013.

individuals wrongly identified as culprits in criminal cases in which an individual is acquitted or a prosecution does not proceed.

The reluctance to make corrections and apologies prominent is at the heart of one key difference between the two Royal Charter drafts put forward in spring 2013. In the version drawn up by the press, independent regulators could only *direct* but not *compel* the nature, extent and location of apologies and corrections. This seems (again) an attempt by the press to reduce the daily impact of regulation on it, which is unfortunate. In terms of crime news, investigative journalism is needed, if only to ensure that crimes cannot easily be covered up because it is convenient to state processes that they should not be scrutinised by the criminal justice process; but restrictions are also needed to achieve a proper balance. The newspaper industry's draft apparently scores on the grounds of guaranteeing press freedom (removing the role of Parliament in particular); but the corollary of freedom is responsibility, and reluctance to acknowledge errors suggests that the industry as a whole has not yet accepted this. It should, instead, be prominent in suggesting how best this could be done on its web editions as well as in print versions, especially when it comes to proper controls on the publication of information relating to cases within the criminal justice system. Such initiatives could, apart from anything else, be a significant newspaper contribution to restoring public respect for the formal criminal justice process by underlining that, if the official system can (and does) make errors, so too does the 'trial by media' process.

This would have the merit of being in line with the spirit as well as the provisions of the Contempt of Court Act 1981, which established that newspapers are guilty of contempt should they publish information which creates a 'substantial risk' that the justice process will be 'seriously impeded or prejudiced'. In this sustained survey of the ways in which crimes have been reported – before, during and after trials – it has to be pointed out that since the mid-1980s media contempt (particularly in the shape of pre-trial press publicity) has reached such levels that trials have collapsed or been halted on a regular basis, as well as, or instead of, such publicity being regulated via contempt of court proceedings. This has happened with summary as well as Crown Court trials. Convictions such as those of Michelle and Lisa Taylor in 1994 for the murder of the former's ex-lover were overturned on appeal because of the 'unremitting, extensive, sensational, inaccurate and misleading' information contextualising their arrest and trial.[12] There is a need for newspapers to

---

[12] This will be discussed in more detail later in this chapter.

accept they have a responsibility to match sensationalism with accuracy to create a balance which has, in the last half century, been lost, but which would genuinely serve the public interest.

It could also serve to reconstruct the trust between journalism and the courts which was such a valuable part of the nineteenth-century and early-twentieth-century model of crime news. The loss of this has had a negative impact on the amount and quality of detail offered to journalists as an automatic part of the criminal justice process, especially as overburdened courts have sought to save time by encouraging the reading of documents, such as witness statements, outside the courtroom. These documents do not then become part of the official court record, available for capture (under certain restraints) by journalists, and there has been no will on the part of the courts to remedy this. As a result, journalists have been encouraged to seek such detail elsewhere, meaning that they are likely to access information without the safeguards that would be imposed by the courts. This can be even more problematic when, because of the lack of specialist newspaper crime reporters sitting in the courts, a journalist may be working on several stories simultaneously and so be unable to afford the time to attend an entire trial. The current emphasis on reporting only serious crime and the length of time such serious cases now occupy means that cases are likely to last for longer than a journalist can afford to stay; and, lacking an appreciation of the criminal justice process, they are less likely to comprehend how important it is to hear a case in its entirety.[13] There is, however, progress on this front in that, while historically access to such testimony has been *ad hoc*, a recent decision should mean that it will be permitted where it is sought for a proper journalistic purpose.[14]

Growing criticism from the media, therefore, about the daily operation of the criminal justice system (despite its own unwillingness to communicate the details of its operation accurately and effectively) has caused concern amongst politicians and legal professionals. Politicians do generally appreciate that there is a problem, but are also aggrieved at being accused of failing in an area where they feel they deserve credit. Legal professionals seem equally exasperated at the public profile they have acquired in the popular press, feeling that they deserve to be better understood. Various efforts over the last two to three years testify

---

[13] See Chapter 6 for an instance when this certainly happened and distorted reportage of a crime.

[14] *R (Guardian News and Media Ltd) v City of Westminster Magistrates Court* [2012] EWCA Civ 420 para. 85.

to consequent efforts by both government and legal professionals to make the law and the criminal justice system more accessible to public understanding, in other words, independently of a media filter such as newspaper reportage. An important tool here has been the Ministry of Justice website, which publishes both searchable legal information on current and pending legislation and a range of links to other useful websites relevant to the criminal law at work. Crucially, one of the tenets of the new Supreme Court when it was created in 2009 (formerly the Appellate Committee of the House of Lords) was that its work should be more publicly accessible than in its previous incarnation. Real efforts have been made to make its decisions, available in a free searchable online format at http://www.supremecourt.gov.uk/decided-cases/, 'user-friendly' for non-lawyers.[15] They open with the majority lead opinion, analysing the main legal issues involved, followed by the lead dissension, instead of the traditional practice of between five and nine individual judicial opinions, ordered consecutively in order of the seniority of the judges.

However, although the style and content of these opinions as well as the judgments of the Court of Appeal Criminal Division are now more comprehensible, it was, up to 2012, only Supreme Court decisions that were freely available and easily accessible to the public. Court of Appeal decisions were only offered on subscription. This was partly because of a contractual arrangement between the Ministry of Justice and BAILII, the British and Irish Legal Information Institute, a charitable body which publishes Court of Appeal decisions but is now reliant on financial donations from law firms and other organisations to support free access.[16] From a human rights perspective, freely accessible Court of Appeal decisions are crucial in providing the public with information which would enable them to read crime reportage critically. Annually the court hears over 300 criminal appeals challenging points of law or sentencing decisions; few are granted further leave to be heard at the Supreme Court because typically such appeals do not constitute a matter of general public importance but a flawed legal, penal or punitive decision affecting a particular individual. Public understanding of this crucial aspect of what can be perceived as malfunctions in the criminal justice process is essential if a greater respect is to be created for its operations. Fundamentally, facilitating

---

[15] And in January 2013 the Supreme Court created its own YouTube channel to release case summaries.

[16] http://www.bailii.org/ew/cases/EWCA/Crim, accessed 19 March 2013.

the dissemination of such decisions is crucial in order to ensure universal judicial and executive consistency in the operation of the criminal justice process.

Another positive move has been a more proactive supply of information from the Ministry of Justice directly to the press, which could then be exploited to inform the public. The official release of more data about crime incidence and court performance allowed media formats to enhance their crime reportage and make it more intelligible. It has been the broadsheets, rather than the mass circulation titles, which have made most use of this resource. *The Guardian*, for example, now hosts a dedicated 'UK Criminal Justice' section on its website providing a medium for informative and interactive crime news streams and a critical platform. In the post-2010 period it has been used to publicise a range of topical issues of concern, such as official responses to the so-called 2011 'riots' and proposed reforms to the provision of legal aid in criminal cases.[17] However, for all the positive developments in terms of improving the communication between legal professionals, the official justice system and the press, they have had little impact on the mass circulation newspapers. In an age when circulation figures for print copies of newspapers are declining overall, the greatest decline is for broadsheets, notably *The Independent* and *The Guardian*.[18] But, despite these improvements in communication, revelations since the summer of 2011 have cast mass circulation crime reportage in the press into disrepute but without redeeming the criminal justice process or the legal profession. The present version of the Charter put forward by the press does not look likely to restore the reputation of the press because of its failure to engage seriously with the issue of complaints against inappropriate or inaccurate reporting and its implicit continuation of the current press belief that it is best placed to judge what is in the public interest and so should be published.

---

[17] http://www.guardian.co.uk/law/criminal-justice, accessed 19 March 2013.

[18] National Readership Survey statistics suggest that, in 2012, 44 per cent of adults were still reading a newspaper daily, but the rise is coming in online newspaper reading. The most read title continues to be the *Sun*, with the *Daily Mail* in second place; with communities of 13.6 million and 10 million print and online UK readers, respectively. *The Guardian*, with the *Observer*, just outscores the *Daily Telegraph*, at 5.2 and 5 million UK readers. Estimations of the online presence of the broadsheets suggest that 2.8 million turn to *The Guardian*, and 2.1 to the *Daily Telegraph*. See D. Ponsford, 'Combined print/online figures make Sun most read title', *Press Gazette*, 12 September 2012.

A 'contemptuous' press or the press in contempt?

Mention has already been made of the Contempt of Court Act 1981, and the previous chapter also explored how, particularly at the start of the twenty-first century, certain elements of the tabloid press had shown themselves increasingly predisposed to further test the boundaries of responsible crime journalism and the Act's provisions regarding the unlawful publication of material that could prejudice live criminal court proceedings. From the trial of Leeds United footballers Jonathan Woodgate and Lee Bowyer in April 2001 to the trial of Levi Bellfield, a number of high profile prosecutions were placed in jeopardy by the details and opinions aired in mass circulation papers. The original Woodgate and Bowyer trial had collapsed after the *Sunday Mirror* published two articles suggesting that their attack on an Asian youth had been racially motivated.[19] At the subsequent contempt of court hearing, the judges presciently alluded to what Leveson would later identify as a core problem with modern investigative reporting. In commenting on the expressions of remorse from the editor and publishers following publication of the articles, they also refused to accept the defence argument that the decision to publish was simply due to 'errors of judgement' on the part of in-house lawyers. Instead, they insisted that 'culpability [for the article tone and content] was much wider'.[20]

In June 2011, Levi Bellfield was eventually found guilty of the abduction and murder of 13-year-old Milly Dowler, snatched while she was walking home from school in Walton-on-Thames in March 2002. Police incompetence, according to the press, had prevented Bellfield from being charged before October 2010, by which time he had already been convicted of two other murders (Marsha McDonnell and Amelie Delagrange) and an attempted murder (Katie Sheedy).[21] What has largely been forgotten, in the furore over the phone-hacking habits of journalists reporting crimes that began to emerge during Bellfield's trial, is that a conclusion on a second charge, for the attempted abduction of

---

[19] See, for example, 'Leeds football case: How tabloid tactics wrecked the trial: The newspaper Rivalry with daily title may have driven decision to publish', *The Guardian*, 10 April 2001. The *Sunday Mirror* articles were withdrawn and, at a retrial, Woodgate was convicted of affray and Bowyer was acquitted. See *Daily Mirror*, 7 April; 10 April; 13 May; 16 May 2001.

[20] See *AG v MGN Ltd (Contempt: Appropriate Penalty)* [2002] EWHC 907.

[21] See, for instance, 'Profile: Levi Bellfield sexual predator who treated women with disdain', *Daily Telegraph*, 24 June 2011; 'Blunders of police who insisted: Milly Dowler's Dad did it', *Daily Mail*, 24 June 2011.

11-year-old Rachel Cowles the day *before* Milly was kidnapped, had to be abandoned. Though jurors went on to deliberate the second verdict, the trial judge, Mr Justice Wilkie, was forced to discharge the whole jury and dismiss that charge because of the 'huge volume' of prejudicial publicity that the tabloid press and other news programmes had transmitted after the first conviction the day before:

> As a result of the trigger being pulled too soon on what would otherwise have been proper and appropriate material, I have been put in a position where I am obliged to discharge the jury from reaching a verdict in her case.[22]

The 'trigger' was under the by-line of *Daily Mirror* reporter David Collins. On 24 June, claiming 'I nailed Milly's killer,' Collins revealed that Bellfield had admitted 'to the Mirror in a chilling phone call that he was near the scene when the 13-year-old was snatched as she walked home from school'. His article concluded, with what (at best) can only have been a careless disregard of the implications of his comments for the ongoing trial, with an effective expectation that the jury would find Bellfield guilty on the second charge as well.[23] One reason why so little attention has been paid to this example of contempt of court is that it was, of itself, very much in line with other pieces published in the tabloids in the preceding 60 years. Instead of being headline-grabbing, it was simply yet another example of how ready investigative journalists were to overstep the boundaries of legality in their will to claim the headlines and the readers that such effective sensationalism could bring.

Amplifying the point made earlier in this chapter, the impression of a survey of contempt of court cases brought against newspapers in the twenty-first century in particular is that the Crown Prosecution Service had largely abandoned pursuing newspapers through the courts for inappropriate investigative journalism that demonstrably had had an impact on the criminal justice process. Where cases had been brought, the impression is also that the judiciary itself had ceased to impose exemplary and deterrent punishments on those convicted of such conduct. Realistically, the seriousness of the contempt of which Bolam

---

[22] 'Media face prosecution for contempt', *The Independent*, 24 June 2011; 'Mail and Mirror face contempt action over Milly Dowler', *The Guardian*, 18 October 2011.

[23] D. Collins, 'I nailed Milly's killer: as Bellfield is convicted, Mirrorman reveals how he trapped him', *Daily Mirror*, 24 June 2011.

was found guilty and consequently jailed in 1949 was very much in line with that committed by Collins and the *Daily Mirror* in 2011. The consequences for them in 2011 were the very opposite of deterrent. In 2012, Sir John Thomas agreed that the Collins article had amounted to a 'serious' example of a prejudicial risk for the jury. Yet, despite the stern words, the proceedings concluded with the awarding of what can only be described as derisory punishment, in the shape of a £10,000 fine.[24] Other examples of contempt which caused the collapse of ongoing trials between 1991 and 2011 included pre-trial coverage of the details of the prosecution case for assault against Geoffrey Knight, known for being the boyfriend of an actress, in 1995. The charge was that pre-trial press coverage had been 'unlawful, misleading, scandalous and malicious' and so 'unfair, outrageous and oppressive' that a fair trial was impossible.[25] However, even though it was agreed that there was an increasing tension between 'the media's wish to publish and the law of contempt', it was decided that no single title could be singled out as having 'created any greater risk of serious prejudice than that which had already been created'.[26] In that sense, the criminal justice process has also failed the victims of criminally bad investigative journalism, but the mechanisms to be exemplary and punitive remain there.

Investigative journalism, phone-hacking and the Leveson Inquiry

Investigative journalism has long been regarded as playing a key role in modern society, with its ability to uncover threats to democracy from political and other corruption to legal and criminal wrongdoing. But from 1885, when W.T. Stead had created his 'Maiden Tribute' articles for the *Pall Mall Gazette*, there had always been concerns about the tactics used by investigative journalists when researching the stories they would subsequently (and sensationally) present for public consumption. During the twentieth century, as investigative journalism had increasingly taken over the field of crime reportage, it had reshaped and redirected its emphasis away from the actual trial procedures to the contextualising human detail of a crime narrative rather than the trial itself, and

---

[24] 'Levi Bellfield: papers guilty of contempt', *Daily Telegraph*, 18 July 2012. The *Daily Mail* was also fined £10,000 for a similar contempt.

[25] ' "Outrageous" press coverage halts trial', *The Independent*, 5 October 1995.

[26] 'Tabloids cleared of contempt in Knights coverage', *The Times*, 1 August 1996.

the impact on how crime stories were popularly read was dramatic. In the nineteenth century, popular expectation was that the key revelations of evidence for or against a defendant would be rehearsed for the first time publicly in a courtroom. Papers, especially those aimed at a working-class audience, would put in an amount of 'human interest' pre-Assize information, but rarely before the committal hearing in the summary courts.[27] The Crippen and George Smith (Brides in the Bath) cases were the first high profile murders for which concern about pre-arrest and pre-trial coverage resulting from investigative journalism carried out by professional journalists was discussed as 'trial by media'. Thereafter, Crippen and Smith-style press coverage of sensational crime stories became the normality. The half century between 1945 and the end of the 1960s constituted the heyday of the specialist crime reporter relying on investigative journalism to create crime news, to the extent of researching and presenting the necessary evidence required for a criminal conviction, as discussed in Chapter 5.

However, that period served to distance even further the concept of crime reportage being something focused on and filtered through the formal criminal justice process. Trial by media before the formal proceedings began was the key feature of contempt of court proceedings from the mid-twentieth century on. Attempts to regulate reportage through legislation other than contempt of court proceedings first appeared in the Judicial Proceedings (Regulation of Reports) Act 1926, which had sought to regulate the ability to publish (in relation to any judicial proceedings, not just criminal trials) information which could 'injure public morals'. The idea that there could be injury to public morals, through the publication of sexually salacious material in general, was largely a historical curiosity by 2010, though it still had some place in regulating reportage of criminal and divorce cases. Other legislation over the course of that century had sought to protect juveniles (Children and Young Persons Act 1933) and racial minorities (Race Relations Act 1968), amongst other groups. Yet, despite this, investigative journalism had continued to expand its hold over crime reportage, though, with the steady demise of the specialist crime reporter, it could at times be difficult to identify clearly whether reportage was intended to be celebrity gossip with a criminal inflection or a crime story inflected by celebrity gossip.

---

[27] The nicely sensational case of Christiana Edmunds, the Brighton Poisoner, is a good example. See 'Attempted Poisoning at Brighton', *Reynolds News*, 20 August 1871, with a mixture of gossip to contextualise the information aired in the courtroom.

This was the background to twenty-first-century developments in investigative journalism when new technology was opening up ever more resources for practitioners to target when researching their stories. With human interest dimensions firmly established as a core plank in journalism's strategy on the public's 'right to know', the opportunities provided by internet use and mobile phones in particular to research potentially sensational stories, including those in the criminal justice arena, were to prove practically irresistible to many editors and journalists conscious of declining print circulation and fierce competition for a diminishing readership. The protests of high profile individuals about invasions of their privacy as a result of stories published about them in the press made it plain, if the public had cared to think along those lines, that journalistic practices had begun to breach the law as well as being, to those so targeted, morally offensive. But the public did not so care to think. There were stories of 'ordinary' citizens claiming harassment and unwarranted intrusion into their lives by investigative journalists which breached the Code of Practice of the Press Complaints Commission. The PCC's own webpage advertises its successes in responding to such claims (by persuading the media under a Desist Notice to refrain from publishing information).[28] Though many of those targeted were (as the Leveson Inquiry revealed) dissatisfied, their protests (when reported, often by television news) won little solid sympathy from the wider public, even though the claims being put forward by individuals suggested the use of practices which were illegal.

Thus, when, in 2006, *News of the World* journalist Clive Goodman was arrested for tapping the private mobile phones of the British Royal Household and, with a co-conspirator Glenn Mulcaire, was convicted and sentenced in January 2007, there was no public outcry. There was general (if cynical) acceptance of the conclusions of the Press Complaints Commission investigation that it had found no evidence to suggest that this was more than a single 'rotten apple' in the *News of the World* barrel of journalists. Subsequent and sustained public discussion of the issue, as ever more celebrities claimed that they, too, had been subjected to phone-hacking, generated little concern, even though there were continuing stories of everyday cases of harassment also. It seems, probably, that, since the majority of the suggested (and self-identified) targets were mainly celebrities, there was no moral panic about the issue. Nor were newspapers worried, as claims generated further sensationalist headlines when figures

---

[28] See 'Examples of Successful Anti-Harassment and Pre-Publication Work', Press Complaints Commission, http://www.pcc.org.uk/aboutthepcc/examplesofsuccessful.html, accessed 19 March 2013.

such as actors Hugh Grant and Jude Law claimed that they, too, had been the victim of phone-tapping. Journalists and editors were at least implicitly encouraged by the stance of the Commission that, while care should be taken and some practices more firmly regulated, there was a 'legitimate place for the use of subterfuge when there are grounds in the public interest to use it and it is not possible to obtain information through other means'.[29] Even when the broadsheet press, in the shape of *The Guardian*, reopened the issue in 2009, there was little discernible mass concern.[30]

What changed public opinion was the revelation that such practices had the real potential to distort the outcome of a major criminal trial. *The Guardian* asserted during the trial of Levi Bellfield that *News of the World* investigative journalists had hacked into Milly Dowler's voicemail during their researches into the case in 2002. This had subsequently interfered with the police investigation and had even raised the spectre that Bellfield might escape conviction.[31] The resulting furore was unequivocally condemnatory. For the first time, there was an extensive public consciousness of the damage that the techniques and strategies evolved by journalists over the previous 100 years could do to the justice process. This was not a case of the law being seen to be 'precious' or misguided during a trial. The police investigation at the time had been incompetent, certainly, but the actions of journalists had enhanced that incompetence, enabling Bellfield to go on to murder at least two more women before being caught. The strength of public feeling was so great that it led to the closure of the 168-year-old *News of the World*, retiring under the headline 'Thank You and Goodbye'.[32]

Since then, there has been an uneasy debate within the media, if largely without mass public support, about the importance of continuing to enable investigative journalism to take place because of the positive things it had also achieved. If it had, in recent years, gone too far, the final

[29] Press Complaints Commission (2007) Report on Subterfuge and Newsgathering (PCC: 15 May 2007).

[30] 'News of the World phone hacking: CPS to undertake urgent review of evidence', *The Guardian*, 9 July 2009.

[31] 'News of the World hacked Milly Dowler's phone during police hunt: Paper deleted missing schoolgirl's voicemails, giving family false hope', *The Guardian*, 5 July, 2011. Although *The Guardian* had to concede in a later article that 'while News of the World reporters probably were responsible for deleting some of the missing girl's messages, police have concluded that they were not responsible for the particular deletion which caused her family to have false hope that she was alive', 10 December 2011.

[32] 'Thank You and Goodbye', *News of the World*, 10 July 2011.

edition of the *News of the World* stressed that it was, amongst other things, its campaigning for action as a result of Sarah Payne's murder that had led to the opening up of public access to a database of sexual offenders.[33] Essentially, the phone-hacking revelations have raised the broader question of public interest as a defence to journalistic subterfuge. While phone-hacking has now been agreed to be indefensible, many crime stories discussed in the previous three chapters would have been unlikely to end up in the criminal courts if journalists had not taken on the role of unofficial detectives to search out crime, and accumulate evidence which could then be used by the official criminal justice system to prosecute the perpetrators. Delimitating public interest is perhaps less complex in the field of crime news, where there is a clear inherent public interest in publication, rather than, say, celebrity 'kiss and tell' stories. As methods to secure information such as entrapment, bribery and offences against the Regulation of Investigatory Powers Act 2000 amount to criminal offences *per se*, many have questioned whether there is any need for any further regulation.[34] Unfortunately, whether a story is in the public interest is something that usually falls to be decided after publication as a matter of defence and is not then *a priori*. Crucially, public interest is construed as 'in the public interest', not 'of interest to the public', despite the claim made by tabloid journalist Paul McMullan to the contrary, that 'circulation defines the public interest'. [35] This would, of course, deem everything published legitimate if the public validated it by buying the newspaper.[36]

McMullan's claim does illustrate the difficulty of a public interest test that embraces both the quality and the tabloid press. What a newspaper such as the *Independent* may deem a matter of public interest may differ from the baser estimations of a tabloid newspaper. Equally, a number of definitional terms in the Code are remarkably broad. But this may be a necessary evil. Research regarding public interest has concluded it is a concept which 'may not have a commonly agreed-upon meaning as far as the general public are concerned'[37] and that the 'precise nature of

---

[33] Ibid. For many, though, that claim was tainted by the revelation that the Payne family's phones had also been hacked.

[34] For example, the evidence given by editor of *Private Eye*, Evidence of Ian Hislop, Leveson Inquiry, 17 January 2011.

[35] Evidence of Paul McMullin, Leveson Inquiry, 29 November 2011.

[36] See http://www.editorscode.org.uk/, accessed 19 March 2013.

[37] D.E. Morrison and M. Svennevig (2002) *The Public Interest, the Media and Privacy: A Report for British Broadcasting Corporation, Broadcasting Standards Commission, Independent Committee for the Supervision of Standards of Telephone Information Services* (Independent Television Commission, Institute for Public Policy Research, The Radio Authority) p. 100.

what constitutes media coverage which is felt to be firmly 'in the public interest' varies greatly from person to person. There is no clear or widely shared definition'.[38]

The aftermath of the Leveson Inquiry

The cessation of one of the oldest Sunday tabloids not only narrowed the market for Sunday red top competitors but led to a general feeling of unease with both how journalists were obtaining their stories and the more fundamental question of how the press should be regulated. For most people, however, the real question during the Leveson Inquiry and after the publication of its Report is what that regulation should be. There is a lack of willingness to listen to arguments from within the media that regulation is not guaranteed to succeed: that the best chance of a real change to the culture of the print press is through self-regulation.[39] In one strongly worded leader, *The Times* warned against statutory regulation defending the positive role played by the press as a check on the activities of the powerful, a role they suggest would be suppressed by government regulation.[40] The *Daily Telegraph* commented that 'The constitutional objection is plain: if politicians regulate newspapers, they will make sure they get the press they want, not the press they deserve.'[41] Interestingly, the Lord Chief Justice, Lord Judge, has, perhaps surprisingly, acknowledged the 'priceless' value of the press despite its apparent shortcomings and has been reluctant to criticise the Press Complaints Commission, asserting that it

> works most of the time [and that while] An independent press ... will also from time to time behave, if not criminally, with scandalous cruelty and unfairness, leaving victims stranded in a welter of public contempt and hatred or uncovenanted distress; that press has the equal capacity to 'reveal a public scandal' which could not otherwise be uncovered.[42]

---

[38] Ibid p. 104.

[39] See, for instance, 'Leveson Inquiry has momentous implications for free speech', *Daily Mail*, 16 November 2012.

[40] *The Times*, 17 January 2012.

[41] 'Our Press Must Remain Free', *Daily Telegraph*, 25 October 2012.

[42] Lord Judge, speech, Human Rights Law Conference, 18 October 2011, reported in full in *The Guardian*, 19 October 2011.

Consequently, any regulation should not 'diminish or dilute the ability and power of the press to reveal and highlight true public scandals or misconduct'.[43]

One worrying aspect of the Leveson Report of relevance to this book is that, while it started with an inquiry into how investigative journalism might have affected the criminal justice process in more cases than that of the trial of Levi Bellfield, the widening of its remit into the criminal activities of journalists and editors overshadowed that original aspect. What has not been prominent in the public discussions is any sense of how crime reportage could be improved in terms of its quality and accuracy, while maintaining the attraction for readers that makes it an important part of the modern media. It is vital for the health of investigative journalism, the legal profession and the public interest (however broadly defined) that there is a strategy for better management of crime reportage in print journalism. This is because it has the potential, otherwise, to get out of control in other ways. A transitional shift is currently evident as examples of 'informed debate' increasingly relocate from the editorials and letters page of the print press to the blogosphere and web.

Current proposals may end in a Royal Charter constraining the print press. However, while an improved code of conduct, and degree of self-regulation, could work to regulate (at least theoretically) the online web presence of various newspapers, there is no practical strategy for controls in respect of bloggers and other online discussants. What amounts to 'crime news' is increasingly driven by these online discussants, who, unconstrained by editorial gatekeeping, can set their own agenda and potentially do far more damage to the presumption of innocence and the right to a fair trial than the combined efforts of investigative journalism in the last quarter century.

The recent prosecutions of police officers for leaking information to the media, especially the print press, also have important implications for any efforts to establish a better quality of crime reportage in terms of public interest, fairness and accuracy. For over a century now, the police have been crucial players in the shape and content of crime reportage made available to the public. If, since the middle of the last century, there have been high profile examples of investigative journalists acting independently of the police to uncover crime (including examples of police corruption), the majority of crime narratives have depended on a flow of information, much of it unofficial, between the police and the media. This has meant that, while in the nineteenth century the

---

[43] Ibid.

preoccupations of lawyers shaped how crime narratives were presented for public consumption, in the twentieth and twenty-first centuries police agendas have drawn attention away from the trial process and towards crime investigation. That is understandable, given the growing importance of the investigative reporter. However, this has got out of hand. Even the junior lawyers entrusted for the most part with the actual reportage from the Victorian courts had sufficient legal knowledge to know how to avoid writing stories that could impede the criminal justice process. But, generally, neither the police nor modern investigative journalists are, as individuals, legal specialists, and are so less well equipped to avoid potentially prejudicial reportage. One indication that the relationship has been damaging to both, in terms of creating a culture which is prejudicial to sound justice delivery, has been the revelations surrounding the so-called 'Plebgate' case. A policeman arrested for misconduct was charged, according to media reports, with disclosing information to the press without authorisation, information which was actually false.[44] The papers relating to Operation Alice, the police investigation of the matter, have been passed to the Crown Prosecution Service, but it seems unlikely that there will be any coherent resolution of the matter in ways which rehabilitate the relationship between the press and the police. Thus, the potential for police information to act to distort the justice delivery process seems likely to remain, as there is no real will on either side to tackle the culture of communication between these two branches of investigation into crime.

Conclusion

The loss of the legal specialists from the stable of reporters, particularly the loss of barrister-created reporting, has inevitably affected the veracity of twenty-first-century crime reportage, which may be incorrectly represented, particularly when details are regurgitated from single and unchecked sources.[45] There is no possibility of returning to a 'golden age' of legally detailed everyday crime reportage; but the way forward, post-Leveson, and under a new Royal Charter, must look to the production of interesting but also accurate journalism, and, for

---

[44] 'Scotland Yard police officer arrested on suspicion of leaking information to the media during "Plebgate" affair', *Daily Mail*, 31 January 2013.

[45] The replication of articles from other newspaper vehicles is, of course not new; the Victorian press regularly published (with attribution) crime news stories that had appeared in other newspapers.

this to be possible, that journalism must be a product of better relations between all the organs of the press (including the tabloids) and the legal profession (and Ministry of Justice from the government side), as well as a more transparent and better-regulated relationship between journalists and the police.

Bibliography

Publications Pre-1914

A Student at Law (1839) *The Fourth Estate: or the Moral Influence of the Press* (London: Ridgeway).

Anon (1872) 'Trial by Judge, and Trial by Jury', *Westminster Review*, April, 289–324.

Anon (1886) *A Generation of Judges by Their Reporter* (London: Sampson Low and Co.).

Anon (1905) *How I Became a Judge, being the Reminiscences of the Honourable Mr Justice Rater* (London: J.B. Nichols and Sons).

E. Austin (1872) *Anecdotage, or Stray Leaves from the Note Books of a Provincial Reporter* (London: F. Pitman).

A. Baker (c.1888) *Pitmans Practical Journalism, an Introduction to Every Description of Literary Effort in Association with Newspaper Production, with Notes on Newspaper Law by Edward a Cope* (London: Pitman & Sons).

C.T. Clarkson and J. Hall Richardson (1889) *Police!* (London: Field and Tuer).

W. Collins (1868) *The Moonstone. A Romance* (London: Tinsley Brothers).

A. Conan Doyle (1891) 'The Man with the Twisted Lip', *Strand Magazine*, 2, 623–637.

A. Conan Doyle (1901) 'The Hound of the Baskervilles', in *The Original Illustrated Strand Magazine Sherlock Holmes* (Ware: Wordsworth, 1989).

J. Curtis (1834) *An Authentic and Faithful History of the Mysterious Murder of Maria Marten* (London: T. Kelly).

J. Dawson (1885) *Practical Journalism. How to Enter Thereon and Succeed* (London: Upcott Gill).

G. Binney Dibblee (1913) *The Newspaper* (London: Williams and Norgate).

C. Dickens (1838) *The Posthumous Papers of the Pickwick Club* (London: Chapman and Hall).

C. Dickens (1853) *Bleak House* (London: Bradbury and Evans).

T. Escott (1911) *Masters of English Journalism. A Study of Personal Forces* (London: T Fisher Unwin).

H. Fenn (1910) *Thirty-Five Years in the Divorce Court* (London: T. Werner Laurie).

A. Forster Boulton (1908) *Criminal Appeals under the Criminal Appeal Act 1907* (London: Butterworth and Co.).

J. Grant (1837) *The Great Metropolis* (London: Saunders and Otley).

J. Grant (1871) *The Newspaper Press, Its Origin, Progress, and Present Position* (London: Tinsley Bros.).

J. Greenwood (1869) *The Seven Curses of London* (London: Fields, Osgood and Company).

J.C. Jeaffreson (1867) *A Book About Lawyers* (London: Hurst and Blackett).

H.S. King (1872) *Two Idle Apprentices, Briefs and Papers, Sketches of the Bar and the Press* (London: King).

J.H. Levy (1899) *The Necessity for Criminal Appeal as Illustrated by the Maybrick Case and the Jurisprudence of Various Countries* (London: P.S. King & Co).

A.W. MacDougall (1891) *The Maybrick Case* (London: Ballière, Tindal and Cox).
A. Plowden (1903) *Grain or Chaff, the Autobiography of a Police Magistrate* (London: T. Fisher Unwin).
R. Renton (1912) *John Forster and His Friendships* (London: Chapman and Hall).
G.W.R. Reynolds (1856) *Mysteries of the Courts of London* (London: John Dicks).
W. Rouse Ball (1879) *The Student's Guide to the Bar* (London: Macmillan).
M. Spielman (1897) *The History of 'Punch'* (London: Cassell and Co.).
J.F. Stephen (1861) 'The Morality of Advocacy', *Cornhill Magazine*, 3, 447–459.
F. Taylor (1898) *The Newspaper Press as a Power Both in the Expression and Formation of Public Opinion. The Chancellor's Essay* (Oxford: B.H. Blackwell).
F.C. Williams (1903) *From Journalist to Judge. An Autobiography* (London: Simpkin Marshall and Co.).

Publications Post-1914

J. Allen and O. Ashton (eds) (2005) *Papers for the People: A Study of the Chartist Press* (London: Merlin Press).
S. Allen (2004) *News Culture*, 2nd edn (Oxford University Press).
A. Aspinall (1945) 'The Social Status of Journalists at the Beginning of the Nineteenth Century', *Review of English Studies*, 83, 216–232.
A. Ballinger (2000) *Dead Woman Walking. Executed Women in England and Wales 1900–1955* (Aldershot: Ashgate).
G. Barak (ed.) (1994) *Media Process and the Social Construction of Crime* (New York: Garland).
A. Bell (1991) *The Language of News Media* (London: John Wiley and Sons).
J. Bengry (2012) 'Queer Profits: Homosexual Scandals and the Origins of Legal Reform in Britain', in H. Bauer and M. Cook (eds) *Queer 1950s: Rethinking Sexuality in the Post-War Years* (Basingstoke: Palgrave Macmillan).
D. Bentley (1998) *English Criminal Justice in the Nineteenth Century* (London: Hambledon Press).
D. Berry (2008) *Journalism, Ethics and Society* (Aldershot: Ashgate).
A. Bingham (2004) *Gender, Modernity and the Popular Press in Interwar Britain* (Clarendon Press).
A. Bingham (2009) *Family Newspapers? Sex, Private Life and the British Popular Press 1918–1978* (Oxford: Oxford University Press).
R.D. Blumenfeld (1930) *R.D.B.'s Diary* (London: William Heinemann).
R.D. Blumenfeld (1933) *The Press in My Time* (London: Rich and Cowan).
L. Brake (1988) 'The Old Journalism and the New: Forms of Cultural Production in London in the 1880s', in J. Wiener (ed.) *Papers for the Millions. The New Journalism in Britain, 1850s to 1914* (Westport, CT: Greenwood Press).
L. Brake and M. Demoor (2009) *A Dictionary of Journalism in Great Britain and Ireland* (Gent: Academia Press).
L. Brake, A. Jones and L. Madden (eds) (1990) *Investigating Victorian Journalism* (Basingstoke: Macmillan).
A. Briggs (1995) *History of Broadcasting: II, The Golden Age of Wireless* (Oxford University Press).
A. Briggs and P. Burke (2009) *A Social History of the Media: From Gutenberg to the Internet* (Cambridge: Polity Press).

L. Brown (1985) *Victorian News and Newspapers* (Oxford: Clarendon Press).

C. Browne (1998) *The Prying Game. Sex, Scams and Scandals of Fleet Street and the Media Mafia* (London: Robson Books).

P. Burden (1982) 'The Business of Crime Reporting: Problems and Dilemmas', in C. Sumner (ed.) *Crime Justice and the Mass Media*, Papers Presented to the 14th Cropwood Round Table Conference (University of Cambridge, Institute of Criminology).

D. Cairns (1998) *Advocacy and the Making of the Adversarial Criminal Trial, 1800–1865* (Oxford University Press).

J.A. Cairns (1922) *The Loom of the Law, the Experiences and Reflections of a Metropolitan Magistrate* (London: Hutchinson and Company).

D. Calcutt (1990) *Report of the Committee on Privacy and Related Matters* (London: HMSO) Cmnd 1102.

E. Carrabine (2008) *Crime, Culture and the Media* (Cambridge: Polity Press).

D. Carswell (2012) *The Trial of Ronald True* (Gale MOML archive first pub. W. Hodge 1950).

C. Carter, G. Branston and S. Allen (eds) (1998) *News, Gender and Power* (London: Routledge).

J. Carter Wood (2012) *The Most Remarkable Woman in England. Poison, Celebrity and Trials of Beatrice Pace* (Manchester University Press).

R. Chadwick (1991) 'Sir Augustus Stephenson and the Prosecution of Offences Act of 1884', in W. Gordon and I. Fergus (eds) *Legal History in the Making. Proceedings of the Ninth British Legal History Conference* (Hambledon: Continuum).

S. Chibnall (1977) *Law-and-Order News: An Analysis of Crime Reporting in the British Press* (London: Routledge).

S. Chibnall (1981) 'The Production of Knowledge by Crime Reporters', in S. Cohen and J. Young (eds) *The Manufacture of News* (London: Constable).

P. Chippindale and C. Horrie (1999) *Stick It Up Your Punter! The Uncut Story of the Sun Newspaper* (London: Simon and Schuster).

R. Cocks (1983) *Foundations of the Modern Bar* (London: Sweet and Maxwell).

S. Cohen (2011) *Folk Devils and Moral Panics* (Basingstoke: Routledge Classics).

S. Cohen and J. Young (eds) (1973) *The Manufacture of News: Deviance, Social Problems and the Mass Media* (London: Constable).

S. Cole (2001) *Suspect Identities. A History of Finger-printing and Criminal Identification* (Harvard University Press).

M. Conboy (2002) *The Press and Popular Culture* (London: Sage).

M. Conboy (2004) *Journalism, a Critical History* (London: Sage).

M. Conboy (2011) *Journalism in Britain: A Historical Introduction* (London: Sage).

C. Critcher (2003) *Moral Panics and the Media* (Buckingham: Open University Press).

T. Crook (2010) *Comparative Media Law and Ethics* (Abingdon: Routledge).

J. Curran (2002) *Media and Power* (London: Routledge).

J. Curran (2002) 'Media and the Making of British Society, c.1700–2000', *Media History*, 8(2), 135–154.

J. Curran and J. Seaton (2003) *Power without Responsibility: The Press and Broadcasting in Britain* (London: Routledge).

L. Curtis (2001) *Jack the Ripper and the London Press* (New Haven, CT: Yale University Press).

A. Dasent (1908) *John Thadeus Delane, Editor of 'The Times': His Life and Correspondence* (New York: Scribner's Sons).

J. Davidson (2008) *Child Sexual Abuse: Media Representations and Government Reactions* (Abingdon: Routledge).

V. Davis (2004) 'Murder, We Wrote', *British Journalism Review*, 15(1), 56–62.

S. D'Cruze (2007) 'Intimacy, Professionalism and Domestic Homicide in Interwar Britain', *Women's History Review*, 16(5), 701–722.

Lord Denning (1955) *Road to Justice* (London: Stevens and Son).

D. Duman (1983) *The English and Colonial Bars in the Nineteenth Century* (London: CroomHelm).

J. Eldridge, J. Kitzinger and K. Williams (2005) *The Mass Media and Power in Modern Britain* (Oxford University Press).

S.M. Ellis (ed.) (1923) *A Mid Victorian Pepys, the Letters and Memoirs of Sir William Hardman, MA FRGS* (London: Cecil Palmer).

C. Emsley (2005) 'Sergeant Goddard: the story of a rotten apple or a diseased orchard?' In A. Srebnik and R. Levy (eds) *Crime and Culture: An Historical Perspective* (Aldershot: Ashgate).

C. Emsley (2009) *The Great British Bobby: A History of British Policing from the Eighteenth Century to the Present* (London: Quercus).

C. Emsley and H. Shpayer-Makov (eds) (2006) *Police Detectives in History 1750–1950* (Aldershot: Ashgate).

M. Engels (1996) *Tickle the Public: One Hundred Years of the Popular Press* (London: Victor Gollancz).

J. English and R. Card (2005) *Police Law* (Oxford University Press).

R. Ericson (1989) 'Patrolling the Facts: Secrecy and Publicity in Police Work', *British Journal of Sociology*, 40, 205–226.

S. Farrall, J. Jackson and E. Gray (2009) *The Social Order and the Fear of Crime in Contemporary Times* (Oxford University Press).

P. Ferris (1972) *The House of Northcliffe: A Biography of an Empire* (Omaha: World Publishing).

S. Firmin (1955) *Murders in our Midst* (London: Hutchinson).

M. Fishman (1981) 'Police News: Constructing an Image of Crime', *Urban Life*, 9, 371–394.

B. Franklin (1997) *Newszak and News Media* (London: Edward Arnold).

B. Franklin (1999) *Social Policy, the Media and Misrepresentation* (London: Routledge).

B. Franklin (2008) *Pulling Newspapers Apart; Analysing Print Journalism* (London: Routledge).

P. Friedland (2012) *Seeing Justice Done. The Age of Spectacular Capital Punishment in France* (Oxford University Press).

J. Galtung and M. Ruge (1965) 'The Structure of Foreign News', *Journal of Peace Studies*, 2(1), 64–91.

D. Garland (2001) *The Culture of Control* (Oxford University Press).

M. Gaskill (2000) *Crime and Mentalities in Early Modern England* (Cambridge University Press).

G. Geis (1961) 'Preliminary Hearings and the Press', *UCLA Law Review*, 8, 397–414.

J. Gerald (1983) *News of Crime. Courts and Press in Conflict* (Westport, CT: Greenwood Press).

M. Ginsburg (ed.) (1959) *Law and Opinion in England in the C20th* (London: Stevens and Sons).

T. Golan (2007) *Laws of Men and Laws of Nature. The History of Scientific Expert Testimony in England and America* (Harvard University Press).

M. Gordon (2002) *The Thames Torso Murders of Victorian London* (Jefferson, NC: Macfarland and Company).

D. Griffiths (2006) *Fleet Street: Five Hundred Years of the Press* (London: The British Library).

H. Gwynne (1915) *Newspaper Editor Files* (St Bride Printing Library), cited in G. Boyce et al. (1978) *Newspaper History from the Seventeenth Century to the Present Day* (Press group of the Acton Society).

J. Hall Richardson (1927) *From the City to Fleet Street* (London: Stanley Paul).

R. Hallworth and M. Williams (1983) *Where There's A Will...The Sensational Life of Dr John Bodkin Adams* (Jersey: Capstan Press).

M. Hampton (2004) *Visions of the Press in Britain, 1850–1950* (Chicago: University of Illinois Press).

C. Harris and K. Stevenson (2009) 'Inaccessible and Unknowable: Accretion and Uncertainty in Modern Criminal Law', *Liverpool Law Review*, 29, 247–267.

P. Hastings (1954) *The Autobiography of Sir Patrick Hastings* (London: Roy Publisher).

R.F.V. Heuston (1964) *Lives of the Lord Chancellors 1885–1940* (Oxford: Clarendon Press).

R. Hoggart (1957) *The Uses of Literacy. Aspects of Working Class Life* (London: Chatto and Windus).

Home Office (1982) *The Investigation of a Series of Major Crimes* (HMSO: Home Office Circular 114/82).

Home Office (1999) *The Stephen Lawrence Inquiry: Report of an Inquiry by Sir William Macpherson of Cluny* Cmnd 4262.

P. Hoskins (1984) *Two Men Were Acquitted. The Trial and Acquittal of Doctor John Bodkin Adams* (London: Secker and Warburgh).

J. Hostettler (2006) *Fighting for Justice. The History and Origins of the Adversary Trial* (Winchester: Waterside Press).

K. Jackson (2001) *George Newnes and the New Journalism in Britain 1880–1910: Culture and Profit* (Aldershot: Ashgate).

L. James (1974) *Fiction for the Working Man 1830–1850* (Harmondsworth: Penguin).

Y. Jewkes (2004) *Media and Crime* (London: Sage).

M. Jones (1981) 'The Relationship between the Criminal Courts and the Mass Media', in C. Sumner (ed.) *Crime Justice and the Mass Media,* Papers Presented to the 14th Cropwood Round Table Conference (University of Cambridge, Institute of Criminology).

Lord Judge (2011) *Practice Guidance: The Use of Live Text-Based Forms of Communication (including Twitter) from Court for the Purposes of Fair and Accurate Reporting* (Lord Chief Justice's Office, 20 December 2011).

J. Knelman (1998) *Twisting in the Wind. The Murderess and the English Press* (University of Toronto Press).

J. Knelman (2003) 'Why Can't a Woman be More Like a Man: Attitudes to Husband Murder 1889–1989', in J. Rowbotham and K. Stevenson (eds) *Behaving Badly. Visible Crime, Social Panics and Legal Responses* (Ashgate, Aldershot).

A. Kronman (1993) *The Lost Lawyer: Failing Ideals of the Legal Profession* (Harvard University Press).

N. Kyle (2009) *A Greater Guilt. Constance Emilie Kent and the Road Murder* (Salisbury: Boolarong Press).

J. Langbein (2003) *The Origins of Adversary Criminal Trial* (Oxford University Press).

A. Lawrence (1903) *Journalism as a Profession* (London: Hodder and Stoughton).

Lord Leveson (2012) *Leveson Inquiry: Culture, Practice and Ethics of the Press*, http://www.levesoninquiry.org.uk/

J. Lewis (1982) *The Victorian Bar* (London: Robert Hale).

J. Lewis, A. Williams, B. Franklin, J. Thomas and N. Mosdell (2008) *Quality and Independence of British Journalism: Tracking the Change over Twenty Years* (Cardiff School of Journalism: Cardiff University).

D. Liddle (2004) 'Anatomy of a "Nine Days' Wonder": Sensational Journalism in the Decade of the Sensation Novel', in A. Maunder and G. Moore (eds) *Victorian Crime, Sensation and Madness* (Aldershot: Ashgate).

E. Marjoribanks (1929) *The Life of Sir Edward Marshall Hall* (London: Victor Gollancz).

T. Martin (2004) *Right to Kill? Tony Martin's Story* (London: Artnik).

P. Mason (ed.) (2003) *Criminal Visions: Representations of Crime and Justice* (Cullompton: Willan).

A. Maunder and G. Moore (eds) (2004) *Victorian Crime, Sensation and Madness* (Aldershot: Ashgate).

A. May (2003) *The Bar and the Old Bailey, 1750–1850* (Chapel Hill: University of North Carolina Press).

I. Mcdowall and Reuters Ltd (1992) *Reuters Handbook for Journalists* (London: Butterworth-Heinemann).

R. McKibbin (1998) *Classes and Cultures. Britain 1918–1951* (Oxford University Press).

R. McWilliam (2007) *The Tichborne Claimant. A Victorian Sensation* (Continuum: London).

J. Meaney (1945) *Scribble Street* (London: Sands).

Ministry of Justice (2010) *Statistical Notice:Anti-Social Behaviour Order Statistics* http://www.statewatch.org/asbo/asbo_statistics_july_2010.pdf

D. Mitch (1992) *The Rise of Popular Literacy in Victorian England* (University of Pennsylvania Press).

B.R. Mitchell (1988) *British Historical Statistics* (Cambridge University Press).

C. Moncrieff (2002) *Living on a Deadline: A History of the Press Association* (London: Virgin Books).

K. Morgan (2002) 'The Boer War and the Media (1899–1902)', *Twentieth Century British History*, 13(1), 1–16.

D.E. Morrison and M. Svennevig (2002) *The Public Interest, the Media and Privacy: A Report for British Broadcasting Corporation, Broadcasting Standards Commission, Independent Committee for the Supervision of Standards of Telephone Information Services* (Independent Television Commission, Institute for Public Policy Research, The Radio Authority).

G. Muhlmann (2008) *A Political History of Journalism* (London: Polity Press).

D. Nash and A.M. Kilday (2010) *Cultures of Shame. Exploring Crime and Morality in Britain 1600–1900* (Basingstoke: Palgrave Macmillan).

R. Negrine (1994) *Politics and the Mass Media in Britain* (London: Routledge).

J. Nicholas and J. Price (1998) *Advanced Studies in Media* (Cheltenham: Nelson Thornes).

T. O'Malley and C. Soley (2000) *Regulating the Press* (London: Pluto Press).

R. Osborne (1995) 'Crime and the Media: From Media Studies to Post-modernism', in D. Kidd-Hewitt and R. Osborne (eds) *Crime and the Media: The Post-Modern Spectacle* (London: Pluto Press).

LeRoy Panek (2011) *Before Sherlock Holmes. How Magazines and Newspapers Invented the Detective Story* (Jefferson, NC: Macfarland and Company).

H. Perkin (2002) *The Rise of Professional Society: England since 1880* (Abingdon: Routledge).

T. Pettit (2010) 'Journalism vs Tradition in the English Ballads of the Murdered Sweetheart', in P. Fumerton, A. Guerrini and K. McAbee (eds) *Ballads and Broadsides in Britain 1500–1800* (Aldershot: Ashgate).

Press Complaints Commission (2007) *Report on Subterfuge and Newsgathering* (PCC: 15 May 2007).

H. Procter (1958) *The Street of Disillusion. The Author's Life as a Journalist* (London: Allan Wingate).

E. Purcell (1916) *Forty Years at the Criminal Bar. Experiences and Impressions* (London: T Fisher Unwin).

L. Radzinowicz (1957) *Sir James Fitzjames Stephen (1829–1894) and His Contribution to the Development of the Criminal Law* (Seldon Society: Spottiswoode, Ballantyne and Co.).

P. Rawlings (1992) *Drunks, Whores and Idle Apprentices* (Abingdon: Routledge).

D. Read (1999) *The Power of News. The History of Reuters* (Oxford University Press).

K. Reid (2003) 'Law and Disorder: Victorian Restraint and Modern Panic', in J. Rowbotham and K. Stevenson (eds) *Behaving Badly: Social Panic and Moral Outrage – Victorian and Modern Parallels* (Aldershot: Ashgate).

R. Reiner (2001) 'The Rise of Virtual Vigilantism: Crime Reporting Since World War II', *Criminal Justice Matters*, 43, 4–5.

R. Reiner, S. Livingstone and J. Allen (2000) 'No More Happy Endings? The Media and Popular Concern About Crime since the Second World War', in T. Hope and R. Sparks (eds) *Crime, Risk and Insecurity: Law and Order in Everyday Life and Political Discourse* (London: Routledge).

R. Reiner, S. Livingstone and J. Allen (2003) 'From Law and Order to Lynch Mobs: Crime News since the Second World War', in P. Mason (ed.) *Criminal Visions* (Cullompton: Willan).

J. Ritchie (1993) *150 Years of True Crime Stories from the News of the World* (London: Michael O'mara Books).

J. Robbins (2010) *The Magnificent Spilsbury and the Case of the Brides in the Bath* (London: John Murray).

D. Rolph (2008) *Reputation, Celebrity and Libel Law* (Aldershot: Ashgate).

D. Rooney (2000) 'Thirty Years of Competition in the British Tabloid Press', in C. Sparks and J. Tulloch (eds) *Tabloid Tales: Global Debates over Media Standards* (Maryland: Rowman and Littlefield Publishers).

N. Root (2011) *Frenzy. Heath, Haigh and Christie. The First Great Tabloid Murderers* (London: Preface Publishing).

A. Rose (1985) *Stinie: Murder on the Common* (London: Bodley Head).

J. Rowbotham (2007) 'Miscarriage of Justice? Post-colonial Reflections on the "Trial" of the Maharajah of Baroda, 1875', *Liverpool Law Review*, 28(3), 377–403.

J. Rowbotham (2009) 'Legislating for Your Own Good: The Lessons of the Victorian Vaccination Acts', *Liverpool Law Review*, 30(1), 13–34.

J. Rowbotham (2012) 'The Shifting Nature of Blame. Revisiting Issues of Blame, Shame and Culpability in the English Criminal Justice System', in J. Rowbotham, D. Nash and M. Muravyeva (eds) *Blame, Shame and Culpability* (Abingdon: Routledge SOLON).

J. Rowbotham and K. Stevenson (2000) 'Societal Dystopias and Legal Utopias: Reflections on Visions Past and the Enduring Ideal of Criminal Codification', *Nottingham Law Journal*, 9(1), 25–38.

J. Rowbotham and K. Stevenson (2002) 'Causing a Sensation: Media and Legal Representations of Bad Behaviour', in (same eds) *Behaving Badly: Visible Crime, Social Panics and Legal Responses – Victorian and Modern Parallels* (Aldershot: Ashgate).

J. Rowbotham and K. Stevenson (eds) (2005) *Criminal Conversations: Victorians Behaving Badly* (Columbus: Ohio State University Press).

J. Rowbotham, K. Stevenson and S. Pegg (2003) 'Children of Misfortune. Media Parallels in the Cases of Child Murders Thompson and Venables, Barratt and Bradley', *Howard Journal of Criminal Justice*, 42(2), 107–142.

J. Rowbotham, D. Nash and M. Muravyeva (eds) (2012) *Blame, Shame and Culpability* (Abingdon: Routledge SOLON).

Royal Commission on the Press (1948) *Minutes of Evidence* (London: HMSO) Cmnd7328.

Royal Commission on the Press (1977) *Report 1974–77* (London: HMSO) Cmnd 6810.

J. Rozenberg (2005) *Privacy and the Press* (Oxford University Press).

A. Sebba (1994) *Battling for News: The Rise of the Woman Reporter* (London: Hodder and Stoughton).

M. Shanley (1993) *Feminism, Marriage and the Law in Victorian England 1850–1895* (Princeton University Press).

H. Shpayer-Makov (2009) 'Journalists and Police Detectives in Victorian and Edwardian England: An Uneasy Reciprocal Relationship', *Journal of Social History*, 42(4), 963–987.

H. Shpayer-Makov (2011) *The Ascent of the Detective: Police Sleuths in Victorian and Edwardian England* (Oxford University Press).

E.A. Smith (1970) *A History of the Press* (London: Ginn and Company).

G. Smith (1996) 'Civilized People Don't Want to See That Kind of Thing: The Decline of Physical Punishment in London 1760–1840', in C. Strange (ed.) *Qualities of Mercy. Justice, Punishment and Discretion* (Vancouver: University of British Columbia Press).

K. Soothill and S. Walby (1991) *Sex Crime in the News* (London: Routledge).

A. Stott (2004) *Hannah More. The First Victorian* (Oxford University Press).

J.A. Strahan (1919) *The Bench and Bar of England* (Edinburgh: Blackwood).

S. Street (2002) *A Concise History of British Radio 1922–2002* (Oxford: Blackwell).

R. Surrette (1998) *Media, Crime and Criminal Justice: Images and Realities* (Belmont CA: Wadsworth).

R. Swift (2005) 'Behaving Badly? Irish Migrants and Crime in the Victorian City', in J. Rowbotham and K. Stevenson (eds) *Criminal Conversations: Victorians Behaving Badly* (Ohio State University Press).

C. Thomas (2010) *Are juries fair?* (London: Ministry of Justice Research Series 1/10).

D. Thomas (2006) *Villain's Paradise. A History of Britain's Underworld* (Harmondsworth: Penguin).

F.M.L. Thompson (1987) *The Rise of Respectable Society 1830–1900* (London: Fontana).

R. Wacks (1995) *Privacy and Press Freedom: Rights in Conflict* (Oxford: Blackstone Press).

C. Walker (2005) 'Small Times, Bad Times', *British Journalism Review*, 16(2), 26–30.

M. Warnock and E. MacDonald (2008) *Easeful Death. Is There a Case for Assisted Dying?* (Oxford University Press).

G. Weaver (2006) *Conan Doyle and the Parson's Son* (Cambridge: Vanguard Press).

D. Webb (2009) 'Caught by the Slip: Part 7 of My Life in a Newspaper Reference Library', *Life Traveller's Tale*, http://intheprint.blogspot.co.uk/

J. Wiener (ed.) (1988) *Papers for the Millions. The New Journalism in Britain, 1850s to 1914* (Westport, CT: Greenwood Press).

J. Wiener (1988) 'How New Was the New Journalism?' In (same ed.) *Papers for the Millions. The New Journalism in Britain, 1850s to 1914* (Westport, CT: Greenwood Press).

J. Wiener (2011) *The Americanization of the British Press: Speed in the Age of Transatlantic Journalism* (New York: Palgrave Macmillan).

M.J. Wiener (1994) *Reconstructing the Criminal: Culture Law and Policy in England 1830–1914* (Cambridge University Press).

D. Williams (2008) *Media, Memory and the First World War* (Montreal: McGill-Queens University Press).

F. Williams (1957) *Dangerous Estate. The Anatomy of Newspapers* (London: Longmans, Green & Co.).

K. Williams (2010) *Read All About It! A History of the British Newspaper* (London: Taylor and Francis).

K. Williams (1997) *Get Me a Murder a Day! A History of Media and Communication in Britain* (London: Hodder).

B. Woffinden (2007) 'Treating contempt with contempt', *British Journalism Review*, 18(2), 5–12.

M. Wolff (1979) 'Urbanity and Journalism. The Victorian Connection. H.J. Dyos Memorial Lecture' (Leicester: Victorian Studies Centre).

Lord Woolf (2003) 'Should the media and the judiciary be on speaking terms?' Speech (University College Dublin: Law Faculty, 22 October). http://www.judiciary.gov.uk/media/speeches/2003/should-media-judiciary-be-on-speaking-terms.

M. Wykes (2001) *News, Crime and Culture* (London: Pluto Press).

M. Wykes and K. Welsh (2008) *Violence, Gender and Justice* (London: Sage).

A. Young (1996) *Imagining Crime: Textual Outlaws and Criminal Conversations* (London: Sage).

Index

Note: Bold terms refer to key topics and locators with 'n' refer to note numbers

Printed and bound by CPI Group (UK) Ltd, Croydon, CR0 4YY